on track ...

The Who

every album, every song

Geoffrey Feakes

sonicbondpublishing.com

Sonicbond Publishing Limited
www.sonicbondpublishing.co.uk
Email: info@sonicbondpublishing.co.uk

First Published in the United Kingdom 2020
First Published in the United States 2020

British Library Cataloguing in Publication Data:
A Catalogue record for this book is available from the British Library

Copyright Geoffrey Feakes 2020

ISBN 978-1-78952-076-7

Typeset in ITC Garamond & ITC Avant Garde
Printed and bound in England

Graphic design and typesetting: Full Moon Media

on track ...
The
Who

every album, every song

Geoffrey Feakes

sonicbondpublishing.com

This book is dedicated to the memories of
Keith Moon, John Entwistle and Doug Sandom

Acknowledgements

A big thank you to Stephen Lambe and all at
Sonicbond Publishing for their support and encouragement
in putting this book together.

Thanks to the Dutch Progressive Rock Page who have published
my album reviews and interviews since 2005.

Gratitude to all the members of The Who, past and present,
and everyone associated with the band.

I would also like to thank all the researchers, journalists,
archivists and fans that have gone before and made
available a wealth of information.

A special thank you to my wife Margaret and her gracious support
through seven months devoted almost entirely to The Who,
their music and this book.

on track ...

The Who

Contents

Forward

My first encounter with The Who was in early 1965 when, at the tender age of ten, I heard the song 'I Can't Explain' on the radio. It was two minutes of catchy, adrenalin-fuelled pop that captured both mine and the record buyer's imagination. It's quite possible however that, unknowingly, I may have crossed paths with the singer ten years earlier. Like Roger Daltrey, I was born in London's Hammersmith Hospital and lived in Shepherd's Bush. As a baby, my mum would often push my pram along Goldhawk Road, the main route that runs along the edge of the suburb and up one of the many side streets. One such street is Percy Road where the ten year old Daltrey lived. My family moved out of London less than a year later so I have no memory of those walks although my mum often talked about them. The street where we lived was Shepherd's Bush Gardens but don't try to find it on any map, it no longer exists. The entire street was demolished in the 1960s to make way for a shopping centre.

The Who, and Pete Townshend's songs in particular, were perfectly in tune with my own development. During the late '60s, radio staples like 'I'm A Boy' and 'Pictures of Lily' struck a chord with my own early teen angst. In 1970, my interests turned to more adventurous rock and The Who duly obliged with *Tommy*, *Who's Next* and *Quadrophenia*. During this period many bands came and went, but few endured like The Who. They redefined the laws of how a pop-rock band should function, especially in the 1960s. While The Who had a commanding frontman, all four band members vied for attention; from the attacking guitar chords and riffs of Pete Townshend to the explosive drumming of Keith Moon to the dexterous bass lines of John Entwistle.

In addition to selling more than 100 million records worldwide in a career spanning six decades, The Who's legacy has been far-reaching. Bands who have acknowledged a debt to The Who include punk rockers the Sex Pistols, the Clash and Eddie and the Hot Rods, punk-pop crossover groups like Blondie and the Ramones, Mod revivalists The Jam, Secret Affair and the Chords and Britpop act Oasis. Many other bands have identified The Who's influence including Rush, Pearl Jam and Green Day.

This book charts The Who's development from the early days as R&B hopefuls the Detours to a rock phenomenon that continues in the 21st century with the latest album *Who*. All too often, the public activities, infighting, fallouts, gossip and myths surrounding the band have been the focus of attention. I examine the individual songs with a chapter dedicated to each studio album. Non-album songs such as singles and bonus tracks on CD reissues are included in the 'Related Tracks' sections. Live albums and soundtracks are also discussed, concluding with a round-up of compilations. If you spot any errors or omissions, please feel free to contact me through the publisher. Happy reading.

Geoffrey Feakes, 30 June 2020

Introduction

When The Who released their twelfth studio album in December 2019, it was welcomed by rock fans and pundits alike. Although the band had remained active as a touring unit, new songs for the first time in thirteen years were something to be savoured. As the two remaining co-founders of the band, Pete Townshend and Roger Daltrey could have hardly realised back in 1964 that 55 years on, The Who would still be alive and kicking.

The origins of the band date back to 1959 when Daltrey, still in his early teens, formed a skiffle group with several friends. Armed with his homemade guitar, he quickly asserted himself as the group's leader and after several name changes they settled on the Detours, taken from the Duane Eddy instrumental 'Detour'. John Entwistle joined the Detours in the summer of 1961, Pete Townshend followed in January 1962, and drummer Doug Sandom was recruited in the summer of '62.

They built up a following playing the pubs and clubs in the suburbs of west London which became their stamping ground. Their repertoire included the current chart hits, rock and roll, R&B, Motown, even trad jazz. The jive and the twist were all the rage, so anything with a solid, danceable beat was fair game. Daltrey took over lead vocals in the summer of '63, relinquishing lead guitar to Townshend who encouraged the Detours to include authentic American blues in their set. Although Daltrey took a little persuading, they were soon belting out convincing versions of songs like Howlin' Wolf's 'Smokestack Lightning'. Playing support to experienced stage acts like Johnny Kidd & the Pirates and later the Rolling Stones, they soaked up the influences and developed their own, high octane sound.

On Valentine's Day, February 1964, after discovering there was a group called Johnny Devlin and the Detours on the scene, they changed their name to The Who. It was short, snappy and would stand out on concert bills and posters. Following a failed audition for Fontana Records, Sandom left the group in April 1964. That same month, they were approached by a cocksure young drummer named Keith Moon. Impressed by his energy and ability, they offered him a job on the spot. He was just the boost they needed and they surged forward with a renewed drive and commitment. Mod aficionado Peter Meaden renamed the group the High Numbers, restyled their look and in July 1964, released the single 'Zoot Suit' b/w 'I'm the Face'. It was promoted as 'The first authentic Mod record', but record buyers were unimpressed. That same month, Kit Lambert and Chris Stamp were looking for a young, up and coming group to film and promote and were impressed by the High Numbers' performance at the Railway Hotel, Wealdstone. They took over the group's management and changed their name back to The Who. With the phrase 'Maximum R&B' and a striking new logo, in November they began a Tuesday night residency at London's Marquee Club and were soon breaking attendance records.

The debut single 'I Can't Explain' was released in January 1965 and breached the UK top ten. Following their flirtation with the Mod subculture, The Who embraced 'pop-art' with eye-catching clothing, including Townshend's famous union-jack jacket. Although three well-received albums followed, *My Generation* (December 1965), *A Quick One* (December 1966) and *The Who Sell Out* (December 1967), it was a run of seven classic singles that captured the public's imagination, in the UK at least. It wasn't until a legendary appearance at the Monterey Pop Festival in June 1967 that America began to sit up and take notice. 'I Can See For Miles' released three months later became the band's only Stateside top-ten hit. The fourth album *Tommy* (May 1969) changed everyone's perception of The Who and rock albums in general. For the band themselves, it was a game-changer, both artistically and financially. Most importantly, *Tommy* marked The Who's transition from a singles group that released the obligatory LPs to an album band. Their success in America was sealed with an iconic performance at the Woodstock festival on 17 August 1969.

The 1970s got off to an impressive start with the acclaimed Live at Leeds (May 1970) and an appearance at the Isle of Wight Festival on 29 August 1970 to a 600,000 strong crowd. *Who's Next* (August 1971) would be their most popular album and *Quadrophenia* (October 1973) was Townshend's homage to the 1960's Mod culture, spawning a 1979 hit movie. More hit singles followed as did the introspective *The Who by Numbers* (October 1975). Three weeks after the well-received *Who Are You* was released in August 1978, Keith Moon sadly died from an accidental overdose of prescription drugs, aged just 32.

Townshend, Daltrey and Entwistle vowed to continue, enlisting drummer Kenney Jones, and were repaid with more sellout tours. The 1980s started well with two albums, *Face Dances* (March 1981), and *It's Hard* (September 1982). When they took the latter on the road, it was billed as the 'Farewell tour'. With the constant grind of touring losing its appeal and Townshend finding it harder to write new Who material, in 1983 they disbanded. They regrouped briefly for the 13 July 1985 *Live Aid* concert and again in 1989 for a 25th Anniversary tour with drummer Simon Phillips replacing Jones. The highlight was a spectacular *Tommy* concert in Los Angeles in August with several notable guest singers. On the 18 January 1990, The Who were inducted into the Rock & Roll Hall of Fame.

When The Who reformed in 1996, it was almost by accident. Townshend was asked to stage a musical version of *Quadrophenia* in London's Hyde Park in June for the Prince's Trust. Joined by Daltrey, Entwistle and drummer Zak Starkey, by the time the show went on the road in October, they were being billed as The Who. Touring continued for the next five years and along with Starkey, keyboardist John Bundrick was a regular part of the stage line-up. A memorable show for everyone involved was the post 9/11 *The Concert for New York City* at the Madison Square Garden on 20 October 2001.

On 27 June 2002, on the eve of a three-month American tour, John Entwistle died from a cocaine-induced heart attack in Las Vegas' Hard Rock Hotel. Bassist Pino Palladino had the unenviable task of being the last-minute replacement, but he rose to the occasion. Another body blow came on 12 January 2003 when Townshend was arrested on suspicion of accessing child pornography on the internet. Daltrey was especially vocal in his defence and when no evidence was found, the charges were dropped.

In 2004 it was business as usual with a headlining performance at the Isle of Wight Festival in June followed by dates in Japan and a return to Australia for the first time since 1968. In July 2005, The Who gave a short, but powerful performance at *Live 8* despite stiff competition from a reformed Pink Floyd. The first studio album in nearly a quarter of a century, *Endless Wire* (October 2006) was released to a positive reception. The supporting tour ran, on and off, for three years, crossing several continents.

On 7 February 2010, The Who's fifteen-minute halftime set during Super Bowl XLIV at Miami's Sun Life Stadium was seen by 100 million television viewers. This was capped on 12 August 2012 when several billion people around the world witnessed The Who during the closing ceremony of the London Olympic Games. In November that same year, they embarked on a nine-month tour with a fresh and spectacular restaging of *Quadrophenia*, playing to more than half a million people across America and Europe.

Daltrey reached his 70th birthday in March 2014 and perhaps unsurprisingly, lengthy touring became problematic and beset with health issues. The Who's 50th anniversary would not pass without due celebration, however. A triumphant world tour included headlining appearances at London's Hyde Park and the Glastonbury Festival in June 2015 and a return to the Isle of Wight Festival in June 2016. 2017 saw a short *Tommy & More* UK spring tour followed by a summer trek around North and South America, including a handful of *Classic Quadrophenia* dates.

The Who Moving On! 2019 tour was interspersed with the recording of the long-awaited new studio album simply titled *Who* (December 2019). Further touring was also planned.

Although *Who* may very well be the final album, with impressive sales figures on both sides of the Atlantic, the near future at least looks bright for The Who. Roger Daltrey celebrated his 75th birthday in 2019 and Pete Townshend did likewise in 2020, but in recent interviews, they both remain optimistic about the future of 'the greatest rock and roll band in the world'.

The Key Players

Not counting touring musicians, The Who family tree is a small one, especially compared with many of their contemporaries. There have been just six official members, including three drummers – Spinal Tap anyone! The core line-up of Roger Daltrey, Pete Townshend, John Entwistle and Keith Moon lasted from 1964 until the drummer's untimely death in 1978. Since then, the band's history has been chequered, but they remain active to this day despite the loss of Entwistle in 2002. When the band reformed in 1996, a conscious decision was made not to recruit new members. Although Zak Starkey and Pino Palladino would become the rhythm section of choice, they are essentially session musicians hired for touring and occasional recording purposes. Other musicians to perform with the band on a long term basis include John Bundrick, Simon Townshend and Loren Gold.

Roger Daltrey (born: 1 March 1944)

1964 – 1983, 1985, 1988, 1989, 1996 – present. Vocals, harmonica, guitar
Roger Harry Daltrey was born in Hammersmith Hospital, west London. Around the age of twelve, he began styling himself after his idol Elvis Presley. Although he was a bright boy, he found school life in his early teens difficult and as an outlet, he and several friends formed a skiffle group, the Sulgrave Rebels who later morphed into the Detours. He was expelled from Acton County Grammar School on his fifteenth birthday following an accident involving an air rifle according to Daltrey. Another story is that he was caught smoking in the boys' toilets.

While serving an apprenticeship in a sheet metal factory, he made his first electric guitar, modelled on a Fender Stratocaster seen in a shop window. He established himself as the Detours' lead guitarist and self-appointed leader. Following the recruitment of John Entwistle and Pete Townshend, they played the west London circuit of pubs and clubs, building up a steady following.

Original singer Colin Dawson – noted for his Cliff Richard impression – departed in January 1963 and his replacement Gabby Connolly – a country and western style singer – followed in the summer, leaving Daltrey to take over lead vocals. Handling sheet metal all day was making it difficult to play guitar and he passed lead duties to Townshend. As the Detours' frontman, Daltrey honed his singing and early role models included local hero Johnny Kidd. He also maintained a reputation as a tough character which dated back to his school days. He later developed his signature stage technique which involved swinging his microphone like a lasso before catching it with his arm outstretched. Although Townshend's development as a songwriter usurped Daltrey's position as The Who's leader, he had a formidable stage presence and when he adopted the role of Tommy in 1969, he became the archetypical rock-god frontman.

As a solo artist, Daltrey is the most prolific and successful in terms of albums and singles. He has also successfully staged performances of the band's work such as *Tommy* at the Royal Albert Hall in 2011. This was part of his annual

Teenage Cancer Trust concerts, a charity he continues to support, earning him a CBE in December 2004. Following the lead role in the 1975 *Tommy* movie, he has enjoyed a parallel career as an actor in both films and television dramas.

John Entwistle (born: 9 October 1944, died: 27 June 2002)

1964 – 1983, 1985, 1988, 1989, 1996 – 2002. Bass guitar, horns, vocals
Affectionately known as 'The Ox' in later years due to his height and stolid stage presence, John Alec Entwistle, like Roger Daltrey, was a – second world – war baby, born in Hammersmith Hospital. He was another Acton County Grammar boy and from an early age, he developed a talent for drawing. He learnt to play trumpet and French horn and joined the Middlesex Youth Orchestra. In 1959, he formed trad-jazz group the Confederates and enlisted schoolmate Pete Townshend. After taking his trumpet playing skills to a rival band, he and Townshend teamed up again in the Aristocats and later, the Scorpions. He decided six-string guitar was the way forward but soon gravitated towards the bass guitar which, due to his large hands, he found easier to play. He would remain a lead instrumentalist at heart however, as evidenced in his later playing style with The Who.

After leaving school aged sixteen, Entwistle obtained a respectable position as a trainee tax officer for the Inland Revenue – the UK's tax collection authority. In the summer of 1961, on his way home from a rehearsal with the Scorpions, he bumped into Daltrey who talked him into joining the Detours. In 1964, he and Townshend pioneered the Marshall stack and were also the first to use eight by twelve cabinets which gave them volume levels unprecedented for a rock group at the time. The Who's reputation as the loudest band in the world came at a cost; when Entwistle died in 2002, he was almost completely deaf. A fervent supporter of touring, in the '60s and '70s, regular stage work honed his bass playing skills. During the '80s and '90s, touring became a financial necessity, but in Daltrey's words 'He lived to play'.

Entwistle was the most musically literate of all The Who members which he believed compromised his spontaneity as a songwriter. Even so, during the 1960s, '70s and early '80s, his songs were welcome fixtures on Who albums and would often provide the B side to Townshend's hit singles. As a musician, he is universally acknowledged as one of the foremost and influential bass players in rock. Many leading exponents of the instrument, especially in the hard-rock and prog-rock genres, have cited Entwistle as a primary influence.

Pete Townshend (born: 19 May 1945)

1964 – 1983, 1985, 1988, 1989, 1996 – present. Guitar, vocals, keyboards
Born in Chiswick Hospital, west London, Peter Dennis Blandford Townshend came into the world at the close of the second world war. Like Roger Daltrey and John Entwistle, he attended Acton County Grammar School, but unlike the singer he went on to pass his final exams. Three months younger than Townshend, Ian Gillan of Deep Purple fame was another Acton County

Grammar boy. At the age of twelve, he met Entwistle and in the summer of 1959, they made their first public appearance as members of the Confederates with Townshend playing banjo. Influenced by skiffle, he abandoned banjo for acoustic, and later electric guitar and Hank Marvin of the Shadows was an early hero. By 1960, he and Entwistle were members of the Scorpions whose repertoire included Shadows' instrumentals. The brash, rhythmic style of rock and roller Eddie Cochran would influence Townshend's later playing in The Who.

Townshend was in his second term at Ealing Technical College & School of Art studying graphic design when, at Entwistle's suggestion, he joined the Detours as a replacement for rhythm guitarist Reg Bowen. When he auditioned in January 1962 aged sixteen, he impressed Daltrey with his technique and inventive chord progressions. In the summer of 1963, Townshend graduated from rhythm to lead guitar and the Detours recorded two of his songs 'Please Don't Send Me Home' and 'It Was You'. Both in the style of the Beatles – it was the height of Beatlemania – they elevated Townshend's status, posing a serious challenge to Daltrey as the group's leader. While opening for the Rolling Stones in December, Townshend took note of guitarist Keith Richards' backstage limbering up exercise which would provide the inspiration for his trademark 'windmill' arm-swinging power chord technique.

One Tuesday in June 1964 during The Who's first performance of many at the Railway Hotel in Harrow, west London, Townshend accidentally punched a hole in the low ceiling with the head of his Rickenbacker guitar. Either through embarrassment, anger or elation, he proceeded to trash his instrument. The following week, he toppled his stack of Marshall amps which was all the encouragement Keith Moon needed to kick over his drum kit. Dubbed 'auto-destruction' by Townshend who believed that art should reflect life, it became a theatrical staple that would close the majority of The Who's shows for years to come.

Doug Sandom (born: 26 February 1930, died: 27 February 2019)
1964. Drums

Douglas Sandom hailed from Greenford in west London. He was a bricklayer by day and a semi-professional drummer by night when he joined the Detours in August 1962. He replaced original drummer Harry Wilson who had been Roger Daltrey's best friend from their first day at primary school. Sandom's first gig with the Detours was at the Paradise club in Peckham, south London. Unlike the rest of the band who were still in their teens and single, Sandom was 32 and married with a son. He passed himself off as being much younger however and he was the resident drummer when the Detours changed their name to The Who in February 1964.

During an audition for Fontana Records, his drumming was criticised, and under pressure from Pete Townshend, Sandom left the group in April 1964. Sandom later said that the age difference had also been an issue. Ironically, a few months earlier, he had defended Townshend when the guitarist was singled out for criticism during another failed audition. Sandom fulfilled his last engagement with The Who on the 13 April at the 100 Club, Oxford Street in the heart of London.

With his easy-going manner and the band's elder member, Sandom had often been the moderator during Townshend and Daltrey's many arguments. His departure, however, was perhaps inevitable; he'd been under pressure from his wife to spend less time with the group and the R&B influences didn't sit comfortably with his drumming style. A solid timekeeper with a professional attitude, his role in the development of the band in their formative years should not be overlooked.

Keith Moon (born: 23 August 1946, died: 7 September 1978)
1964 – 1978. Drums, vocals

Keith John Moon, the youngest of the four core members, was born in Central Middlesex Hospital, north-west London. Even as a boy he was an extrovert and his hyperactive activities marked him out from the rest of his schoolmates. His prophetic secondary school reports were also an indicator of things to come. He received his first drum kit at the age of sixteen; a Premier brand kit which he would favour throughout his later tenure with The Who.

Moon played in numerous bands in the local Wembley area including the Altones, the Escorts and most notably, Mark Twain and the Strangers in 1962. In the summer of 1963, while a trainee electrician, he joined the semi-professional group the Beachcombers who specialised in Hank Marvin and the Shadows covers. His induction into The Who came during a gig at the Oldfield Hotel, Greenford in late April 1964. Two weeks after Doug Sandom's departure, session drummer Dave Golding was filling in that evening. Moon, aged seventeen, was still a member of the Beachcombers at the time. During an interval in The Who's set, a young man approached the band and claimed that his mate was a better drummer than Golding. Up steps Moon and he's invited to join them for Bo Diddley's 'Road Runner'. He broke the bass drum pedal in the process, but they knew they had their new drummer.

Although his unconventional, attacking style was unique, it's generally acknowledged that in the early '60s, Moon was influenced by the showmanship and vitality of American jazz drummer Gene Krupa. He also took lessons from an unconventional source, Screaming Lord Sutch and the Savages' drummer Carlo Little who Moon admired for his similarly powerful technique. Until his untimely death in September 1978, Moon relished his role as The Who's self-imposed court jester. It was often difficult to separate fact from fiction with tales of wrecked hotel rooms and cars in swimming pools. The media fuelled the myth and, in the public domain where he was dubbed 'Moon the Loon', he was better known for his antics off, rather than on stage. Which is a pity because as every self-respecting rock fan of a certain age knows, he was one of the most individual and entertaining musicians to have sat behind a drum kit.

Kenney Jones (born 16 September 1948)
1978 – 1983, 1985, 1988, 2014. Drums

Kenneth Thomas Jones came to The Who with a solid musical pedigree. He was a highly respected drummer having played in both the Small Faces fronted by Steve Marriot and the Faces backing Rod Stewart. He was approached to join in November 1978 following the death of Keith Moon. For Pete Townshend, he was the obvious replacement following his role as principal drummer on the soundtrack for the 1975 *Tommy* film. When Jones received the call, he was on the verge of forming the band Lazy Racer with producer, musician Glyn Johns. His position as a full time Who member was made official in January 1979 and he made his stage debut at London's Rainbow Theatre on 2 May.

A disagreement over the sharing of advances from The Who's record deal with Warner Brothers at the beginning of 1980 sparked tensions between Jones and Roger Daltrey. In Daltrey's opinion, Jones is a great drummer, but he was the wrong drummer for The Who. The situation wasn't helped when Jones replaced the traditional floor tom-toms with smaller concert toms which produced a voguish, '80s sound. Ironically, the friction between Jones and Daltrey and the friendship he developed with the easy-going Entwistle mirrored his predecessor's relationships within the band. Compared with Moon, his drumming was more economical, maintaining a rigid tempo which he believed provided a solid platform for Townshend and Entwistle to be adventurous with their playing. For Jones, The Who's appearance at *Live Aid* in July 1985 was one of the highpoints of his tenure with the band. Although he found The Who technically and physically demanding and the material complex compared with his previous work, he stated in his 2018 autobiography *Let The Good Times Roll* that they were the most exciting band he'd played with.

My Generation (1965)

Personnel:
Roger Daltrey: lead vocals, harmonica, tambourine
Pete Townshend: electric guitar, backing vocals, lead vocals on 'A Legal Matter'
John Entwistle: bass guitar, backing vocals
Keith Moon: drums
Additional personnel:
Nicky Hopkins: piano
Produced by: Shel Talmy
Engineered by: Glyn Johns
Recorded at: IBC Recording Studios, London, April – October 1965
Release date: UK: 3 December 1965, USA: 25 April 1966
Record label: UK: Brunswick, USA: Decca
Highest chart places: UK: 5, USA: Did not chart
Running time: UK: 36:13, USA: 33:35

When The Who entered IBC Studios, London on 12 April 1965 to begin work on their first album, it must have been with a mixture of confidence and trepidation. As a unit, Roger Daltrey, Pete Townshend, John Entwistle and Keith Moon had been performing continuously for almost a year and the debut single 'I Can't Explain' was riding high in the UK charts. Located in the heart of London south of Regent's Park, IBC was home to many major UK recording acts during the '60s and '70s including the Kinks and the Rolling Stones.

In 1964, in their haste to secure the services of producer Shel Talmy and a major label, Decca, The Who's managers Kit Lambert and Chris Stamp had unwittingly agreed to a recording contract that tied the band to Talmy for five years. In addition to the first two Kinks albums, Talmy had produced the hit singles 'You Really Got Me' and 'All Day and All of the Night' so he seemed the ideal choice for The Who. Talmy by all accounts wasn't a hands-on producer, allowing engineer Glyn Johns to work closely with the band. Johns had assisted Talmy on the Kinks' recordings and would soon become a successful producer in his own right.

With Lambert's encouragement and supply of tape recorders, Townshend spent late nights producing home demos of each song. It set a precedent for future Who albums. On the demos where he would sing and overdub all the instruments, thus ensuring the songs were recorded as he intended. Once presented to the rest of the band, they would be rehearsed and perfected before entering the studio. As a result, they were recorded with very few takes. Thanks to Townshend's demos and a week of rehearsals, the time spent recording the album was fairly short. The protracted recording period was a result of commitments elsewhere – The Who were rarely off the road in 1965.

Daltrey wanted the album to reflect the band's setlist which mostly comprised R&B, soul and Motown covers. The album was slated for release in the summer but when nine completed tracks were presented to Beat

Instrumental magazine in July for appraisal it was given a thumbs down due to a lack of originality. The album was temporarily shelved while The Who went back out on the road. They returned to the studio on 13 October for a six-hour midnight session which included the title song and the final tracks were recorded on 10 and 12 November. Several R&B covers had been replaced with what Lambert called 'hard pop' and the finished album includes an impressive nine out of twelve original songs, unprecedented for a debut release at the time.

The Who were on the ascendency in 1965 and in addition to live performances, they made numerous promotional appearances on radio and TV. Personality-wise, they remained as dysfunctional as ever with dynamic live performances underpinned by an undercurrent of behind the scenes rivalry and aggression. Things came to a head on 27 September 1965 in Aalborg, Denmark. In Daltrey's view, the playing had become louder and more erratic on the tour, which he blamed on drugs. He stormed backstage and flushed Moon's stash of pills down the toilet. When the outraged drummer retaliated, he was punched by Daltrey who as a result, was fired from the band. Around two weeks later, Lambert and Stamp persuaded the other three to allow Daltrey to return. They reluctantly agreed on the proviso that there would be no more physical assaults.

When the album was finally released in the UK in December, Townshend and Daltrey voiced their disapproval of the finished results, especially the production. Despite their misgivings, *My Generation* is acknowledged as a classic mid-'60s slice of energised pop-rock. It would also be the last time that Townshend would write anthems like 'My Generation', 'Anyway, Anyhow, Anywhere' and 'The Kids Are Alright' intended to empower The Who's youth audience. It was well received by the press and the record-buying public, breaching the top five UK chart.

For the American market where it was released in April 1966, it was retitled *The Who Sings My Generation* and the Bo Diddley tune 'I'm A Man' on side two replaced by the Townshend original 'Instant Party (Circles)'. The poor chart performance was indicative of Decca's lack of faith and promotion. As part of the British Invasion which began with the Beatles in early 1964, many lesser acts were enjoying unprecedented popularity in the USA, a situation The Who would not fully address until 1967.

The overhead cover photo on the UK release of *My Generation* was taken at Surrey docks in south-east London by photographer David Wedgbury. Townshend's union jack jacket is draped over Entwistle's shoulders, and appropriately, they are standing next to four drums of propane which, exposed to air, can form an explosive mixture. For the American cover of The Who Sings *My Generation*, Wedgbury chose a more famous London landmark. The band are pictured looking suitably moody in front of the tower of Big Ben.

'Out in the Street' 2:31 (Pete Townshend)

When the album was released, The Who already had three UK hit singles under their belt so record buyers had a pretty good idea of what to expect. As such, they wouldn't have been surprised by the opening song. The guitar intro leading into Daltrey's vocal and a full band arrangement of the chorus is perhaps a little too close to 'Anyway, Anyhow, Anywhere' for comfort. Both songs were recorded during the initial 12 to 14 April 1965 sessions. A solo guitar intro would become a trademark of Who songs during the '60s. Townshend's playing is ragged in places but well suited to the song's gritty R&B flavour. Only the faux Beach Boys-style harmonies around the 1:30 mark sound out of place.

Lyrically it's pretty basic with variations on the same lines and little in the way of a coherent narrative. Townshend disowned the lyrics, saying that they had been rewritten by Lambert who wasn't happy with the original lines. Bruce Springsteen's 1980 song with the same title paints a more focused picture of carefree life on the street. Under the extended title 'Out in the Street (You're Going to Know Me)', it was the American B side to the 'My Generation' single.

'I Don't Mind' 2:36 (James Brown)
To reflect the band's stage set, the album as originally planned was heavily reliant on cover versions. This is one of three non-original songs to survive from the early sessions. The harmonies are more finely tuned on this slow blues ballad and Daltrey's sultry vocal does justice to the original. The recording was edited for the album and the full-length version surfaced as a bonus track on the 2002 'Deluxe Edition' of *My Generation*. The original version by James Brown and the Famous Flames reached number four in the R&B Billboard chart in 1961. The unusual chord progression appealed to Townshend who was experimenting with different chords and guitar rhythms at the time.

'The Goods Gone' 4:02 (Pete Townshend)
Although the longest track on the album, this is another song that would have to wait until the 2002 reissue for the full recording to be heard. Townshend singled Daltrey out for praise, whose singing is barely recognisable at the bottom end of his vocal range. Like 'Out in the Street', lyrically this is repetitive and tells a simple tale of love that's gone sour. Townshend's guitar playing is particularly impressive with a high ringing tone and a jazz-influenced solo at 1:55. At the time, Townshend was in awe of guitarists like Jimmy Page, Eric Clapton and Jeff Beck and believed he was unable to compete on their level. As a result, he mostly avoids solos on the album. It was lifted for the B side to 'La-La-La-Lies', the final single from the album.

'La-La-La-Lies' 2:17 (Pete Townshend)
This is one of Townshend's least favourite songs on the album. It sounds like a deliberate commercial stab with the production, Daltrey's singing and the backing harmonies mimicking the popular Merseybeat sound of the time. The

lyrics are pure cliché; the protagonist is confident that the feelings he shares for the girl by his side will withstand the lies being spread by a jealous ex-partner. Moon's inventive, tom-toms biased drumming lifts the song above the ordinary and it also benefits from Nicky Hopkins' lively piano accompaniment.

Without the approval of the band, 'La-La-La-Lies' was released as a single on 11 November 1966 by Brunswick. It was a last-ditch attempt to exploit The Who's newfound popularity on the rival Reaction label. It was in competition with The Who-sanctioned 'Happy Jack' hit and failed to chart in most regions.

'Much Too Much' 2:47 (Pete Townshend)
Opening the song acapella style, high harmonies are once more to the fore. They also provide the memorable choral hook and contrast with Daltrey's laidback drawl which seems to be aping Mick Jagger. The melody in the verses also bears a marked similarity to 'I Can See For Miles'. In Townshend's songs, relationships are never straightforward, and here the protagonist is telling his partner that her love is too overbearing.

'My Generation' 3:18 (Pete Townshend)
The title song is one of The Who's most famous and regularly features in 'greatest rock songs of all time' lists. Townshend's original conception, however, is a far cry from the rebellious anthem. It started out as a folk style offering influenced by Bob Dylan and the slow, talking blues of Jimmy Reed. It went through several changes during the demo stages and during the second, Townshend introduced a stutter to emulate blues singers like John Lee Hooker and Sonny Boy Williamson. When recorded by Daltrey, the stutter mimicked the articulations of a Mod under the influence of pills. On first hearing, the song's aggressive tone and stuttered 'f-f-f-fade' left many anticipating a stronger 'F' word. Which is perhaps why the single was initially banned by the BBC although they claimed the song was offensive to people with a genuine stutter.

The song title was inspired by a trilogy of plays 'The Generations' about the British working class by dramatist David Mercer, one of Townshend's lecturers at Ealing Art College in 1963. The words, including the infamous line 'Hope I die before I get old', were written hurriedly in the back of a car and Townshend has been defending them ever since.

The R&B influences are ripe in the call and response verses and handclaps used to punctuate the stop-start vocal sections. Townshend's Rickenbacker guitar phrase that holds the song together is simple but effective. Following Moon's explosive drum break, the two guitar parts at the end feature overdubbed feedback. For his groundbreaking bass solo, Entwistle made several, unsuccessful attempts using a Danelectro bass and ended up using a Fender Jazz instead. His nonchalant stance on stage undermined his dexterous playing with all four fingers of the right hand moving at a rapid rate. Unusually, the song has three upward key changes, which gives it that propulsive edge. These were added by Townshend during his third demo, and he has stated that this was another idea borrowed from the Kinks. He also cited Mose Allison's 'Young Man Blues' which was regularly played live by The Who as an inspiration.

Released as the third single on 29 October 1965 – a full month before the album – it sold around 300,000 copies and reached number two in the UK chart. It was kept off the top spot by the Seekers' bland 'The Carnival Is Over' which was the antithesis of The Who's song. Nonetheless, it was their best-selling record thus far and remained in the charts for a total of ten weeks. When it was released in America on 20 November, it stalled at a miserable 74 on the Billboard chart due to a lack of promotion and Decca's apathy towards the band. 'My Generation' is a near-perfect representation of The Who's '60s live sound, and unsurprisingly, it quickly became the closing number in their set. During the climax, Townshend would often pound his Rickenbacker down onto the stage to achieve the tortured sounds and then spear the neck of the guitar into his speaker cabinet. A near fifteen-minute version appears on the 1970 *Live at Leeds* album. In the '70s, it was often performed as part of an extended medley in a slow blues style as 'My Generation Blues'.

'The Kids Are Alright' 3:04 (Pete Townshend)

Perhaps more than any other song, 'The Kids Are Alright' is the closest The Who came to a Mod anthem and no better way of launching side two of the debut album. With its carefree attitude – 'I don't mind other guys dancing with my girl' – this is Townshend identifying with the band's teenage audience. It's one of his earliest compositions where musically, he has one foot in the seventeenth century. Lambert introduced Townshend to some of his favourite classical composers, most notably Henry Purcell. As a result, the guitarist began to incorporate a baroque influence with the suspended chords in his songs. 'The Kids Are Alright' is an early example, as is 'I'm A Boy' released the following year. A classical harmonic style is evident in the chorus and the song's buoyant, wide-eyed charm also brings to mind the Beatles in their mid-'60s, pre-cynical, period. Moon's brisk drumming, however, keeps the song firmly grounded in Who territory. The rich choral harmonies are closer to the uniquely British church choir tradition than the sunny, west-coast style of the Beach Boys.

It was released as a belated single in the UK by Brunswick Records on 12 August 1966. This was part of Shel Talmy's tit-for-tat dispute with The Who and their new label Reaction. With no promotion from the band who disowned the single, it faltered at 41 in the UK chart while 'I'm A Boy', released by Reaction two weeks later, reached number two. Although it's not in the same league as 'I'm A Boy', 'The Kids Are Alright' deserved to do better given that it's one of The Who's best remembered and most radio-friendly songs from this era. The single release in America in July 1966 with 'A Legal Matter' as the B side stalled outside the Billboard top 100.

Unsurprisingly, it was another stage favourite. When it was played live in later years, the song was often extended with an improvised section at the end. It was performed during the 50th anniversary 2014 to 2016 tours. An excerpt from the song features at the end of the song 'Helpless Dancer' on the 1973 *Quadrophenia* album. It also provided the title for the 1979 Who documentary and companion soundtrack album.

The Rockin' Vickers, who featured future Motorhead frontman Ian 'Lemmy' Kilmister on guitar, lifted 'The Kids Are Alright' for their song 'It's Alright'. This was possibly at the suggestion of Shel Talmy who produced both versions. It's Alright' was released as a single in March 1966 but disappeared without a trace. The Kids Are Alright' was one of Keith Moon's favourite Who songs and appears on his 1975 solo album *Two Sides of the Moon*. It's also been covered by countless other artists including Eddie and the Hot Rods, Green Day and Pearl Jam.

'Please, Please, Please' 2:45 (James Brown, Johnny Terry)

Like 'I Don't Mind' on side one of the vinyl LP, this song was included as a concession to Daltrey who felt the album should be more representative of the band's R&B roots and live repertoire. The original version was also another James Brown and the Famous Flames song. It was their debut single and reached number six in the American R&B chart in the summer of 1956. Like 'I'm A Man', 'Please, Please, Please' is built around a stop-time arrangement although this is more in the walking blues style. Nicky Hopkins' ever-present piano embellishments stand out and Moon ends the song with a roll across the snare drum.

'It's Not True' 2:31 (Pete Townshend)

A forerunner of the off the wall compositional style that would propel songs like 'Substitute', 'I'm A Boy' and 'Happy Jack' into the charts the following year. Here, the protagonist is refuting rumours regarding his status and family background. Like several of Townshend's early songs, lines like 'I weren't born in Baghdad, I'm not half-Chinese either' seem almost politically incorrect by current standards. Townshend had pretty much disowned the song by the time the album was released. It's fairly typical early Who fare however with a catchy choral hook and Moon, Entwistle and Nicky Hopkins maintaining the song's jaunty, foot-tapping momentum.

'I'm a Man' 3:21 (Bo Diddley AKA Ellas McDaniel)

The album's third and final cover. It was the flipside to a number one hit on the Billboard R&B chart for Bo Diddley in 1955 when the future members of The Who were still in short trousers. The Muddy Waters influenced stop-time blues pattern clearly left an impression which they recreate to perfection. The same year The Who recorded the song, it was also a popular stage number for the Yardbirds. It was allegedly omitted from the American release *The Who Sings My Generation* because of its sexual content, which is surprising given the song's vintage and the fact that the Yardbirds had a Stateside hit single with their version in 1965. A six-minute version recorded at New York's Radio City Music Hall in 1989 is included on the 1994 *Thirty Years of Maximum R&B* box-set.

'A Legal Matter' 2:48 (Pete Townshend)

This has the distinction of being the first Who song to feature Townshend on lead vocals. It's an atypical song – which is perhaps why Daltrey didn't sing it – about a man, desperate to avoid wedlock, who's being pursued by a girl for breach of promise. Daltrey's first marriage was short-lived at the time and he was divorced five years later. Townshend later admitted that although he was a twenty-year-old eligible bachelor when he recorded the song, he was more in need of a maid than a wife. He did, however, get married on 20 May 1968 – the day after his 23rd birthday – to fashion designer Karen Astley.

Townshend's falsetto – and slightly accented – delivery has a vulnerability that's absent from Daltrey's machismo, R&B inflected style elsewhere on the album. It includes other Who anomalies; the twangy guitar picking is in the country-style supported by Nicky Hopkins' swinging, boogie-woogie piano. Drums and bass are simple but very effective. The song goes full circle, beginning and ending with the same ringing guitar line. The guitar part and the song's jaunty style is especially reminiscent of the Rolling Stones' 'The Last Time' released as a single in February 1965.

'A Legal Matter' was rush-released as a single on 7 March 1966 by Brunswick in response to The Who's independent single 'Substitute' released a few days earlier on the Reaction label. Not an obvious single despite being a decent song, it unsurprisingly faltered at 32 in the UK chart whereas 'Substitute' reached number five. In America, it was released by Decca as the B side to 'The Kids Are Alright' A-side in July 1966 and typically failed to chart.

'The Ox' 3:50 (Pete Townshend, John Entwistle, Keith Moon, Nicky Hopkins)

Surprisingly, the album concludes with an instrumental which borrows Entwistle's nickname for the title. It's modelled on the Surfaris' surf-rock instrumentals 'Waikiki Run' and 'Wipe Out' – especially the relentless drumming – although it's more west London than west coast California. It thunders along at a lively pace and the band improvised in the studio to capture the sound and energy of a stage performance, perhaps more so than any other track on the album. Moon in particular, who had a penchant for surf music, excels on this track with his tom-toms dominating along with Nicky Hopkins' stunning, rhythmic piano fills. Townshend's tortured guitar tones pre-empt Jimi Hendrix who burst onto the scene a year later.

In August 1966, 'The Ox' was the B side to the European single release of 'The Kids Are Alright'. The 2009 deluxe edition of *The Who Sell Out* includes the jingle 'Top Gear' derived from this track.

Related Tracks

The tracks in this section were recorded between 1964 and 1966 with several from the *My Generation* sessions. With the exception of the High Numbers' songs, they were produced by Shel Talmy, unless stated otherwise.

'Zoot Suit' 1:57 b/w 'I'm the Face' 2:32 (Peter Meaden)

Publicist Peter Meaden penned the lyrics to both sides of the High Numbers only record in the hope they would become Mod anthems. That wasn't to be and the single released on 3 July 1964 by Fontana Records was destined to become a collector's item, selling only half of the 1000 copies pressed. It was recorded at Philips' studios, Marble Arch in June with Chris Parmenter and Jack Baverstock producing.

The tune for 'Zoot Suit' is borrowed from a song called 'Misery,' released by American R&B group the Dynamics in 1963. Although Zoot suits originated in America in the 1940s, the name was adopted for a very different style worn by fashion-conscious Mods in the '60s. Townshend adapted the line 'I wear a Zoot suit jacket with side vents five inches long' nine years later for the *Quadrophenia* song 'Cut My Hair'. The tune for 'I'm The Face' was lifted from the song 'I Got Love If You Want It' which appeared on the Kinks' eponymous debut album that same year. It was written by American blues artist Slim Harpo who originally released it as a single B side in 1957. 'Face' is a term used by mods to reference one of their own who dresses sharp and acts cool.

'Zoot Suit' is an agreeable pop song with Townshend's tremolo guitar playing displaying his Hank Marvin influences. 'I'm the Face' is closer to the early Who R&B sound with fine harmonica from Daltrey and piano from Allen Ellert. Townshend's twangy guitar break, on the other hand, is closer to west-coast surf rock. Both songs are crisply produced and worthy precursors of the '60's Who sound. The single was reissued as a limited edition picture disc in March 1980. Both songs appeared on the 1994 *Thirty Years of Maximum R&B* box-set and 'I'm the Face' was included on the 1974 *Odds & Sods* LP.

'Here 'Tis' 2:08 (Ellas McDaniel)

A lively R&B tune recorded as the High Numbers. Townshend's jangly guitar and Daltrey's spirited vocal and harmonica do full justice to the 1962 Bo Diddley original. It was recorded in June 1964 during the same sessions as 'Zoot Suit' and 'I'm the Face' but went unreleased until the 1994 *Thirty Years of Maximum R&B* box-set. It was also covered by the Yardbirds.

'I Can't Explain' 2:04 (Pete Townshend)

A calculated song to introduce The Who to the singles chart and a deliberate Kinks pastiche designed to appeal to Shel Talmy. It did the trick, in early November 1964 The Who entered Pye Records Studio, London to record their debut record with Talmy at the helm. The session lasted just two hours and as was typical for unproven bands at the time, the producer brought in additional musicians as an insurance measure. This included twenty-year-old Jimmy Page, one of London's hottest young session guitarists. Justifiably, Townshend insisted that he play lead and Page was relegated to doubling the rhythm guitar parts although his contributions did not make the finished recording. Talmy enlisted vocal trio the Ivy League to sweeten the backing harmonies as he wasn't impressed by The Who's own attempts. Perry Ford plays piano.

The song's premise is simple enough; the young protagonist is frustrated over his inability to articulate his true feelings to the girl he loves. It has also been suggested, not least by Townshend himself, that drugs might be the cause of his dilemma. Daltrey was unsure of the lyrics at first; the song's vulnerability didn't quite suit his machismo stage persona. He would have similar doubts about later Who songs but, as is the case here, he would soon grow into, and inhabit the songs.

Although this is the band's debut record, from the very go, it's characteristic Who. Entwistle's bass lines are tight, underpinning Townshend's blistering Rickenbacker twelve-string chords and Moon's rampant drum barrage. As acknowledged by Townshend, the staccato riff owes a good deal to the Kinks' 'You Really Got Me' which topped the UK singles charts in September 1964. Daltrey turns in an assured and attacking vocal performance offset by the – not overly – sweet harmonies which add a touch of the west coast surf sound. In addition to lead vocals, Daltrey plays tambourine.

The Who's debut single was released on 15 January 1965 in the UK. Competition that month included the number one hits 'I Feel Fine' by the Beatles and 'Go Now' by the Moody Blues. Following initial sales, 'I Can't Explain' stalled and began to slide back down the charts. An appearance on the TV pop weekly *Ready Steady Go!* and three consecutive appearances on BBC1's *Top Of The Pops* prompted a resurgence of sales, eventually peaking at number eight on the 8 April 1965. In America, it was released in December 1964, but due to a lack of promotion by Decca – which would be a sign of things to come – it stalled at 93 in the Billboard chart. Despite the song's success, it earned The Who just 1,000 pounds as a result of the meagre two and a half per cent royalty rate in Talmy's contract. After much persuasion from Lambert and Stamp, this was increased to four per cent for later records, but this was still way below what most bands were earning.

The staying power of the band's debut single is exemplified by the fact that 'I Can't Explain' would nearly always be the opening song for The Who's shows for years to come. Townshend played guitar on a cover version by Yvonne Elliman, released as a single in August 1973 and a track on her *Food Of Love* album. His riff was sampled by Fatboy Slim for 'Going Out Of My Head' which featured on the DJ's 1996 album *Living Through Chemistry* and released as a single in 1997.

'Bald Headed Woman' 2:32 (Shel Talmy)

A traditional blues song and a rather drab one at that, this was not only the B side to 'I Can't Explain', but also a track on the Kinks' 1964 self-titled debut album. In a shrewd move, Talmy took the credit for writing the song, thus earning royalties on the back of Townshend's successful A side. Although Jimmy Page's guitar soloing on 'I Can't Explain' is pure myth, he did add lead lines to this song with Townshend playing rhythm. It required his fuzz box, which he refused to allow Townshend to use. Daltrey's rampant harmonica solo is better than his deep and bluesy vocal drawl. Like 'I Can't Explain', the Ivy League provide backing vocals.

'Anyway, Anyhow, Anywhere' 2:41 (Pete Townshend, Roger Daltrey)

Released on 24 May 1965 in glorious mono, 'Anyway, Anyhow, Anywhere' was The Who's second single. The song's title and attitude were influenced by jazz saxophonist Charlie Parker whose, free improvisational style impressed Townshend. The song, like 'My Generation', is full of bluster and bravado, providing an ideal vehicle for Daltrey's macho, no-nonsense persona. Compared with 'I Can't Explain', it has a harder edge, designed to introduce record buyers to their rawer, live sound. For a while, it was adopted as the theme song for *Ready Steady Go!* When the song was performed on the show in July 1965, they appeared in their 'pop art' style stage wear for the first time including Townshend's union jack jacket. The performance is one of the highlights of the 1979 *The Kids Are Alright* documentary.

During rehearsals, Daltrey altered some of Townshend's verses to project a tougher image. As a result, it was the first, and last credited songwriting collaboration between the pair. It was recorded in April during the initial sessions for *My Generation*. When it was presented to Decca in America, they thought the tapes were faulty due to the ear-piercing feedback from Townshend's Rickenbacker. Marketed by Lambert and Stamp as 'the first pop art record', it reached number ten in the UK, but unsurprisingly, given Decca's lack of confidence, it failed to chart in America.

The experience and confidence gained through constant gigging pays dividends here. For its time, 'Anyway, Anyhow, Anywhere' is unconventionally structured. The call and response verses and chorus are almost indistinguishable while the bridge occupies more than half the song. Townshend's opening guitar salvo is in 6/4 while the rest of the song is in more common 4/4 time. The unaccompanied, opening guitar figure, followed by Daltrey's short, acapella vocal section before Moon leads the full band in would become a familiar trait of Who songs that can also be found in 'The Kids Are Alright'. Moon's precision drum volleys are superbly underpinned by Entwistle. Townshend's solo begins with a trademark windmill-arm power chord followed by creative use of distortion and feedback. A second, overdubbed guitar and Hopkins' tasteful piano playing add weight and substance to the song. As such, it wasn't the easiest of Who songs to pull off live and following 1965, it rarely featured in the setlist. The controlled feedback is one of the earliest examples on record even though the Beatles' 'I Feel Fine' is often credited as the first popular song to employ the technique.

'Daddy Rolling Stone' 2:49 (Otis Blackwell)

The B side to the UK release of the 'Anyway, Anyhow, Anywhere' single. It resurfaced on the 1994 *Thirty Years of Maximum R&B* box-set and an alternate, marginally longer version appeared on the 2002 reissue of *My Generation*. Composer Otis Blackwell wrote hits for rock and roll artists like Elvis Presley and Jerry Lee Lewis, but this is one of his lesser-known tunes. An early stage favourite, Daltrey's confident singing, drenched in reverb, demonstrates just how adaptable his voice was in those days. It brings to mind Van Morrison's performance of 'Baby Please Don't Go', a UK hit for Them in February 1965.

'Anytime You Want Me' 2:38 (Jerry Ragovoy, Garnet Mimms)

The American and Australian B side to 'Anyway, Anyhow, Anywhere'. The writer, American soul singer Garnet Mimms was popular in the 1960s and '70s. It's a slow ballad with a walking bass line, piano, sweet harmonies and a soulful vocal from Daltrey. This, along with an acapella version, was a bonus track on the 2002 deluxe edition of *My Generation*.

'Shout and Shimmy' 3:20 (James Brown)

The UK B side of the 'My Generation' single. It was recorded in April 1965 for the album but was displaced following the decision to include more original songs. Like the other covers recorded at the time, it was regularly performed live before the setlist was re-appraised in 1966 to include more of Townshend's songs.

Like the 1962 original by James Brown and The Famous Flames, The Who's raucous, good-time version unashamedly borrows from the Isley Brothers' 1959 R&B stomper 'Shout' which was a 1964 UK hit for Lulu and the Luvvers. The Who resurrected 'Shout and Shimmy' for the 1979 documentary *The Kids Are Alright* although it didn't appear on the companion soundtrack album. It remained unreleased in America until it surfaced as the opening track on the 1985 compilation *Who's Missing*.

'Circles (Instant Party)' 3:12 Pete Townshend)

Recorded on 13 January 1966, 'Circles' was the final session with producer Shel Talmy. It was the proposed follow up single to 'My Generation' for release on the Brunswick label. The Who had other ideas and independently recorded and released 'Substitute', breaching their contract with Talmy. 'Circles' was retitled 'Instant Party' for the B side to the UK 'A Legal Matter' single. It made its American debut in April 1966 as the closing track on *The Who Sings My Generation* album.

29

The song certainly lives up to its name, swimming around the listener to dizzy effect with Entwistle's French horn doubling the vocal lines. The bass salvos and Moon's drumming are stunning, especially during the extended instrumental sequence at 1:58. Moon is also included in the backing vocals.

For The Who produced version of 'Circles', see the *Ready Steady Who* EP chapter.

'Instant Party Mixture' 3:24 (Pete Townshend)
This is not to be confused with the song 'Instant Party' – AKA 'Circles'. Produced by Shel Talmy, it was recorded in January 1966 as the intended B side for the proposed Brunswick single 'Circles'. It's an entertaining pastiche of Dion's 'Runaround Sue', an international chart-topper in 1961. The doo-wop harmonies, spoken interruptions from Townshend, Moon and Entwistle, handclap rhythm, nonsense lyrics, and throw away ending all add to its charm.

'Leaving Here' 2:12 (Brian Holland, Lamont Dozier, Eddie Holland)
Recorded in March 1965, this first appeared on the 1985 *Who's Missing* compilation and later, on the 1998 remaster of *Odds & Sods*. Together with 'Lubie (Come Back Home)' and 'Motoring', it was intended for the debut album, originally scheduled for release in the summer of '65. All three were jettisoned in favour of original compositions from Townshend. It was also a contender as the follow-up single to 'I Can't Explain' and several versions were recorded. None were released and ironically fellow Mod group The Birds had a UK hit with 'Leaving Here' in 1965. An alternate version appears on the 1994 *Thirty Years of Maximum R&B* box-set and it was also a bonus track on the 2002 reissue of *My Generation*.

The Eddie Holland original released in December 1963 was a minor Stateside hit. It was also treated to an unlikely cover by UK metal rockers Motorhead in 1977.

'Lubie (Come Back Home)' 3:37 (Paul Revere, Mark Lindsay)
The original version of this song was released as a single in March 1964 by Paul Revere and the Raiders under the title 'Louie, Go Home'. In 1964, a young David Bowie recorded a cover of the same song. It was the B side to his debut single 'Liza Jane', released under the name Davie Jones with the King Bees. The Who's version was recorded at IBC Studios in April 1965. This is another song that first appeared on the 1985 *Who's Missing* LP and featured as a bonus track on the 2002 deluxe edition of *My Generation*.

'Motoring' 2:52 (Ivy Jo Hunter, Phil Jones, William "Mickey" Stevenson)
This less familiar Motown song was recorded in April 1965 during the *My*

Generation sessions to appeal to The Who's Mod following. It didn't see the
light of day until 1987 however, courtesy of the *Two's Missing* compilation.
It was also another bonus song on the 2002 reissue of *My Generation*. The
original version by Martha Reeves & The Vandellas was the B side to the 1965
hit single 'Nowhere to Run'.

'Good Lovin' 1:49 (Rudy Clark, Arthur Resnick)
The Who recorded their version of this song in June 1965 for the BBC radio
program *Top Gear*. It would later appear on the *BBC Sessions* collection
released on 15 February 2000. An energetic rock and roll tune, Daltrey is in
excellent, soulful form with rousing vocal backing. In 1966, the Young Rascals
enjoyed a number one American hit single with their version.

'Just You and Me, Darling' 2:01 (James Brown)
Another 1965 recording for the BBC included on The Who's *BBC Sessions*
in 2000. Daltrey delivers a pretty convincing James Brown impression and
Townshend's twangy guitar break is suitably edgy.

Ready Steady Who (EP) (1966)

Personnel:
Roger Daltrey: lead vocals, backing vocals
Pete Townshend: guitar, lead vocals, backing vocals
John Entwistle: bass, backing vocals, brass
Keith Moon: drums, lead vocals, backing vocals
Produced by: Kit Lambert, The Who
Engineered by: Paul Clay
Recorded at: Pye Studios, Olympic Sound Studios, IBC Recording Studios, London,
12 February – 11 October 1966
Release date: 11 November 1966
Record label: Reaction/Polydor
Highest chart place: UK: 1
Running time: 11:05

On the 18 October 1966, The Who pre-recorded a sixteen-minute sequence for the UK TV music show *Ready Steady Go!* It was broadcast on the 21 October, but ITV refused permission for the recording to be used for a proposed EP. Five studio tracks were compiled instead and The Who's first EP preceded the second album, *A Quick One,* by just four weeks. Although only 'Circles' featured on the LP, the others surfaced as bonus tracks on the 1995 CD. It was released in the UK only on seven-inch vinyl; the EP format wasn't popular in America.

In December 1966, *Ready Steady Who* spent two weeks at number one in the UK chart before briefly making way for a Jim Reeves Christmas EP. Three months earlier, Reeves' 'Distant Drums' had kept The Who's 'I'm A Boy' single off the top spot. *Ready Steady Who* returned to the top for a further two weeks in January 1967. It was finally usurped by the Beach Boys' *Hits* EP which coincidentally closes with 'Barbara Ann', the final song on *Ready Steady Who*.

'Disguises' 3:10 (Pete Townshend)

Regarded by many as one of The Who's most underrated songs despite the EP's chart success. It was initially recorded at IBC/Pye Studios, London on 14 June 1966 along with 'I'm a Boy' and completed on 31 July. They are the earliest recordings to be credited to Kit Lambert as producer. Both songs were written for the aborted concept album 'Quads'. Like 'I'm a Boy', the protagonist is in a confused state of mind, gender-wise, and disguises are a metaphor for his girlfriend's elusive personality.

The song has a hypnotic, psychedelic vibe with a touch of raga rock – played by Entwistle on French horn – during the instrumental break. At Lambert's suggestion, unusual instrumentation like claves are incorporated; even at this early stage, he was attempting to compete with the Beatles. A circular, rhythm guitar and bass pattern drive the song and the free-form vocal coda clearly owes a debt to the Fab Four. 'Disguises' debuted in America on the 1968 compilation *Magic Bus: The Who on Tour*. A cover version by Mod revivalists The Jam appeared on the B-side of their 1981 single 'Funeral Pyre'.

'Circles' 2:27 (Pete Townshend)

The Who's own version of a song they originally recorded with Shel Talmy in January 1966 – see previous chapter. This version was recorded shortly after and production is credited to The Who. Under the alternating titles 'Circles' and 'Instant Party' it made its debut in the UK on 4 March 1966 as the B side to the 'Substitute' single before being replaced by the non-Who track 'Waltz for a Pig'. Arrangement wise there is little to distinguish this version from Talmy's although it's taken at a faster tempo and features a lead vocal from Townshend in the middle-eight. Entwistle's horn is also more prominent in the mix and the harmonies are tighter.

'Circles' was also recorded by the unlikely named Fleur-De-Lys who released their single version – produced by Jimmy Page – on 18 March 1966.

'Batman' 1:22 (Neal Hefti)

The opening track on side two of the EP was recorded, with and without vocals, on 30 and 31 August 1966 at IBC/Pye Studios. During the same sessions, they also cut 'Barbara Ann', 'Heat Wave' and the Everly Brothers' 'Man With Money'. *Batman* was a hugely popular TV show in the 1960s thanks to its kitsch portrayal of the caped crusader. The theme's light-hearted tone struck a chord – or rather three chords – with several bands including the Kinks and The Jam. Twangy guitar and propulsive bass are to the fore and the drums are rampant if a tad sloppy. 'Batman' occasionally provided a rousing opening to The Who's stage set in 1966.

'Bucket T' 2:07 (Don Altfield, Roger Christian, Dean Torrence)

'Bucket T' and 'Barbara Ann' are two of Keith Moon's favourite songs and were included to placate the drummer. He was also permitted to sing on this song and the four-part harmonies, complete with American accents, are not a million miles from Jan and Dean's original. It also benefits from Entwistle's trumpet and tuba solos. Following its release as a single in several European countries, it was an unexpected number one hit in Sweden in February 1967 thanks to an appearance on local TV. 'Bucket T' was recorded at IBC/Pye Studios on 11 October 1966. The song's debut release in America was on the 1968 compilation album *Magic Bus: The Who on Tour*.

'Barbara Ann' 1:59 (Fred Fassert)

Although the original version was a top twenty US hit for the doo-wop group the Regents in 1961, it's the Beach Boys' 1966 hit that informs The Who's version of 'Barbara Ann'. Again, the massed harmonies are by no means shabby and the pace of the song makes the Beach Boys' version seem almost pedestrian. Moon's cymbal splashes are everywhere and his falsetto lead vocal on the choral hook 'Ba Ba Ba Ba Barbara Ann' is conspicuously low in the mix. During the instrumental break, the acoustic guitar on the Beach Boys' version is replaced with a slide whistle solo, probably for the first, and last, time on a pop record. 'Barbara Ann' was regularly performed live by The Who and featured in the setlist of their first tour of North America in 1967. The song was performed again by Moon for the 1979 *The Kids Are Alright* documentary.

Related Tracks

'My Generation / Land of Hope and Glory' 2.05 (Pete Townshend, Edward Elgar)

Classical music purists should look away now. This unlikely pairing was recorded in October 1966 for a special edition of *Ready Steady Go!* It was rejected, and a combined 'My Generation / Rule Britannia' was used instead. The programme had provided plenty of exposure for The Who but was taken off the air in December that year. Although intended for the *Ready Steady Who* EP, it went unreleased until the 1995 reissue of *A Quick One* as a bonus track. Basically, this is a stripped-down version of 'My Generation' that morphs into a deliberately ramshackle 'Land of Hope and Glory'. If for no other reason, the bass and drums barrage that links the two sections makes this worth hearing.

A Quick One (1966)

Personnel:
Roger Daltrey: lead vocals, trombone on 'Cobwebs and Strange'
Pete Townshend: guitar, backing vocals, co-lead vocals on 'A Quick One, While He's Away', tin whistle on 'Cobwebs and Strange'
John Entwistle: bass, backing vocals, lead vocals on 'Boris the Spider', 'Whiskey Man' and co-lead vocals on 'A Quick One, While He's Away', French horn, trumpet on 'Cobwebs and Strange'
Keith Moon: drums, lead vocals on 'I Need You', tuba on 'Cobwebs and Strange'
Produced by: Kit Lambert
Recorded at: IBC Studios, London, Regent Sound Studios, London and Pye Studios, CBS Studios, London, September – November 1966
Release date: UK: 9 December 1966, USA: May 1967
Record label: UK: Reaction/Polydor, USA: Decca, MCA
Highest chart places: UK: 4, USA: 51
Running time: UK: 31:48, USA: 32:18

1966 was a particularly good year for classic albums with *Pet Sounds*, *Revolver*, *Aftermath*, *Face to Face* and *Blonde on Blonde* amongst many others. Although dismissive of the Beach Boys and the Beatles, Pete Townshend viewed the Rolling Stones and the Kinks as kindred spirits and revered Bob Dylan. The Who's second album may not have scaled the same heights as some of the competition, but like the band's lead singer, *A Quick One* punches well above its weight.

In early 1966, prior to the release of the fourth single 'Substitute', The Who signed to Robert Stigwood's Reaction Records. It was the first move to break their unfavourable recording contract with producer Shel Talmy. Later, The Who's management New Action came to a settlement that gave Talmy a lucrative five per cent from their recordings over the next five years. This would include best-selling albums *Tommy* and *Who's Next* even though Talmy had no involvement with the recordings. Although The Who were still tied to Decca Records in America, *A Quick One* was released on the Reaction/Polydor label in the UK and Europe.

The publishing deal arranged with Essex Music by Chris Stamp was that each band member would contribute two songs for which they would receive an advance of £500. Although neither Roger Daltrey, John Entwistle or Keith Moon had any songwriting experience, It was designed to encourage their creative input and boost their income. With composer royalties from the first album and singles, Townshend was earning far more than his bandmates. The resulting album is far more cohesive than one might expect. The pressure was on Townshend to provide the hit singles which he dubbed 'power pop'. From 1965 to '67 he averaged around one every four months, the same rate as Lennon & McCartney and Jagger & Richards.

Compared with the first album, *A Quick One* was recorded over a comparatively lean two month period in the Autumn of 1966. Kit Lambert perfected his craft as a producer as the album progressed and he utilised several studios around London. It was Townshend however, who produced the first song of 1966, 'Substitute' and once again, it was his accomplished demos that provided the basis for the recordings. He also assisted the others, including Daltrey's 'See My Way' which was demoed in Townshend's home studio. Despite contributions from all members, Townshend's songs dominate and there is just one cover version.

As was common practice at the time – even for the Beatles – the album was rebranded for the American market with a different title (*Happy Jack*), track listing and cover artwork. In the UK, singles and albums were regarded as separate entities, but in America, albums were often marketed to capitalise on the success of a recent hit song, in this case 'Happy Jack', their highest charting US single at the time.

To downplay the Talmy-produced *My Generation*, Townshend described *A Quick One* as the first real Who album. It was certainly a superior piece of work and the music press agreed. In the UK, *Melody Maker* called it 'An incredible new album' and in America, *Crawdaddy* was equally smitten. According to Townshend, Paul McCartney was very enthusiastic about *A Quick One* and claimed the album inspired the Beatles later work. In 1967, Townshend also cited McCartney as a source of inspiration, singling out 'Eleanor Rigby'.

The Who capitalised on their run of UK hit singles with TV appearances in Britain and France, headlining package tours in the UK, a performance at the *NME* Poll Winners Concert on 1 May, BBC radio sessions and countless interviews. They played an average of fifteen dates per month in 1966, including several treks around mainland Europe. Now a major headlining act, they were especially popular in Germany, Austria and Scandinavia. Stamp directed several promotional films of The Who around London and gigs were filmed for broadcast on American and Canadian television. With 'My Generation' already established as the show closer, and several of Townshend's songs in the setlist, The Who's live performances in 1966 still relied on cover versions.

The pop-art cover artwork for *A Quick One* was by renowned illustrator Alan Aldridge. The colourful image depicting the four members of The Who in performance is less detailed and bolder in style than much of his later work. The eye-catching effect is heightened by the song titles streaming in stylised lettering from the instruments, or in Daltrey's case, mouth. By the close of 1966 when the album was released, Townshend declared that The Who had finished with pop-art and that the Mod subculture was outdated. For the next album, he would set his musical sights higher still. There was also the not inconsiderable matter of North America to address.

'Run Run Run' 2:44 (Pete Townshend)
The improvement in production on this album is apparent from the start. The song's main riff and choral hook is basic, but it's a compelling slice of pop-rock

nonetheless. The main point of interest is the instrumentation with Entwistle's upfront bass line vying with Townshend's guitar for attention. After frequent live performances, the playing by both men had improved considerably since the previous album. In the song, the protagonist is giving sound advice to a girl who's plagued with bad luck. He clearly doesn't have her best interests at heart because there's a sting in the tale with the final line 'Whenever you run, I'll be following you'.

'Run Run Run' had been recorded earlier in 1966 by two London based Mod groups, the Birds featuring Ronnie Wood on guitar and The Cat with John 'Speedy' Keen on drums and Chris Thomas on guitar. Townshend produced The Cat's version and Thomas returned the favour when he produced Townshend's solo albums in the 1980s. Keen reciprocated by supplying the opening song 'Armenia City in the Sky' for *The Who Sell Out* album.

'Boris the Spider' 2:29 (John Entwistle)

This has the distinction of being Entwistle's first individual composition on a Who album. It also remains his best-known song and was regularly in demand by audiences during The Who's live performances. It was also allegedly Jimi Hendrix's favourite Who song, which irked Townshend given the depth of his own compositions and his admiration for the American guitarist.

Entwistle had already written and demoed 'Whiskey Man' for the album, and when Townshend asked if he had another song available to fulfil the band's publishing deal, 'Boris the Spider' was virtually made-up on the spot. Entwistle later admitted that it was the fastest song he ever wrote. He already had a title, he and his Rolling Stones drinking buddies Bill Wyman and Charlie Watts had spent an evening concocting suitable Christian names for animals. Entwistle remembered horror movie legend Boris Karloff and decided that his was an appropriate moniker for a 'creepy, crawly' creature like a spider. Townshend was particularly impressed by the haunting chords which fuelled his own songwriting. The Who recorded the song in early October 1966 with the bassist also providing the lead vocals – it's hard to imagine either Daltrey or Townshend singing it.

The main riff was reused by Entwistle in the sequel 'My Size' which opened his 1971 solo album *Smash Your Head Against the Wall*. It was written to appease Entwistle's manager who wanted 'Boris the Spider' on the album. Despite the song's sinister overtones and Entwistle's deep, gravelly vocals in the chorus accompanied by trebly bass, the song has a child-friendly innocence that brings to mind spooky nursery rhymes and Halloween. For the 'creepy crawly' bridge, he reverts to singing in falsetto.

While it's undoubtedly a novelty song, 'Boris the Spider' has an endearing charm that's sustained it over the years, even after Entwistle's passing in 2002. Townshend later admitted that as The Who's principal songwriter, it was band politics and his own vanity that prevented 'Boris the Spider' from being released as a single. It did appear in that format in 1967 with an unlikely cover version by American psychedelic rockers the Kords although it failed to trouble the charts. Encouraged by 'Boris the Spider', every future Who album in his lifetime, with the exception of *Quadrophenia*, would include at least one Entwistle composition.

'I Need You' 2:25 (Keith Moon)

Even if fans anticipated something out of the ordinary from Moon, this song still surprised. It's melodic and his restrained lead vocal is not too bad either. With busy drumming to the fore, guitar is virtually absent, leaving harpsichord – beautifully played by Entwistle – to provide the lead fills. The production is spacious and the stereo panning is superb, especially during the bridge which features harpsichord, sound effects and a John Lennon style spoken voice. It's a not too veiled sideswipe at the Beatles' secret band language devised to exclude outsiders from their conversions. Depending upon who you believe, the man responsible was either Who road manager Neville Chesters, a Yorkshireman affecting a Liverpool accent or Gordon Molland, a Liverpudlian roadie doing a John Lennon impression.

'Whiskey Man' 2:57 (John Entwistle)

A fine example of Entwistle's droll sense of humour and an ode to an imaginary drinking partner. The song was inspired by the 1966 western *Ride Beyond Vengeance*, released in the UK as *Night Of The Tiger*. In the film, the town drunk Elwood Coates, played by Claude Akins, has an imaginary friend called 'Whiskey Man'. Entwistle's incessant riff is simple but effective and not too far removed from Duane Eddy's 1959 take on the 'Peter Gunn' theme. It underscores his tuneful and double-tracked lead vocal with colourful French horn embellishments during the bridge. Moon is uncharacteristically restrained for the most part. 'Whiskey Man' was the B side of the 'Happy Jack' single release in America in March 1967. It was also released in Japan as an A side, backed by 'Boris the Spider'.

'Heat Wave' 1:57 (Brian Holland, Lamont Dozier, Edward Holland)

With Daltrey conspicuously absent from the previous three songs, he comes into his own here. He cruises his way through this Motown classic with engaging vocal support from Townshend and Entwistle. 'Heat Wave' was a popular stage number for The Who, often opening the set, so its inclusion is not wholly surprising. An earlier version had been recorded for the *My Generation* album but was omitted to make room for more of Townshend's songs. The original was a big hit in America for Martha and the Vandellas in 1963 and was a particular favourite with Mods. The Who's cover inspired a version on the 1979 album *Setting Sons* by The Jam. 'Heat Wave' is absent from the *Happy Jack* album – the American version of *A Quick One* – where it was displaced by the title song.

'Cobwebs and Strange' 2:31 (Keith Moon)

To close side one of the LP, a Who instrumental. It was originally titled 'Showbiz Sonata' and was changed to 'Cobwebs and Strange' in deference to Entwistle's 'Boris the Spider'. Although credited to Moon, the tune and treatment were lifted from the 1960 TV theme 'Eastern Journey' performed by big-band drummer Tony Crombie. Here, Moon matches him for sheer energy and dexterity. In many ways, with its banjo and marching band sound, it's also a throwback to Townshend and Entwistle's early dalliance with trad jazz and skiffle.

To capture the effect of a marching brass band in the studio, producer Lambert had The Who parading up and down past a microphone with Moon playing orchestra cymbals, Townshend pennywhistle, Daltrey trombone and Entwistle trumpet. The backing track was played from a monitor at the far end of the studio which they couldn't hear and therefore were unable to keep in time. As a result, the marching was abandoned, and the piece recorded stationary. Moon also overdubbed drums, Townshend banjo and recorder, and Entwistle tuba. As a tribute to Moon, in 1993 Townshend used 'Cobwebs and Strange' to introduce his band during the *Psychoderelict* solo tour.

'Don't Look Away' 2:54 (Pete Townshend)

To open side two, an uncharacteristically bright and poppy affair from Townshend. Daltrey's double-tracked lead vocals and the backing harmonies are impeccable and a testimony to the album's crystal clear production values. Townshend's atypical, bright guitar picking during the instrumental bridge is in the country rock style of James Burton and Chet Atkins. Love never runs smoothly in Townshend's songs and here he's baring his heart and soul to a girlfriend who's about to walk out on him.

'See My Way' 1:53 (Roger Daltrey)

Daltrey's only song contribution to a Who album is lean in every respect. It's almost a philosophical version of the previous song, he and his partner do not share the same point of view so it's inevitable that they should part. It's a pretty decent tune with a pulsating bass riff and uplifting horn embellishments from Entwistle. At the time, it promised a bright future for Daltrey as a songwriter, but that wasn't to be. It was recorded at Townshend's flat in Wardour Street, London with the guitarist's assistance. Overdubs were added later at IBC Studios. The galloping riff was inspired by Buddy Holly and Daltrey insisted that Moon play in the style of the Crickets' drummer Jerry Allison. Unable to recreate the sound on his normal kit, Moon achieved the desired effect by playing the rhythm on cardboard boxes.

'So Sad About Us' 3:04 (Pete Townshend)

The album's most memorable song and, with the exception of 'A Quick One,

While He's Away', its main claim to fame. If there was ever a hit single that
never was, this is it. With chiming guitars, a driving rhythm, multi-tracked
vocals and infectious choral hook, this is pop perfection. The brief but rising
'La la la la la la' vocal bridge is simply stunning. It was written at the home
of Townshend's friend 'Speedy' Keen and continues the theme of a broken
relationship from the previous two songs.

'So Sad About Us' was recorded as a single by The Merseys earlier the same
year with Lambert producing and released on 29 July 1966. It failed to match
the success of their previous single 'Sorrow' – later covered by David Bowie.
'So Sad About Us' has been covered by several artists, including The Jam as
the B side to their 1978 hit 'Down in the Tube Station at Midnight'. The song's
potential as a Mod anthem was clearly not lost on Paul Weller.

'A Quick One, While He's Away' 9:10 (Pete Townshend)

Lambert encouraged Townshend to write something more ambitious than the
three-minute pop song and the result was 'A Quick One, While He's Away'.
They were also short of material for the album and this filled the ten-minute
deficit. Dubbed a 'mini-opera', in reality, it's six songs stitched together to form
a not entirely convincing story of loneliness, infidelity, guilt and forgiveness.
Consciously or not, Townshend channelled several childhood memories and
anxieties into this piece, including abandonment, isolation, loneliness and
abuse. These themes would return to the composer during his later work,
especially the rock opera *Tommy*. On a purely musical level, it works superbly,
moving through a variety of moods, melodies and tempos.

I 'Her Man's Been Gone' 0.22

In the opening movement, the heroine of the story – who isn't named – has
been left alone by her lover who's been away for almost a year. It's sung in rich
a-cappella harmonies.

II 'Crying Town' 1:37

Her desperation takes hold. Accompanied by a circular, ringing guitar motif,
Daltrey sings in a deliberately slow, accented drawl, a cross between Mick
Jagger and Bob Dylan.

III 'We Have a Remedy' 1:21

She attracts the attention of several admirers. Daltrey reverts to the upper end
of his register backed by sweet harmonies and chiming guitars.

IV 'Ivor the Engine Driver' 1:53

At the suggestion of her friends, the girl becomes involved with a train driver
named Ivor. He was partly inspired by *Ivor the Engine*, a popular British
animated television series set in Wales. It was first broadcast in 1959 and would

have been watched by a young Townshend. Entwistle sings against a brisk, martial-like rhythm and Moon's splashing cymbals.

V 'Soon Be Home' 1:26

Her lover is returning by horse, suitably accompanied by a slow, cowboy-like theme to mimic the horse's plodding pace. Like the opening sequence, it's sung by the full band in Beach Boys style harmony.

VI 'You Are Forgiven' 2:31

She confesses her infidelity to her lover who forgives her. The final sequence is led by Townshend's power chords and lead vocal with great counterpoint backing, building to a satisfying finale. It has a classical harmonic style but costs prevented the use of strings so they compromised with the chiming vocal line 'Cello, cello, cello' instead. When the rising coda was performed on stage, it was always an intense, emotionally charged moment for Townshend.

'A Quick One, While He's Away' made its debut live appearance at the Saville Theatre, London in January 1967. It was also performed in America later that year including the Monterey Pop Festival. It formed The Who's ten-minute slot during *The Rolling Stones Rock and Roll Circus* extravaganza on 11 December 1968. Despite an impressive line-up of acts, The Who billed as special guests stole the show from everyone, including the Stones who hadn't played live since April 1967. The 1970 *Live At Leeds* version is first rate, albeit slightly truncated and Townshend introduces the song as 'Tommy's parents'. The word 'girl' is also substituted with 'Girl Guide', perhaps in recognition of Townshend's bitter experiences as a Sea Scout. It was dropped from the setlist soon after but was resurrected in its entirety during the 50th-anniversary tour. It's not an obvious song to cover but American rockers Green Day did just that in 2009. They also performed the song live.

Related Tracks

'Substitute' 3:47 (Pete Townshend)

If the first three Who singles were essentially youth anthems, 'Substitute' heralded a more personal, introspective side to Townshend's songwriting. For me, it's the first in a quartet of classic singles – which includes 'I'm a Boy', 'Pictures of Lily' and 'I Can See For Miles' – released in 1966 and '67. 'Substitute' came about simply because Townshend liked the rhythmic quality of the word as sung by Smokey Robinson in 'Tracks Of My Tears', his favourite song at the time. The riff was lifted from a song called 'Where Is My Girl' by Robb Storme & The Whispers, a record that Townshend had reviewed for UK music weekly *Melody Maker*. In a move to break free from their recording contract with Shel Talmy, 'Substitute' was recorded on the 12 February 1966 at

Olympic Studios, London with Townshend producing for the first time. It was released on the Reaction label in the UK on 4 March and Atco in the USA one month later.

The story behind the single – or the B side at least – is a convoluted one. It had been announced that the follow up single to 'My Generation' would be the Talmy-produced song 'Circles' on the Brunswick label. The band released 'Substitute' instead with a re-recorded version of 'Circles' on the B side, retitled 'Instant Party'. Talmy claimed copyright infringement and a high court injunction forced the withdrawal of 'Substitute'. To sidestep the ruling, 'Substitute' was re-released the following week with a new B side, 'Waltz for a Pig' credited to The Who Orchestra. With no new songs at their disposal at such short notice, it was, in fact, a jazz-pop instrumental recorded by the Graham Bond Organisation featuring Jack Bruce and Ginger Baker.

The Motown style bass riff in 'Substitute' which drives the verses is especially reminiscent of the Four Tops' 'I Can't Help Myself'. Tambourine high in the mix is another Tamla influence. Townshend also claimed it was a spoof of the Rolling Stones' 'Nineteenth Nervous Breakdown' and both singles were released just a week apart. The song is built around a twelve-string acoustic guitar which, unaccompanied, also opens the song. Like 'My Generation', Entwistle's bass provides the solo during the instrumental break and Moon became so excited during the inventive drum fill, he lets out an impromptu yell at 2:38. Such was his state of mind at the time, he couldn't remember the session and accused the band of using a replacement drummer.

'Substitute' reached number five in the UK singles chart, consolidating The Who's growing reputation as hitmakers. It also did well in most European countries. The North American release was edited down to three minutes, losing the second verse. It also featured a different vocal and the line 'I look all white, but my dad was black' was replaced with the nonsensical 'I try going forward, but my feet walk back'. Despite the reworking, it disappointingly failed to chart either side of the border.

Compared with the three previous singles, 'Substitute' is an introspective, inward-looking song with a depreciating tone that borders on self-loathing. The words contrast with the song's otherwise upbeat tone and roll off Daltrey's tongue at a rapid, almost tongue-twisting rate. It featured prominently in the 1966 setlist and TV appearances and The Who's first full-scale tour of North America the following year. It would regularly open The Who's shows as it did at the Monterey Pop Festival in June 1967.

'I'm a Boy' 2:34 (Pete Townshend)

The band's seventh single was recorded at IBC Studios, London on 31 July 1966. It's one of the first Who songs produced by Kit Lambert. The day before the recording, The Who aired 'I'm a Boy' at the Windsor Jazz & Blues Festival. It was released in the UK on 26 August and reached number two on the 29 September which, along with 'My Generation', is The Who's highest UK chart placing for a single. It was kept off the top spot by housewives' favourite Jim Reeves' perennial 'Distant Drums'. Like 'My Generation', 'I'm a Boy' spent a total of ten weeks in the chart. It was released in America on 10 December but criminally failed to chart due to a lack of airplay. The song's left of field subject matter seemingly did not appeal to US radio stations.

'I'm a Boy' was salvaged from Townshend's first attempt at a rock opera, tentatively titled 'Quads', set in the year 2000 where parents can choose the sex of their children. The mother in the story gives birth to three girls and a boy instead of four girls as she requested. The backstory goes some way to explaining the song's unconventional lyrics about a boy who's dressed as a girl and denied the activities normally associated with his gender. While the overall tone is light-hearted, there is a subtext of sexual identity, the anxiety of puberty, even child abuse – 'I'm a boy but if I say I am I get it'.

The song is bursting with vitality with a ridiculously catchy tune played with a rare intensity. The subject matter is also pretty extraordinary for its time. It was Townshend's most complex single to date. The drum sound is hard, almost brittle. Daltrey, who was used to singing in the testosterone-driven R&B style, found it difficult when faced with the lyrics. He would have similar issues with subsequent singles like 'Happy Jack' and 'Pictures of Lily'. Townshend leads the way by singing the angelic first verse with Daltrey coming in on the hard-hitting second, 'My name is Bill and I'm a headcase'. This line is backed by an unusual – for The Who – 2/4 'oom-pah-pah' beat with Entwistle's inventive bass prominent, accompanied by Moon's crashing cymbals. They harmonise seamlessly during the chorus. Like 'The Kids Are Alright' the previous year, the guitar and harmony vocal sections have a classical baroque influence. This is underlined by Entwistle's ripe, French horn embellishments.

'I'm a Boy' would become a popular stage song and was regularly performed during The Who's first tour of North America in 1967. It was played during the legendary concert at Leeds University on 14 February 1970 although it's absent from the original *Live at Leeds* LP. A different version of 'I'm a Boy' was recorded on 3 October 1966 and features on the 1971 compilation *Meaty Beaty Big and Bouncy*. It's more than a minute longer with an extended guitar solo and richer, Beach Boys-style harmonies although it lacks the edge of the original.

'In the City' 2:21 (John Entwistle, Keith Moon)

The B' side of 'I'm A Boy' was recorded during the same sessions. It was also a bonus track on the 1995 CD reissue of *A Quick One*. As unlikely as it may seem, Entwistle and Moon failed to notify the other two about the session and as a result, they are responsible for the backing track with Townshend adding guitar later. It's a celebration of California with references to surfing, swimming, drag racing and pretty girls. This is mirrored in the treatment with sunny counterpoint harmonies, ringing guitar and Entwistle's unusual, but effective, tuba accompaniment. It lacks that Beach Boys sparkle however and is not one of The Who's most memorable efforts. Although it's a different song, The Jam's 1977 debut single took its title from this track.

'Happy Jack' 2:14 (Pete Townshend)

'Happy Jack' was a single release in the UK on 3 December 1966, less than a week before *A Quick One* hit the shops. In North America it was held over until 18 March 1967 to coincide with The Who's first Stateside visit. It was also the title song on the *Happy Jack* album – the American version of *A Quick One* – released the following month. It was recorded at CBS Studios on the 9 and 10 November.

The song's light-hearted tone and quirky lyrics recall Townshend's happy childhood memories of holidays spent on the Isle of Man in the 1950s. His father Cliff played the summer season as alto saxophonist in the Squadronaires dance band. It relates the story of Jack, a fictional character who lives on the island's beaches where he's taunted by the local children. Entwistle has a rare lead vocal outing on a Townshend song, singing the first verse, although Daltrey takes over from there. Rather like Jack, who 'would take the wrong key', Moon was not known for his singing skills and was excluded from the studio while the other three recorded the backing vocals. Townshend spotted the drummer lurking in the control room and his spontaneous 'I saw yer' made it onto the final recording as the song ends.

It's in 2/4 march time with an extra beat in each line of verse. The opening guitar phrase is very distinctive, as is the choir-like backing voices. The prominent bass riff, along with clattering drums, carries the song. Moon attacks the song with gusto acting as a lead instrumentalist while still holding down the beat. There is a flamenco influence in the guitar solo, a stylistic leftover from Townshend's original demo.

'Happy Jack' spent seven weeks in the UK chart, reaching number three. The third of three top five hits in 1966, The Who matched the Rolling Stones and outdid the Beatles who released just two singles that year. Even though it was The Who's most successful single so far in the USA, it wasn't the big hit they hoped for, peaking at number 24 in the Billboard chart. It fared much better north of the border, reaching number one in May 1967 in a year The Monkees dominated the Canadian charts. It was also a top ten record in several other regions including Australia and many parts of Europe.

Unsurprisingly, it was destined to become a popular stage song, especially in America where, in 1967, it featured in their short – 40 minutes – but memorable set as support act to Herman's Hermits. 'Happy Jack' is included on the expanded 1995 CD version of *Live at Leeds*, appropriately sandwiched between 'Substitute' and 'I'm A Boy'. A particularly strong performance filmed at the London Coliseum on 14 December 1969 is included on the 1994 *Thirty Years of Maximum R&B* Live video. An early treatment of 'Happy Jack' with Townshend on acoustic guitar and Entwistle on cello surfaced as a bonus track on the 1995 CD reissue of *A Quick One*.

'I've Been Away' 2:08 (John Entwistle)

The UK B side to the 'Happy Jack' single. It was recorded at Regent Sound Studios in one quick, 30 minute take in early November 1966. Townshend and Daltrey did not participate in the session and it features Entwistle on vocals, bass and piano with Moon on drums. Entwistle's protagonist has been framed and is wrongly imprisoned for a crime committed by his brother Bill. Atypical for a Who song – although this could hardly be called that – it's in 3/4 waltz time, emphasised by the lilting piano.

'Man With Money' 2:45 (Don Everly, Phil Everly)

Recorded in August 1966, this went unreleased until it surfaced as a bonus track on the 1995 *A Quick One* CD. It concludes with a fine example of Townshend's trademark guitar solo used during live performances with a sustained power chord followed by vibrato and string glissandi. The original was an album track for the Everly Brothers, and the B-side of their 1965 single 'Love Is Strange'. In their early days, The Who were influenced by the Everlys and regularly included their songs in the setlist.

'Pictures of Lily' 2:44 (Pete Townshend)

The Who's tenth single was released in the UK on 22 April 1967. It followed nine weeks later in the USA, six days after their 18 June appearance at the Monterey Pop Festival. It was The Who's first release on Track Records, the independent label formed by their management New Action Ltd. The label's debut release, Jimi Hendrix's 'Purple Haze', preceded 'Pictures of Lily' by five weeks. Like many of The Who's singles from this era, the speedy turnaround between recording and release is impressive.

The song is a simple tale of a boy who is given pictures of scantily clad ladies by his father to help him sleep at night. In addition to advancing his sexual awareness, the boy develops an infatuation for a girl in the photos even though she is long since dead. The song's title and chorus was inspired by a picture of music hall actress Lillie Langtry – or Lily Bayliss depending on Townshend's memory – that his then-girlfriend Karen Astley had on her bedroom wall. A collection of titillating, vintage postcards were used to promote the single in the UK although Decca considered them too risqué for the American market. Townshend described the song as 'a ditty about masturbation' and it's a throwback to his own adolescence when he and Entwistle, like many schoolboys of a certain age, collected erotic pictures.

Given the subject matter, Daltrey perhaps understandably found it difficult to relate to the song and initially felt uncomfortable singing it. His feelings were shared by American radio stations who refused to play the single at the risk of offending their sponsors. As a result, it stalled just outside the Billboard top 50. In the UK it was another top-five hit, peaking at number four. It drew unanimous approval from the UK music press, who generally – and quite rightly – regarded 'Pictures of Lily' as The Who's finest single thus far.

Undaunted by the criminally poor showing in the charts, the song was played during The Who's first tour of North America in the Summer of 1967. Moon's customised 'Pictures of Lily' Premier drum kit was unveiled for the tour. In addition to a nude image from the UK promotion, the vivid artwork on the nine-piece kit includes the words 'Keith Moon Patent British Exploding Drummer'. The panoramic logo on the twin bass drums left no one in doubt as to the identity of the band.

'Pictures of Lily' boasts a bright, infectious melody, contrasting with Townshend's apocalyptic power chords. Entwistle typically pins down the beat, maintaining time, allowing Moon's explosive drumming to explore every corner of the song. Entwistle's short French horn solo was intended to evoke the first world war when Langtry was still very popular. Fittingly, it ends on a triumphant high and along with 'I Can See For Miles', it was the last of Townshend's 'power pop' singles before he tackled weightier subjects like *Tommy*.

'Doctor, Doctor' 3:02 (John Entwistle)
The B-side to the 'Pictures of Lily' single. It also appeared as a bonus track on the 1995 reissue of *A Quick One*. Like the A-side, It was produced by Kit Lambert and engineered by Alan McKenzie at IBC/Pye Studios, London on 5 April 1967. It's another tongue in cheek offering from Entwistle, dedicated to hypochondriacs everywhere. Again, his pulsating bass line is to the fore, and his falsetto singing stretches his upper vocal range to the absolute limits.

The Who Sell Out (1967)

Personnel:
Roger Daltrey: lead vocals
Pete Townshend: guitar, piano, organ, backing and lead vocals on 'Odorono', 'Our Love Was', 'I Can't Reach You' and 'Sunrise'
John Entwistle: bass, horns on 'Armenia City in the Sky', 'Someone's Coming' and 'Top Gear', backing and lead vocals on 'Medac' and 'Silas Stingy'
Keith Moon: drums
Additional personnel:
Speedy Keen: vocals on 'Armenia City in the Sky'
Al Kooper: organ on 'Rael 1'
Produced by: Kit Lambert
Engineered by: Kit Lambert, Damon Lyon-Shaw, Mike Ross Trevor, Chris Huston, Mike Weighell
Recorded at: IBC, Pye, De Lane Lea and CBS Studios, London, Talentmasters Studios, New York, Gold Star, Los Angeles, May – November 1967
Record label: UK: Track Records, USA: Decca Records
Release date: 15 December 1967
Highest chart places: UK: 13, USA: 48
Running time: 38:46

If 1967 was the summer of love, peace and harmony, there was very little to show for it in The Who's live performances and songs. Recording of their third album began in May, following a short tour of Scandinavia. Several studio locations around London were utilised with Kit Lambert again producing. Like the first album, the recording schedule was punctuated by concert commitments, TV appearances and radio sessions. Both John Entwistle and Keith Moon sustained injuries in late May which delayed recordings. A ten-week tour of North America did not curtail the process, however.

Following two years of lacklustre record sales Stateside, '67 was the year The Who made a concerted effort to crack America. On the 21 March, they made their first Atlantic crossing for a week of package shows in New York. While in America, Pete Townshend changed to Fender guitars for live work. He found that Stratocasters, in particular, were more durable than the Rickenbakers he had played up to that point and cheaper to buy in the States. The Stratocaster was also Jimi Hendrix's instrument of choice.

The Who returned to the USA in June to play several dates, including an all-conquering appearance at the Monterey Pop Festival on the 18 June. They were less than happy with the performance, blaming the hired equipment. As a result, for The Who's first proper tour of the USA and Canada beginning on 13 July, they flew over their own Marshall equipment and Moon's new customised 'Pictures Of Lily' drum kit. They were the unlikely support act to UK lightweight-pop group Herman's Hermits who had a run of hits during the '60s both sides of the Atlantic. Two infamous incidents, in particular, occurred during the ten-week trip, both, unsurprisingly, involving Moon. The first was on the 23 August during his 21st birthday party at the Holiday Inn, Flint, Michigan and allegedly involved a car and the hotel's swimming pool. There's no doubt as to the validity of the second incident, however, which was captured for prosperity on American TV. At the end of the tour on the 15 September, The Who's recorded appearance for *The Smothers Brothers Comedy Hour* climaxed with an explosion that left Townshend visibly shaken and temporarily deaf in his right ear.

Despite frantic activities both on and off stage, during the American jaunt, The Who managed to record several tracks for the still-unnamed album. On the days they were not performing, the band stopped off at various studios along the way. The Who's management was keen to have an album in the shops by Christmas – which they achieved by just ten days. Townshend wrote several songs for the album during the tour, quite a feat considering the obvious distractions. However, with subjects as diverse as souring relationships, body decoration, masturbation, deception and over population, he felt that the songs did not gel. In the wake of *Sgt. Pepper's Lonely Hearts Club Band* released in May 1967, Townshend decided a linking theme was needed.

In defiance of the BBC's monopoly of the airwaves, Pirate Radio took to the seas in the early '60s. These offshore stations were instrumental in advancing the sales of British pop music in the mid-'60s, including The Who. In August 1967, they were outlawed by the UK government's Marine Broadcasting Bill. As a mark of solidarity, Townshend and Chris Stamp devised a concept whereby the album would simulate a typical Pirate broadcast with the songs linked by advertisements and jingles. Each band member was photographed in a mock ad for products ranging from Odorono deodorant (Townshend), Heinz baked beans (Daltrey), Medac acne cream (Moon) and Charles Atlas bodybuilding course (Entwistle). The resulting album cover and title was a tongue in cheek homage to consumerism and far removed from the psychedelic imagery popular with The Who's contemporaries in '67.

It was the first Who album release on Track Records. Obtaining permission to include the various products on the album and artwork delayed The Who's album by four weeks. Reviews were mostly positive, acknowledging the boldness of the advertising concept. For some, however, it didn't go far enough while for others, it was too radically removed from their previous work and a distraction from The Who's reputation as a high energy stage act.

The album peaked at number thirteen in the UK chart, a disappointment considering the amount of work that had gone into making the album an artistic success. With a wealth of classic albums in 1967 including *Sgt. Pepper*, *Days of Future Passed*, *The Piper at the Gates of Dawn* and *Disraeli Gears*, perhaps record buyers had had their fill by mid-December. A high of 48 on the Billboard chart was even more disappointing, but it did linger in the American chart for 23 weeks. Although the trips across the Atlantic had failed to turn in a profit, they had sown the seeds for a successful relationship between The Who and their American audience that would last indefinitely.

'Armenia City in the Sky' 3:48 (Speedy Keen)

To open the album, a rare instance of a song written specifically for The Who by someone outside the band. As a later member of Thunderclap Newman, John 'Speedy' Keen would enjoy a number one UK single in 1969 with the Townshend produced 'Something in the Air'. This was Lambert's second Who album as producer and he was experimenting with several studio effects including backwards guitar to compete with George Martin and the Beatles.

It's introduced by a short radio-style jingle that counts down the days of the week. We then enter a psychedelic landscape of disorientating, swirling sounds with backward instruments, distortion and a relentless chugging rhythm. Daltrey's unnatural sounding vocal for the verses was processed through an effects filter with Keen taking over for the high, and quite memorable chorus. Lyrically, the song is a close cousin of 'Lucy in the Sky with Diamonds' released earlier that same year on *Sgt. Pepper*. John Lennon denied the LSD connection in the Beatles' song but here, the aural allusions to an acid trip are ripe. A short jingle for Radio London leads into...

'Heinz Baked Beans' 1:00 (John Entwistle)

The Who wrote and recorded a dozen or more jingles which were eventually pared down to those on the album. The majority were dreamt up by Entwistle and Moon during a drinking session in a pub near De Lane Lea Studios. This is actually a segment of the instrumental 'Cobwebs And Strange' from the previous album with comical voiceovers by Moon and Entwistle. The penultimate line 'What's for tea daughter?' always brings a smile to my face. The 'More music' jingle leads into...

'Mary Anne with the Shaky Hand' 2:28 (Pete Townshend)

A thinly veiled allusion to masturbation, this song goes hand in hand – if you excuse the pun – with 'Pictures of Lily'. Led by acoustic guitar and ethnic percussion, it has a poignancy and charm that's hard not to like. Vocally, it's Daltrey and Townshend meets Simon and Garfunkel with exquisite results. It was occasionally performed in the summer of 1968, during the 1989 tour and was resurrected acoustically in 1999.

Several versions of this song were recorded and released. The acoustic album version was the third, recorded at De Lane Lea Studios in London on 24 October 1967. Two earlier, electric versions were recorded at Talentmasters Studios in New York on 6 and 7 August with Al Kooper on organ. The first was released by Decca as the American and Australian B side to 'I Can See For Miles' and was remixed into stereo for the 1998 *Odds and Sods* CD. The second was a bonus track on the 1995 album *The Who Sell Out* CD. A jingle for Premier drums leads into...

'Odorono' 2:34 (Pete Townshend)

Armed with the album's concept, Townshend wrote this song about a singer who fails her audition when the handsome impresario Mr Davidson discovers she suffers from body odour. Townshend's plaintive tenor vocal has a sincerity that's at odds with the lightweight – almost comical – subject matter. The treatment with chugging, dual rhythm guitars and delicate wordless harmonies gives the song an added poignancy. I had long believed that 'Odorono' was a Townshend invention until later discovering that it was a real antiperspirant once sold in America. It's one of the few mock adverts on the album that was developed into a fully-fledged song. An alternate jingle for Radio London leads into...

'Tattoo' 2:51 (Pete Townshend)

This, along with 'Substitute' and 'Relax', was one of the few songs from *The Who Sell Out* regularly played on the subsequent North America tour in the spring of 1968. It was performed until the mid-'70s and occasionally resurfaced in later years. A live version appears on the 1995 CD reissue of *Live at Leeds*.

Using tattoos as a metaphor, it's a song about adolescent rites of passage, peer pressure and masculinity. Sung in the first person, the protagonist and his brother are tattooed to prove they are real men. In keeping with the album, it ends on a light-hearted note with 'Now I'm older, I'm tattooed all over, my wife is tattooed too'. When writing the song, Townshend recalled the men from his boyhood whose arms were covered in tattoos and his concerns that one day he would look the same. He was pleasantly surprised when Daltrey agreed to sing the song believing he would refuse on the grounds that it did not suit his macho image. 'Tattoo' is beautifully constructed. A lean arrangement of rippling acoustic and electric guitars underpin Daltrey and Townshend's thoughtful vocals with heavenly wordless backing. A Radio London jingle advising the listener to go to the church of their choice leads into...

'Our Love Was' 3:23 (Pete Townshend)

This is another song that was subject to several recording attempts. This version was cut at Columbia Studios, Los Angeles in September 1967. For some unknown reason, on the American release, it was listed as 'Our Love Was, Is'. It's another stripped-back arrangement with Townshend's vocal at its most vulnerable. He sings about a so-so relationship that blossoms into true love. Acoustic and electric guitars are panned to the extreme left and right in the stereo image. Moon and Entwistle's contributions are suitably restrained and the 'Love love love long' bridge at 1:29 is an absolute joy. Like 'Tattoo', this is a fine example of Townshend's maturing talents as a songwriter. He even throws in a pretty decent guitar solo at 2:09. A brief medley of jingles including Rotosound Strings leads into...

'I Can See For Miles' 4:05 (Pete Townshend)

The only song from the album released as a single. It remains my favourite Who single from the '60s and probably my favourite period. 1967 was a landmark year for singles in general and 'I Can See For Miles' has stood the test of time along with the best of them. Sadly, however, it never achieved its full potential sales-wise, especially in the UK where it just made the top ten following its release on 13 October. It was rush-released in America on 18 September to capitalise on The Who's Stateside tour, reaching number nine in November. It would be the highest chart placing in the USA for a Who single. At the time, Townshend believed it to be the ultimate Who record and was convinced that it would be their first number-one single. He was therefore understandably frustrated by what he perceived to be a rebuff by the record-buying public, particularly when it dropped out of the UK chart after just four weeks. Disillusioned, the subsequent Who singles of 1968 would display nowhere near the same craft or effort. As a result, UK sales suffered further.

By way of consolation, when classical composer William Walton heard 'I Can See For Miles' through his godson Kit Lambert, he said the song 'indicated real greatness'. Townshend later said that Walton's praise gave him the confidence to begin work on *Tommy*. His timing was right given that 1968 was the year that albums in general outsold singles for the first time.

'I Can See For Miles' had a long gestation period. Recording began with the backing tracks at CBS Studios, London in May 1967. Vocals and overdubs were added at Talentmasters Studios, New York in August during a break in The Who's ten-week tour of North America. The finishing touch was provided at Gold Star, Hollywood where it was mixed and mastered. They made good use of the studio's echo chamber which was favoured by Phil Spector amongst others. Recorded the previous year, Townshend was particularly proud of his demo which was very close to the finished song. He considered it to be the ace up his sleeve and deliberately held it back for a rainy day when The Who's fortunes needed a boost. He also wanted to be sure that Lambert had developed sufficiently as a producer to do the song justice.

The song is a heady rush that generates excitement with an underlying hint of menace. The arrangement is meticulously understated with stunning production. Multiple guitar parts were overdubbed although the track never sounds cluttered. The cool detachment of Daltrey's delivery is a masterclass in contained anger. The song is driven by Entwistle's pumping single bass note, and Moon's fills add to the song's tension and its slow build. On the stereo version – the original single was mono – Townshend's two electric guitars are positioned in the extreme left and right channels while his acoustic hovers discreetly in the centre. Although not a technically advanced player, Townshend makes the best of his abilities by hammering out a one-note solo. Some have interpreted the song as an acid trip set to music, but to my ears, it's a menacing threat from a man whose partner has been unfaithful. Townshend put it bluntly in December 1971 when he said the words 'are about a jealous man with exceptionally good eyesight. Honest'.

'I Can See For Miles' has rarely been performed live, due in part to the layered guitar parts and complex vocal harmonies. Moon also found it hard to replicate his unorthodox drumming. Ironically, it was played with more regularity after Kenny Jones joined the band. Deservedly, it was performed during the 50th-anniversary tours.

'Can't Reach You' 3:03 (Pete Townshend)

Townshend has written many songs on long plane flights, including this one which opens side two of the original LP. The evidence is there in the first verse, which relates to flying and the distortion of time as a result of crossing time zones. Townshend also sings the line 'You fly your plane right over my head' in what may be a spiritual journey as he tries to reach a heavenly like deity. Written in 1967 on piano, it pre-empts his discovery of Meher Baba later that same year. This is another sensitive arrangement with Townshend once again on – reverb-drenched – lead vocals. He's also responsible for the delightful piano accompaniment.

Backed with 'Our Love Was', it was released as a single in Australia and what a fine couplet they made even though they didn't set the charts alight. On some reissues of *The Who Sell Out*, it's listed as 'I Can't Reach You'. The line 'See, feel or hear from you' at the end of the chorus was adapted for 'See Me Feel Me' on *Tommy*.

'Medac' 0:57 (John Entwistle)

Sung by Entwistle in typically whimsical fashion, this is a pubescent tale of young Henry Pond who cures his acne problem with Medac cream. In America, the song was retitled 'Spotted Henry' to avoid potential litigation from the German pharmaceutical company of the same name.

'Relax' 2:41 (Pete Townshend)

Another song with spiritual overtones that has close similarities to the Beatles, in this case, 'Tomorrow Never Knows' released the previous year. Compare for example Townshend's opening lines 'Relax and settle down, let your mind go round' with Lennon's 'Turn off your mind relax and float downstream' and 'Lay down on the ground and listen to the sound' with 'Lay down all thoughts, surrender to the void'. The two songs also share a psychedelic vibe. Opening with Townshend's magisterial organ tones, he and Daltrey combine voices for the trippy verses. Townshend takes the lead at 1:10 for the lengthy bridge and the guitar solo at 1:46 is as gritty as anything he's committed to vinyl thus far. When performed live, the song was anything but relaxed. It became a hard-rock onslaught with Townshend's extended solo incorporating feedback and lengthy, Hendrix style improvisation. Another jingle for Rotosound Strings from Entwistle and Moon leads into…

'Silas Stingy' 3:07 (John Entwistle)

Although it was performed on the 1968 summer American tour, this is one of Entwistle's most understated and underrated songs. It has a medieval ambience thanks to Townshend's discreet, church-like organ, horns and spiralling harmonies – a multi-tracked Entwistle. It's another of his bizarre character creations, a Scrooge-like person obsessed with money. Lyrically, it's in the same nursery-rhyme style of 'Boris the Spider' with a child-friendly chorus 'There goes mingy Stingy'. Like Townshend's character Happy Jack from the previous year, Silas is tormented by the local children for his peculiar appearance. Although the song is based on George Eliot's novel *Silas Marner*, at the time Entwistle was labelled a miser by the rest of the band when he saved hard to buy his first house.

'Sunrise' 3:06 (Pete Townshend)

Performed solo by Townshend at IBC Studios, London on 2 November 1967, 'Sunrise' was the last track recorded for the album. He penned the song for his mother to prove that he could write a real love song. That said, things are not always as they seem in a Townshend ballad and the lines 'You take away the breath I was keeping for sunrise' and 'My morning put to shame' are open to interpretation. While he can be justifiably proud of the song and his performance, there was a dissenting voice regarding its inclusion. Moon felt it didn't belong, perhaps because The Who's recording of his own song 'Girl's Eyes' didn't make the album.

Townshend played 'Sunrise' on a Harmony twelve-string guitar, double-tracked with six-string, and it's a foretaste of his solo work during the 1980s. He incorporates jazz chords, inspired by two tutor books by American guitarist Mickey Baker he was studying at the time. He was also influenced by jazz exponents Kenny Burrell and West Montgomery.

'Rael (1 and 2)' 5:44 (Pete Townshend)

'Rael' started life as another attempted rock opera, but during the recording and mixing in New York and London, it was eventually condensed to less than six minutes. Although shorter than 'A Quick One, While He's Away' that closed the previous album, it's weightier in terms of subject matter. Townshend's writing and the band's playing had also matured significantly during the twelve months that divided the two albums. Al Kooper's simmering organ opens the song and along with the vigorous, martial rhythm, he accompanies the see-sawing melody. Daltrey sets the scene and his singing has a distinct Beach Boys inflection. Brain Wilson's influence is evident throughout the song, in the unorthodox instrumentation, ambitious arrangements and lush harmonies. Moon's inspired drumming informs the entire track, ably supported by Entwistle's thundering bass lines.

This is one of the earliest rock songs to tackle environmental issues and over-population. During the 1960s and '70s, the population explosion in China was a real concern and resulted in the instigation of the one-child policy in 1979. Townshend believed that China's Cultural Revolution that began in May 1966 and 'Maoism' posed a threat to western civilisation. His story takes things to the extreme. 'Rael' is set in 1999 where the Red Chinese have become leaders of a world that's so overpopulated, each person is confined to just one square foot of earth.

The story's protagonist Damon was named after The Who's recording engineer Damon Lyon-Shaw. Rael as a name dates back to biblical times and in Hebrew means 'Lord of the light'. The name was adopted by Peter Gabriel for the hero of Genesis' 1974 concept album *The Lamb Lies Down On Broadway*. Gabriel chose the name for his Puerto Rican character, believing it to be of Spanish origin.

Musically, Townshend absorbed classical music as well as the work of his future father-in-law Edwin Astley. He wrote and arranged music for films and British television series during the 1950s and '60s and arranged the strings on The Who's 1978 album *Who Are You*. Townshend installed a piano in his home studio and studied orchestration which would manifest itself on the next album in particular. In some respects, 'Rael' is a dry run for *Tommy*, containing in the instrumental bridge two themes that would be reprised in 'Sparks' and 'Underture'. Lambert and Townshend had originally envisaged 'Rael' as an orchestrated opera with Arthur Brown, who had recently signed to Track, as the title character. The idea was dropped for practical reasons.

On the 1994 *Thirty Years Of Maximum R&B* box-set and the 1995 *The Who Sell Out* CD, this track was renamed 'Rael 1'. A 50-second coda – sung rather weakly by Townshend – dropped from the original version was included as a bonus track under the title 'Rael 2'. The 2009 deluxe edition combined the two tracks and reverted back to the original title 'Rael 1 and 2'. It also includes the one-minute bonus track 'Rael Naive', a variation of 'Rael 2'. 'Rael' made its stage debut in October 1967 in the UK, two months before the release of the album. Unprepared for this new and, by Who standards, complicated piece, it left some audiences members dumbfounded.

Related Tracks
Included in this section are non-album songs recorded or released in 1967 and 1968 plus bonus tracks included on the 1995 and 2009 CD reissues of *The Who Sell Out*. The 2009 2CD release also includes alternate versions and mixes of songs that appeared on the original album.

'The Last Time' 2:59 b/w 'Under My Thumb' 2:44 (Mick Jagger, Keith Richards)
On the 29 June 1967, Mick Jagger, Keith Richards and art dealer Robert Fraser were jailed following a highly publicised drugs bust. The recording of these two Rolling Stones songs was hastily arranged by Townshend to provide financial support. As had been anticipated, the sentences were quashed soon

after, but the publicity generated did neither the Stones or The Who any harm. Entwistle, who married Alison Wise on 23 June, was on honeymoon at the time, so Townshend plays bass as well as guitar and keyboards on both tracks.

'Someone's Coming' 2:33 (John Entwistle)
The UK B side of the 'I Can See for Miles' single. It was also the B side of the American release of the 'Magic Bus' single. Here, Entwistle's protagonist is maintaining a secret, nightly tryst with a girl despite her parent's objections to the relationship. The song is based on his schoolboy courtship of fourteen-year-old Alison Wise. Given the song's personal nature, it's surprising that Daltrey provides the lead vocals for the first time on an Entwistle song. The bassist was responsible for the brass arrangement which embellishes the entire song with lead guitar conspicuously absent.

'Dogs' 3:04 (Pete Townshend)
It had been eight months since the release of 'I Can See For Miles' and The Who were in desperate need of another UK hit single. 'Dogs' was recorded at Advision Studios on 22 May 1968, just two days after Townshend's wedding. It was one of the first studios in London to house eight-track equipment. Townshend had developed an interest in greyhound racing, a very British working class sport that remains popular to this day. With his friends Chris Morphet and Richard Stanley, he attended several race meetings around London and 'Dogs' developed from there. Although I was too young to remember, in the 1950s, my father could be found most weekends alongside the greyhound track at the White City Stadium near Shepherd's Bush, an area very familiar to The Who.

'Dogs' music-hall style wasn't a particularly good fit for The Who and when it was released as a UK single on 14 June 1968, it limped home to a sorry 25th position in the chart. It was the first Who sanctioned single written by Townshend to stall outside the UK top ten. Created specifically for the Anglophile market, unsurprisingly America passed on 'Dogs' having released 'Call Me Lightning' three months earlier. Daltrey adopts a mock cockney accent for the verses and the bridge could have been recorded on the football terraces. It's the type of novelty song better suited to the Small Faces. Townshend plays piano and harmonica with Moon on percussion. Although it has a certain charm, 'Dogs' is probably The Who's most disposable single of the 1960s and one of the few to be omitted from the 1971 compilation *Meaty Beaty Big and Bouncy*.

'Call Me Lightning' 2:25 (Pete Townshend)
The demo for this song was one of the first recorded by Townshend back in the winter of 1964. It's included on the 1987 *Another Scoop Compilation* and is a superb example of how well recorded and produced those early demos were with layered guitars and vocal harmonies. The song is

performed in a cod rock and roll doo-wop style. Townshend was trying to appease not only Daltrey's need for macho lyrics but also Moon's craving for surf music and fantasy sports car imagery. Following the initial recording in London, it was completed at Gold Star Studios, Hollywood in late February 1968 with Lambert producing.

In America, it was a single A-side released on 16 March 1968, reaching number 40 on the Billboard chart. The release was timed to coincide with the North American spring tour even though it hardly featured in the setlist. The song was perhaps a little outdated for the UK market and was relegated to the B side of the 'Dogs' single. It also featured on the American only album *Magic Bus: The Who on Tour* released in September 1968.

'Glittering Girl' 2:56 (Pete Townshend)
Recorded in London circa July 1967, this surfaced as a bonus track on the 1995 CD reissue of *The Who Sell Out*. Townshend's raw singing, backed by Entwistle, is clearly a guide vocal and the song never progressed further than the rough mix stage.

'Melancholia' 3:17 (Pete Townshend)
'Melancholia' was recorded on 29 May 1968, a few days after 'Dogs', and although it went unreleased until the 1994 *Thirty Years Of Maximum R&B* box-set, in many ways, it was a superior song. Townshend wrote and recorded the demo the previous year and decided it wasn't appropriate for The Who at that time. Despite the sad tone, like the majority of Townshend's songs, 'Melancholia' is in a major key. It's a very mature sounding Who, with a restrained vocal from Daltrey and sweet harmonies, although it's Moon's superbly judged drumming that stands out. Only Townshend's raucous, Hendrix style solo at 2:41 seems out of place.

'Magic Bus' 3:15 (Pete Townshend)
One of Townshend's leftover compositions from late 1965. His demo from early 1966 with acoustic guitar bouncing off percussive sounds, loses a little of its charm when transferred to the full band arrangement. Like 'Dogs', it was recorded in late May 1968 at Advision Studios, London for possible single release. Following the poor chart showing of 'Dogs', 'Magic Bus' was released in the UK on 11 October. To launch the single, The Who hired a vintage bus and their journey around London was filmed for promotional purposes. Despite the hard sell, it stalled at 26 in the UK chart. As 'Dogs' had bypassed America completely, Decca released 'Magic Bus' on 27 July to coincide with The Who's 1968 summer tour of North America. It was performed during the tour and reached number six in Canada and 25 in the USA. It was also performed during the UK autumn tour. With its party atmosphere and good time feel, 'Magic Bus' would become a much in demand stage favourite, and along with 'My Generation', would regularly close The Who's shows.

Although The Who and Lambert were spending more time in the studio in perfecting singles, 'Magic Bus' was recorded in half a day. The slight melody is driven by acoustic guitar, loud percussion claves and Townshend and Daltrey's choral chants. Like the Rolling Stones' cover of 'Not Fade Away' from four years earlier, 'Magic Bus' is based on a single note Bo Diddley beat from the 1950s. When performed live, it could be extended indefinitely with an eight-minute version closing the *Live at Leeds* set. The nonsense words are loaded with veiled drug references such as 'Thruppence and sixpence every day, just to drive to my baby', a reference to the rising price of LSD.

'Magic Bus' featured on the American only album *Magic Bus: The Who on Tour* released in September 1968 by Decca. The bogus title and timing of the album, was designed to capitalise on two recently completed Who tours of North America. It's not one of Townshend's favourite songs but it became one of the most requested in The Who's repertoire. Entwistle also baulked at playing it live given the song's repetitive riff. Prior to The Who's recording, 'Magic Bus' was given to a group called the Pudding and their version was released by Decca in the UK in April 1967.

'Dr. Jekyll and Mr Hyde' 2:27 (John Entwistle)
Recorded in January 1968, this was the B side on two singles; in America 'Call Me Lightning' was the A-side and in the UK it was 'Magic Bus'. It was written as a result of Entwistle's rooming with Moon during the 1967 American tour with Herman's Hermits. Naturally, drinking to excess is a key factor in the lyrics, changing the bassist into Mr Hyde. Suitably, the song has a sinister, melodramatic tone that only Entwistle could conjure. His rumbling bass riff is front and centre and Moon adds a manic drum break and ghoulish laugh towards the end.

'In the Hall of the Mountain King' 4:19 (Edward Grieg)
Grieg's famous piece from the *Peer Gynt Suite* was recorded in April 1967 during *The Who Sell Out* sessions for an aborted EP of instrumentals. It subsequently appeared on the 1995 CD reissue. The Who's arrangement was inspired by Johnny Kidd & the Pirates' live performance of the piece. As you would expect, it plays fast and loose with Grieg's work although the melody is still intact under a barrage of improvisation, feedback and eerie wordless vocal backing. It concludes with Entwistle's vocal hook from 'Boris the Spider' but he sings 'Radio London' instead.

'Early Morning Cold Taxi' 2:55 (Roger Daltrey, Dave Langston)
Despite the joint credit, this was composed by Dave Langston who at the time was trying to develop a writing partnership with Daltrey. It was recorded in May 1967 during *The Who Sell Out* sessions, but because of the song's true authorship, it never made it onto the album. It subsequently appeared on *Thirty Years Of Maximum R&B* and *The Who Sell Out* expanded CD. It's a

mid-paced pop song with a catchy hook and engaging harmonies but a tad lightweight by The Who's standards. Langston later worked on Entwistle's solo albums and several Who-related projects.

'Girl's Eyes' 3:28 (Keith Moon)

Recorded in May 1967, another abandoned song from *The Who Sell Out* sessions that surfaced as a bonus track on the 1995 CD and *Thirty Years Of Maximum R&B*. Moon's tasteful words relate to a female fan who 'Can't tell a note from a symphony'. The song has a sunny vibe with the melody and combined voices of Moon and Entwistle bringing the Mamas and the Papas to mind. Townshend's acoustic guitar solo and Moon's drumming vie for attention in the instrumental coda.

'Summertime Blues' 2:35 (Eddie Cochran)

The Who recorded two studio versions of this rousing live favourite in May and October 1967. Both went unreleased until the 2009 deluxe edition of *The Who Sell Out* and a longer version appears on the 1998 CD reissue of the *Odds & Sods* compilation. 'Summertime Blues' quickly became a live staple. It was performed during The Who's legendary performance at the Monterey Pop Festival in June 1967 and was played on the subsequent North American tour.

'Jaguar' 2:51 (Pete Townshend)

Although mainly instrumental, this features Moon on lead vocals extolling the virtues of Jaguar motor cars which have 'Grace, space and pace'. Townshend sings the choral hook. Driven by rhythm guitar, bass and drums, the rapid pace brings to mind 'Rael' and later, 'Sparks' on the Tommy album. Recorded on 20 October 1967, it was originally intended as a pivotal track on *The Who Sell Out* but finished up as a bonus track on the 1995 CD instead. It's late replacement on the original album was 'Sunrise'. Despite its relegation, it's a powerful song and Townshend later said that 'The Who made a good job of it'.

'Coke After Coke' 1:05, 'Things Go Better with Coke' 0:30

Two advertising jingles for Coca-Cola recorded in 1967 for American radio that went unused. Both are bonus tracks on *The Who Sell Out* 2009 2CD.

'Sodding About' 2:47 (John Entwistle, Keith Moon, Pete Townshend)

An aptly titled, raucous instrumental jam. It was the band's way of letting off steam during *The Who Sell Out* recording sessions and is a bonus track on the 2009 2CD. It nearly made it onto the 1998 reissue of *Odds and Sods* but was dropped at the last minute. Also known as 'No Title', it's appeared on Who bootlegs under several different titles.

'John Mason Cars' 0:40, 'Premier Drums' 0:43 (Moon), 'Odorono' 0:24, 'Top Gear' 0:52

These jingles or, in the case of 'John Mason Cars', failed jingles were recorded in October 1967 for *The Who Sell Out*. They're all included as bonus tracks on the 2009 2CD reissue. 'Top Gear' was recorded on 10 October during a session for the BBC radio program of the same name.

'Great Shakes' 1:01

One of the most fully realised jingles recorded by The Who. It features a full band arrangement with a narration from Moon expounding the qualities of milkshakes. Like the Coca-Cola jingles, it was intended for American radio but didn't appear until *The Who Sell Out* 2009 2CD as the final, hidden track.

'Fortune Teller' 2:18 (Naomi Neville)

The Who's studio version of this song first saw the light of day on the 1994 *Thirty Years Of Maximum R&B* box-set. The three-part harmonies are superb and Moon's drumming keeps things moving at a brisk pace. A stage favourite, live versions were included on the CD reissues of *Live at Leeds* as well as *Live at Hull 1970* and *Live at the Fillmore East 1968*. The original was released as a single by American R&B singer Benny Spellman in 1962. It's also been covered by the Rolling Stones, the Hollies, the Merseybeats, Robert Plant and Alison Krauss amongst others.

'C'mon Everybody' 1:55 (Eddie Cochran, Jerry Capehart)

A live recording from April 1968 that featured on the *Live at the Fillmore East 1968* album, released in April 2018. As you would expect, this is a no holds barred, rock and roll blast from The Who. Although they sound a little rough around the edges, Daltrey gives a more than convincing performance of this classic. The original was a UK hit single for Eddie Cochran in 1959 and has been covered by just about everybody from Led Zeppelin to the Sex Pistols. It was a UK top five hit for the latter in 1979.

Tommy (1969)

Personnel:
Roger Daltrey: vocals, harmonica
Pete Townshend: vocals, guitars, piano, organ, banjo
John Entwistle: bass, French horn, vocals
Keith Moon: drums, vocals
Produced by: Kit Lambert
Engineered by: Damon Lyon-Shaw
Recorded at: IBC, London, September 1968 – March 1969
Record label: UK: Track Records, USA: Decca
Release date: UK: 23 May 1969, USA: 17 May 1969
Highest chart places: UK: 2, USA: 4
Running time: 75:15

Following several earlier attempts to write and record a full-scale rock-opera, Pete Townshend's dream was realised in 1969 with the release of the double LP *Tommy*. He conceived his magnum opus the previous year in between extensive overseas touring, especially in America and Canada. In 1968, The Who were the fourth biggest draw behind Cream, Jimi Hendrix and the Doors. On 20 May, Townshend married Karen Astley and they moved into a Georgian house facing Eel Pie Island on the River Thames in Twickenham. He installed a studio with a variety of instruments and two-track recording equipment which would later be replaced by eight-track. Over the next fourteen years, The Who's demos would be devised and recorded here. John Entwistle also installed a home studio. 1968 was the year that albums in general outsold singles for the first time, so clearly, the band were right to channel their energies into the next album.

Encouraged by the teachings of Meher Baba who Townshend had discovered in 1967, his original idea was to record an album of thematically linked songs based on man's search for spiritual enlightenment. He christened his hero Tommy, a suitable name for an everyman figure. The provisional title was 'Amazing Journey' and the Hermann Hesse-like story slowly evolved. When interviewed by *Rolling Stone* during a North American tour in the summer of '68, Townshend explained the storyline in detail. The working title was now 'The Deaf, Dumb and Blind Boy' and he spent his evenings in hotel rooms writing songs and outlining story ideas. Once again, he received enthusiastic support from Kit Lambert, who, as a classical music buff, first suggested a rock opera.

The recording of *Tommy* began on 19 September 1968 in Studio A at IBC Recording Studios in central London. It was recorded on eight-track – all they could afford at the time – with Lambert once again producing. Like *The Who Sell Out*, the recording process was a protracted one, over a six month period. The sessions were very structured, eight hours a day, Monday to Friday and although scheduled to finish at 10.00 pm, they often ran into the early hours.

With the exception of brief visits to Bremen and Paris for TV recordings, The Who restricted their stage and promotional activities to the UK. In March 1969, the album was mixed in Studio B at IBC by engineer Damon Lyon-Shaw and assistant Ted Sharp. Overall, the sound has a lighter touch than previous Who albums. Townshend initially felt that Lambert had sacrificed the band's dynamic instrumental sound in favour of the vocals although he later concluded that this was a wise decision given the importance of the narrative. Roger Daltrey felt that the songs were outside his vocal comfort zone, but he rose to the occasion, giving his most sublime and assured vocal performance thus far.

Part of March and April 1969 was spent in intense rehearsals for their most ambitious stage undertaking yet. With the exception of festivals, *Tommy* was played almost in its entirety – minus 'Cousin Kevin', 'Underture', 'Sensation' and 'Welcome'. Trimmed to an hour in length, it was the centrepiece of their shows which now ran to two and a half hours, twice as long as the pre-*Tommy* sets. On stage it gelled, and in terms of pure dynamics, outshone the album. It also transformed Daltrey's stage persona. Townshend replaced his trusty Fender guitars with Gibson SGs which in 1972 he would replace with the heavier Les Pauls. The 1969 *Tommy* tours included three visits to North America as well as dates in the UK and mainland Europe. In more recent times, such as the 2017 *Tommy & More* tour, the opera would be performed in its entirety.

When The Who performed at the legendary Woodstock festival during the early hours of Sunday morning on 17 August 1969, Daltrey looked every inch the iconic rock frontman – aided by the rising sun which spread its rays during the 'See Me, Feel Me' finale, he was dressed in his full *Tommy* regalia with a buckskin leather fringed jacket and a large crucifix around his neck. A performance in Amsterdam on 29 September saw the first of several unique *Tommy* shows in European opera houses. Despite the time spent in the recording studio, The Who gave a total of 112 live performances in 1969.

On its initial release in May 1969, the album was a slow starter in the UK but eventually climbed to number two. Thanks to regular airplay, it was an instant success in America and was The Who's first – of many – Stateside gold records, remaining in the charts for 47 weeks. Although it received its fair share of praise, and UK music weekly *Melody Maker* awarding *Tommy* album of 1969, it left some critics and pundits perplexed. While many saw The Who as a noisy pop group capable of producing the occasional engaging single, this was very different. It was disparaged by some music critics for its highbrow notions which they felt did not belong in pop. Its merits as an opera has been extensively debated over the years as has its – for some – elusive storyline and absence of a clear plot. Even without hearing the album, the more reactionary press claimed the suffering of a deaf, dumb and blind person was in bad taste.

As social commentary taken to the extreme, *Tommy* works brilliantly, commenting on everything from dysfunctional families to child abuse to media hype to blind adulation and misguided hero worship. Like all great albums, it succeeds on a musical and emotional level. Even the release of the Pretty Thing's album *S.F. Sorrow* – often cited as the first rock opera – six months earlier couldn't diminish its impact.

Tommy is complemented by Mike McInnerney's superb cover artwork featuring a lattice effect globe. The original gatefold LP sleeve opened out with a third flap to give full scope to his artistic creation. The elaborate packaging also included an eight-page booklet incorporating Kit Lambert's explanatory storyline. He later developed it into a film script but failed to gain the support of the record company or Townshend, putting an irreversible strain on their relationship.

'Overture' 5:21 (Pete Townshend)

This – mostly – instrumental track is the first of three on the album. It's an overture in the true sense, containing themes that would later appear as fully developed songs. These include '1921', 'We're Not Gonna Take It', 'See Me, Feel Me', 'Listening to You', 'Pinball Wizard' and 'Sparks'. They are underpinned by the bass line from 'Go to the Mirror!', Entwistle also providing rich French horn embellishments, while Townshend adds magisterial organ during the 'Listening to You' section. His primary instrument, however, which features throughout the album, is a Gibson J-200 acoustic guitar. It's the only backing for the vocal coda which sets the story in World War One where Captain Walker is missing in action. His guitar picking here is superb, incorporating various styles including, blues, jazz and flamenco. On the original LP, the 'Overture' stops at the 3:50 mark and the vocal section is part of the second track 'It's a Boy'.

Although this track was considered groundbreaking for a rock album, the Moody Blues opened their 1967 concept album *Days Of Future Passed* with the overture 'The Day Begins'. The Who's overture was Lambert's idea although his desire to have it similarly orchestrated was vetoed by the band. They wanted an album they could faithfully recreate on stage. With the exception of 'Sally Simpson' and parts of 'Amazing Journey', this is the only track on the album to feature a narrator. The others are sung from the perspective of characters in the story. When an all-star version was performed in London on 9 December 1972 with the London Symphony Orchestra, Townshend unwisely elected to narrate throughout the opera, with embarrassing results.

An unlikely cover version of 'Overture' was a single by American instrumentalists Assembled Multitude which reached number sixteen on the Billboard chart in July 1970. In response, The Who's original was used as the B side for the 'See Me, Feel Me' single released on 9 October 1970.

'It's a Boy' 0:38 (Pete Townshend)

Townshend's strummed acoustic guitar and falsetto vocal continue into the second track announcing Tommy's birth. A grandiose choir-like section proclaims 'A son! A son! A son!'.

Like the other band members, Townshend grew up in war-torn London and the devastation lived on in the memories of his parents' generation. He, therefore, felt it prudent to avoid the second world war and set his story in the aftermath of the 1914 to 1918 war. In his 1975 film of *Tommy*, Ken Russell reset the story in the post-world war two years.

'1921' 3:14 (Pete Townshend)

Acoustic guitar again takes the lead as Tommy's mother and her lover confidently predict it's going to be a good year. Their optimism is short-lived, Tommy's father, Captain Walker, returns and kills the lover in a fit of anger. None of this is described in the song, but the repeated line 'What about the boy?' tells us that something is wrong. Tommy has witnessed the murder reflected in a mirror and is browbeaten by his parents into silence. Traumatised, he loses not only his ability to speak but his hearing and sight as well. The multi-tracked chorus marks Daltrey's first appearance on the album while Townshend sings the verses which, given the subject are very melodic. Piano and guitar engage harmoniously while bass and drums are discreetly subdued.

When Townshend was a young boy, his mother had taken a lover, but the relationship ended when she and his father got back together again a few years later. As one of a number of plot holes in *Tommy*, there's no explanation as to where Captain Walker has been for the past three years since the ending of the war. Tommy's sensory shutdown is later explained as psychological and his condition is integral to the story. It represents a state of spiritual isolation with no concept of reality and for Townshend, 'His limitations are symbolic of our own'.

'Amazing Journey' 3:25 (Pete Townshend)

Written prior to *Tommy*, this is one of the key songs, providing an insight into the way Tommy's character will later develop. Now ten-years-old, he exists in his own inner world and conjures up wondrous images in his mind, including a god-like figure. In the song, the lines alternate between Tommy's perspective 'me', and that of a narrator 'he'. It's the album's first proper rock song with Daltrey singing lead. His double-tracked vocals are untypically angelic, perfectly conveying the innocence of the young Tommy. As Townshend later commented, Daltrey 'discovered his falsetto voice he used so brilliantly on *Tommy*'. The song's trippy ambience is enhanced by Lambert's backward tape effects although the track belongs to Moon. His superlative and very busy drumming leads while bass and guitar maintain the rhythm.

'Amazing Journey' is an excellent live song and has made regular appearances over the years, including the 50th-anniversary tours. It's usually paired with 'Sparks', even when the stripped-down version of *Tommy* is performed.

'Sparks' 3:45 (Pete Townshend)

This instrumental is another piece that works well on stage, especially when performed back to back with 'Amazing Journey'. Tommy has developed a heightened sense of touch and finds he can communicate through vibrations as he stands transfixed by his reflection in the mirror. Townshend incorporates a dramatic theme from 'Rael' on the previous *The Who Sell Out* album. The lead bass motif stands out while Townshend plays mostly acoustic rhythm. There are again some interesting effects such as backward guitars which all add to the track's energetic thrust.

At one point, around the summer of 1968, Townshend envisaged that *Tommy* would include instrumental interludes with sound effects to link the songs. The idea was abandoned, and as a compromise, he incorporated the two instrumentals, 'Sparks' and 'Underture'. While neither advance the story in any particular way, they are both superior instrumentals. In 1962, a booklet of Meher Baba's sayings were compiled by Delia DeLeon entitled *Sparks* which inspired the title of this track.

'The Hawker' 2:15 (Sonny Boy Williamson II)

Closing side one of the original double LP, 'The Hawker' is the album's only non-original song. It was adapted from 'Eyesight to the Blind', released by American bluesman Sonny Boy Williamson in 1951. Townshend discovered the song through a jazzy interpretation by Mose Allison. He also considered incorporating Allison's own song 'Young Man Blues', but the idea was dropped.

Although not written for *Tommy*, the lyrics slot neatly into the narrative. Townshend set them to a new arrangement, adding an inventive guitar solo. Daltrey rises to the occasion with a spirited, soulful vocal, backed by an electric guitar and banjo rhythm. The Hawker is peddling fake remedies and claims that his gipsy wife can cure Tommy. He's the first of several dubious characters that cross paths with the boy, none of whom have his best interests at heart.

The husky-voiced Richie Havens gives a memorable performance of this song on the 1972 *Tommy* orchestral album. Eric Clapton was an inspired choice to perform the song in the 1975 film, given his affinity for the blues. In a display of quirky cinematic license, writer/director Ken Russell turned the character of the Hawker into a Marilyn Monroe worshipping preacher.

'Christmas' 5:30 (Pete Townshend)

It's Christmas day but unlike other children, Tommy is oblivious to the festive occasion or its religious significance. His parents are becoming increasingly frustrated over his disability and state of mind, with the desperate plea 'How can he be saved?' Townshend sings the strident 'Tommy can you hear me?' refrain for the first time while Daltrey introduces the opera's haunting core theme 'See Me, Feel Me'. Even though he lacks the ability to speak or show feelings, Tommy's subconscious mind is trying to reach out for help and understanding. In the 1975 film version of 'Christmas', Alison Dowling provides young Tommy's singing voice and her angelic delivery of 'See me, feel me, touch me, heal me' sends shivers down the spine every time.

Compared with the tracks on side one, 'Christmas' is closer to a typical Who sounding song. Despite the title and subject, musically, it makes few concessions to the festive season. It does have a lively, upbeat feel however with meticulous drumming from Moon. The backing vocal 'gobble-gobble-gobble-gobble' adds a note of levity, mimicking the hapless bird that provides the centrepiece to a traditional Christmas dinner.

'Cousin Kevin' 4:03 (John Entwistle)

This song and 'Fiddle About' are stark reminders of Entwistle's down to earth style compared with Townshend's sometimes abstract, spiritually guided songs. Lyrically, they leave little to the imagination and are firmly grounded in reality. Townshend admitted that he didn't have the stomach for writing explicit songs of child cruelty and handed the task to Entwistle, knowing that he would bring the right element of sadistic cynicism to the story. When writing the songs, Entwistle presumed that Cousin Kevin was the son of Uncle Ernie which goes some way to explaining Kevin's motivations. Like Ernie, he takes advantage of Tommy's autism to mistreat him.

Entwistle sings the song in a key that would have been too high for Daltrey. In unison with Townshend, he conveys the sadistic intent of Kevin with convincing menace and would reprise the role for Lou Reizner's 1972 orchestral version of *Tommy*. In Ken Russell's 1975 film, Paul Nicholas plays the part superbly and was one of the few cast members adept at both acting and singing. Following its initial outing in 1969, 'Cousin Kevin' was dropped from The Who's staging of *Tommy*.

'The Acid Queen' 3:31 (Pete Townshend)

Tommy's trials continue with an encounter with the Acid Queen, thanks to his parents misguided attempts to find a cure. She's the gypsy wife of 'The Hawker' and continuity wise, it would have made more sense for that song to lead into this one. On the 1975 film soundtrack, 'Acid Queen' directly follows 'Eyesight to the Blind'. The Acid Queen falsely claims that she can heal Tommy when in reality, she's a prostitute selling sex and drugs. For Townshend, her character represents the social pressures placed upon young people and the erroneous message that drugs and alcohol abuse and sexual permissiveness are merely a rites of passage.

'The Acid Queen' has a strong, vibrant melody and singing from a female perspective, Townshend is convincing. He's backed by electric guitar and piano and the song features a superb instrumental sequence at 2:09 that builds to an emotional peak. Townshend was writing and singing from experience being no stranger to hallucinogens. He suffered a particularly bad acid trip in 1967 on a flight back to the UK following The Who's appearance at the Monterey Pop Festival. His abusive Granny Denny was also the daughter of a gypsy which may have inspired the character. Mary Clayton gives a soulful performance as the Acid Queen in the orchestral version of *Tommy*. And who can forget Tina Turner's scenery-chewing turn in the film version.

'Underture' 10:10 (Pete Townshend)

Following *Tommy's* unsavoury encounter with the Acid Queen and LSD, this instrumental underscores his hallucinogenic trip. Like 'Sparks' on side one, 'Underture' reprises the suspenseful acoustic guitar line and bass riff from 'Rael'. Townshend plays acoustic guitar throughout and Moon's wall to wall drumming and echoing tympani rolls add to the track's impact. It brings side two of the original album to a dramatic and satisfying close. It's the longest track on the album by some distance. Although sequences are repeated, it never feels overweight nor does it outstay its welcome. A ten minute instrumental was however deemed excessive for live audiences and until 2017, 'Underture' remained mostly studio-bound. An extract from The Who's performance at Woodstock is included on the *Thirty Years of Maximum R&B* box-set.

Townshend and Entwistle had wanted to put more overdubs on the album, but due to the protracted recording process, they ran out of studio time. 'Underture' especially would have benefitted from a fuller arrangement. On the 1972 *Tommy* album, it boasts the combined might of the London Symphony Orchestra and Chamber Choir to grandiose effect.

'Do You Think It's Alright?' 0:24 (Pete Townshend)

Tommy's parents express their doubts about the suitability of Uncle Ernie as a minder for the boy which they, or rather Daltrey and Townshend, exchange in both close and counterpoint harmony.

'Fiddle About' 1:26 (John Entwistle)

The second of two contributions from Entwistle and given the subject of sexual abuse, this is the album's most disturbing song. He treads a thin line between humour – the song's overly melodramatic style – and a vivid portrayal of a child molester. Entwistle avoids graphic detail with the oft-repeated line 'Fiddle about' providing the lyrical thrust. Fortunately for Tommy, immersed in his own inner world, he's oblivious to the depredation to which he's being subjected.

Entwistle certainly gets under the skin of Ernie with a credible vocal performance that builds to an intense peak. When Moon took over the role on stage, the characterisation became pure pantomime which added an element of – albeit warped – humour to The Who's shows. He reprised the role in the 1975 film to screen stealing effect. His buddy and fellow drummer Ringo Starr was equally effective on the 1972 orchestral *Tommy* album although he was replaced by Moon when it was transformed to the stage. Like much of *Tommy,* there is an autobiographical element to this song. At the age of four, Townshend was sent to live with his Granny Denny, who he believes subjected him to similar sexual abuse. She was also prone to random relationships with men who would often come to the house at night.

'Pinball Wizard' 3:01 (Pete Townshend)

Tommy was almost complete by the end of 1968 when Townshend played some of the tracks to friend and critic Nik Cohn. He was an influential correspondent for the *New York Times* and a pinball fanatic and suggested the opera needed something to lighten the mood. To appease Cohn, in the space of one evening Townshend wrote 'Pinball Wizard'. Pinball requires concentration and quick reactions which Tommy masters through his keen sense of touch and sensitivity to vibrations. It's his first experience of triumph in an otherwise remote existence. Tommy, however, was born during World War one and the version of the game as described in the song with flippers and digit counters did not come about until the late 1940s by which point he would have been in his thirties.

Typical of his demos, the song's structure, arrangement and key changes were faithfully reproduced by the band while putting their own stamp on it. As the obvious single, 'Pinball Wizard' preceded the album by two months. It was recorded on 7 February 1969 at Morgan Studios, London and released exactly a month later. Townshend's ploy to insert a deliberately commercial song into his otherwise weighty work paid off. It reached number four in the UK and remained in the chart for a total of eight weeks. It was The Who's biggest hit since 'Pictures of Lily' two years earlier. When it was released in America on 22 March, it peaked at nineteen on the Billboard chart. It received unanimous approval from critics on both sides of the Atlantic including – unsurprisingly – Cohn. It would be the last classic Who single of the 1960s.

'Pinball Wizard' is sung from the perspective of a pinball champion who has just been beaten by Tommy and enthusiastically extols his rival's skills. The extended instrumental intro boasts probably the best known acoustic guitar riff in the history of rock. Townshend's frantic, flamenco-style strumming, has Baroque influences. On his demo, the intro is even longer. It perfectly captures the vigorous pace of a pinball game. The sweet sound of the acoustic guitar is punctuated by electric power chords and like 'My Generation', features subtle upward key changes. The first verse doesn't begin until half a minute into the song and the drums don't enter until the end of the verse. The call and response bridge 'How do you think he does it' works a treat and after the song effectively restarts at 2:14, Daltrey's vocal range is tested to its upper limits.

Irrespective of the numerous stage performances of *Tommy*, 'Pinball Wizard' has remained a staple of The Who's repertoire since 1969. The only version to rival The Who's for adrenaline is Elton John's rousing performance on the *Tommy* film soundtrack. He's backed by his own band comprising Davey Johnstone (guitar), Dee Murray (bass) and Nigel Olsson (drums) who really nail the song, playing out with the main riff from 'I Can't Explain'. Released as a single on 26 March 1976, it reached number seven in the UK chart. A less likely cover was MOR act the New Seekers' version of 'Pinball Wizard' b/w 'See Me, Feel Me'. It reached number sixteen and 29 respectively on the UK and US singles charts in March 1973.

'There's A Doctor' 0:25 (Pete Townshend)

Another short introductory link. Tommy's father – voiced by a harmonious Townshend, Daltrey and Entwistle – has found a doctor who may be able to cure Tommy. The bouncing piano line reflects the song's optimistic tone.

'Go to the Mirror!' 3:50 (Pete Townshend)

The specialist concludes that the boy's condition is psychological. Tommy is transfixed by his own reflection in the mirror, which may hold the key to a cure. Although the melody is slight, the central riff to this song is great and carries Daltrey's vocals with it. He sings the role of the doctor, leaving Townshend to counter with Tommy's refrain 'See me, feel me, touch me, heal me' between verses. The uplifting 'Listening to you' theme is heard for the first time and brings the song to a memorable close. Curiously, on the 23 May 1969, 'Go to the Mirror!' was released as a single in Australia with the more radio-friendly 'I'm Free' as the B side. In the 1975 film, Ken Russell secured the services of Jack Nicholson to play the doctor. The vocally challenged actor wisely adopts a clipped, semi-spoken delivery.

'Tommy Can You Hear Me?' 1:36 (Pete Townshend)

This jaunty singalong features three-part harmonies, backed by acoustic guitar and a nimble bass line. When 'I'm Free' was later released as a single in parts of Europe, this provided the B side.

'Smash the Mirror' 1:35 (Pete Townshend)

Tommy's mother realises that he can see his reflection. Unable to communicate with him, out of frustration and anger, she smashes the mirror. Daltrey's soulful vocal is supported by a funky guitar line and syncopated drumming. For the high vocals during the 'Rise, rise, rise, rise' sequence at 0:42, Townshend enlisted his younger brothers Paul and Simon to provide backing. The crash of breaking glass at the end is a rare sound effect on the album.

'Sensation' 2:32 (Pete Townshend)

With his inner block broken by the smashing of the mirror, Tommy's primary senses return. His spiritual awakening mirrors Townshend's discovery of Meher Baba in 1967 and becomes, in Townshend's words, 'A universally conscious person'. Tommy goes further by declaring himself a Messiah-like figure and his sense of elation is reflected in the song's jubilant tone. Townshend adapted 'Sensation' from a pre-*Tommy* song called 'She's a Sensation'. It was written about a girl in Melbourne during a 1968 Australian tour. She had been hanging out with the Small Faces and clearly left an impression on Townshend. A simple change to the lyrics and 'She's a sensation' became 'I'm a sensation'.

Although 'Sensation' is sung from Tommy's perspective, it's Townshend, not Daltrey, who provides the lead vocals and he does a fine job. On the 1972 orchestral album and the 1975 film version, it's sung by Daltrey. The song has an uplifting, feel-good factor with superb French horn and piano embellishments to heighten the melody. Only the ending lets the side down, fading disappointingly all too soon. Surprisingly, it was excluded from the subsequent *Tommy* tours but made a welcome return in 1989 during The Who's 25th-anniversary reunion tour. 1989 also marked the 20th anniversary of *Tommy*.

'Miracle Cure' 0:10 (Pete Townshend)
A newspaper vendor voiced by Daltrey, Townshend and Entwistle announces Tommy's miraculous rehabilitation.

'Sally Simpson' 4:10 (Pete Townshend)
Tommy has become a Messiah adored by his fans. Similar to a rock star, his sermons are large scale events with support groups, music, a DJ, merchandise and police controlling the crowds. Sally Simpson is a devoted follower and in defiance of her parents, she attends one of his meetings. In her attempts to get closer to Tommy, she is thrown from the stage by security and is permanently disfigured. Despite a slight melody, 'Sally Simpson' features engaging piano arpeggios with lively acoustic guitar and drums providing a shuffle groove. Lyrically, it's probably the most descriptive and self-contained song on the album and is almost a separate story unto itself. Daltrey's singing is assured, backed by Townshend for the rousing chorus.

Townshend was inspired to write the song following an incident during a Doors concert at New York's Singer Bowl on 2 August 1968. As the support act, The Who had already completed their set and Townshend was watching from the sidelines. During a stage invasion, a girl in her attempt to evade capture fell from the stage, badly injuring herself. The 2003 CD reissue of *Tommy* contains the bonus track 'I Was'. It's a seventeen-second wordless chant believed to have been intended as a linking piece for this song or 'Tommy's Holiday Camp'.

'I'm Free' 2:40 (Pete Townshend)
Along with 'Pinball Wizard' and 'See Me, Feel Me', this is one of the best-known songs from the album and one of The Who's best period. Tommy is rejoicing in his newfound freedom and calling upon his disciples to follow him to spiritual enlightenment. According to Townshend, 'I'm Free' was influenced by the Rolling Stones' 1968 hit 'Street Fighting Man'. It certainly shares that same spirit of elation with piano, a solid six chord electric guitar riff and a

memorable acoustic solo at the midway point. The guitar riff intro from 'Pinball Wizard' is reprised at 2:05 during the 'How can we follow?' outro. According to Entwistle, Moon struggled with the intro on this track and as a result, he and Townshend play some of the drum parts.

'I'm Free' works as a standalone song and on 5 July 1969, it was justifiably released as a single in America and parts of Europe – although not the UK. It peaked at 37 on the Billboard chart. Lou Reizner's arrangement from the 1972 *Tommy* album was released as a single in 1973 with Daltrey backed by the London Symphony Orchestra. It reached number thirteen in the UK chart. As well as an essential part of the *Tommy* repertoire, 'I'm Free' regularly featured in The Who's setlist, particularly in the 1970s. The song inspired the best sequence in the 1975 film version. Daltrey is filmed running through a variety of different scenes and backdrops to exhilarating effect, pre-empting MTV and pop videos of the 1980s.

'Welcome' 4:30 (Pete Townshend)
Tommy invites followers from all walks of life to hear his divine message and his popularity grows. As with 'I'm Free', Daltrey assumes the voice of Tommy joined by Townshend at 2:47 for the 'The more at the door' sequence. Entwistle plays Tommy's polite helper who delivers the spoken line 'Excuse me sir, there's more at the door'.

'Welcome' is a fairly lightweight song, to begin with at least, with chiming acoustic guitar and banjo. The tempo rises a few notches around the halfway mark with lively jazz-inflected piano and a memorable, Latin flavoured instrumental bridge at 1:38. It concludes with a classical piano style flourish. Moon criticised the album for many of the songs sounding 'soft' and although I disagree, I'm sure he had 'Welcome' in mind. It's not a song that would have transferred readily to the stage and not surprisingly, it wasn't played during the subsequent 1969 and '70 *Tommy* tours.

'Tommy's Holiday Camp' 0:57 (Keith Moon)
This was a late entry into the story. After the theme of Tommy as a pinball hero had been introduced, Moon suggested that a holiday camp, with its arcades, would be a more fitting environment rather than a church-like setting. It also introduces an element of commercialism that parallels the trappings of the pop industry familiar to The Who. It has a lively tune with fairground style Wurlitzer organ, banjo and a comical Goons show-ish vocal from Townshend as Uncle Ernie. Although Townshend wrote the song, Moon received the credit for suggesting the idea.

'We're Not Gonna Take It' 7:08 (Pete Townshend)
Although Tommy wants his followers to find their own path to enlightenment, they insist on slavishly following his example. He responds with moral guidelines on how to live their lives which includes renouncing vices like alcohol and drugs.

These are rejected, and they rebel against Tommy. There are parallels here with the teachings of Meher Baba and the fate of Jesus in the canonical gospels of the New Testament. The 'We're Not Gonna Take It' section that occupies the first half of the song was written before *Tommy* as an anti-fascist statement. The original message, a rejection of political rhetoric, is similar to that of 'Won't Get Fooled Again', released two years later. At 3:30 it segues into the haunting 'See Me, Feel Me' bridge. This builds into the stirring 'Listening to You' coda which Townshend had originally written as a prayer to Baba.

'We're Not Gonna Take It' provides a powerful ending to *Tommy* and is probably Townshend's most accomplished song at that point in his career. On stage, it proved to be an emotional finale, even when the opera was performed in its abridged form. 'Listening to You' was often played faster, as evident on the *Live at Leeds* reissue where it builds to a feverish peak before ending with the central riff from 'We're Not Gonna Take It'. The Who performed 'See Me, Feel Me/Listening To You' as the finale to the closing ceremony of the 2012 London Olympic Games. An edited version of 'We're Not Gonna Take It' was released as the B side to the American single 'I'm Free' in July 1969. 'See Me, Feel Me' was released as a single edit on 10 October 1970. Although it failed to chart in the UK, it reached number twelve on the Billboard chart and number four in Canada. At half the length of the album track, it's the version usually included on Who compilations.

Related Tracks
In addition to Townshend's 5.1 remix of the original eight-track masters, the 2003 deluxe edition of *Tommy* includes seventeen bonus tracks. The non-album tracks and outtakes are discussed here. The other bonus tracks are rough, incomplete or alternate versions of songs that appear on the original album. The other non-album songs in this section were recorded in 1969 and 1970.

'Cousin Kevin Model Child' 1:24 (John Entwistle)
A linking song recorded as an introduction to 'Cousin Kevin' dropped from *Tommy* at the last minute during the mixing and mastering stage. Despite the credit, it was actually written by Townshend and sung by Moon. It swings in a twelve-bar blues style with a galloping rhythm and Moon adopting an American accent. It surfaced for the first time in 1998 on the *Odds & Sods* expanded CD and is included as a bonus track on the 2003 reissue of *Tommy*.

'Trying to Get Through' 2:51 (Pete Townshend)
An outtake from *Tommy*, this would have been sung from the perspective of his parents. The strident riff had evolved both on stage and in the studio. Townshend provides the lead vocal and under his direction, the band attempt to work it up into a viable song. Moon runs out of steam around the two-minute mark and it was never completed.

'Dogs Part Two' 2:26 (Keith Moon)

This was recorded on the 12 February 1969 at IBC Studios, London. It was the B-side to the 'Pinball Wizard' single released on 7 March in the UK. It's essentially a drums driven, loose jam and despite the title, it bears no resemblance to The Who's 1968 UK single 'Dogs'. On the original UK release, it was credited to 'Moon/Towser/Jason'. Towser was the name of Townshend's Spaniel at the time and Jason was Entwistle's Wolfhound.

'The Seeker' 3:10 (Pete Townshend)

The Who's eighteenth single and their first release of the 1970s was recorded at IBC Studios, London on 19 January 1970. Although Lambert is credited, it was produced by the band with Damon Lyon-Shaw engineering. The Who's first recording since *Tommy*, it was released on 20 March in the UK and the 25 April in America as a stopgap to fill the void before the next studio album. It's a straightforward – for The Who – riff-based song with a running bass line in the verse. Although it's not exactly heavy metal, it does venture into the heavy rock territory of the early '70s. On his original demo, Townshend played the rapid lead guitar part on acoustic which gives it a Spanish flamenco flavour absent from The Who's version. Moon's drumming is uncharacteristically straight forward, lacking his usual flair and attack. His lack of spirit is perhaps understandable given the tragic circumstances relating to the death of his driver Neil Boland just two weeks earlier. Guitar breaks alternate between a Chuck Berry style and a banjo style. Regular Who session man Nicky Hopkins adds piano fills.

At the time, this was one of Townshend's least favourite Who singles. He said it suffered from too many recording attempts. Lyrically, he's searching for the true meaning of life and references his contemporaries Bob Dylan, the Beatles, and Timothy Leary. It was written during one of The Who's visits to America in 1969. In the swamplands of Florida at three in the morning, a drunk Townshend, in a state of despair, came up with the words. Townshend's demo version was one of his contributions to the Meher Baba tribute album *Happy Birthday* released in February 1970. He confessed that he preferred the demo to The Who's version.

'The Seeker' reached a rather average nineteen in the UK singles chart before swiftly dropping out again. A high of 44 in the American Billboard chart was even more disappointing although, to be fair, it's not one of The Who's strongest efforts. They performed the song in the UK but rarely in America. It was resurrected for the 50th-anniversary tour and the 2017 North and South American tour where it followed 'I Can't Explain' as the second song in the set.

'Here for More' 2:56 (Roger Daltrey)

Recorded in February 1970, this was the B side of 'The Seeker' single. It's a rare song from the pen of Daltrey whereas Entwistle was usually responsible for

The Who's B sides. It's a fairly lightweight, un-Who like offering with acoustic rhythm guitar and electric country-style picking from Townshend.

'Young Man Blues' 2:51 (Mose Allison)

The original studio version of 'Young Man Blues' is commonly referred to as 'Version one'. It was recorded in September 1968 to provide a stop-gap single while The Who were working on *Tommy*. It didn't appear until *The House That Track Built* sampler album released in September 1969 and much later, the 2003 deluxe edition of *Tommy*. A slower 'Version two' appeared on the *Odds & Sods* expanded CD in 1998. The Who had been performing the song since 1964 and the definitive, near five-minute version, was recorded live on 14 February 1970. It was selected as the opening track on the original *Live at Leeds* LP released on 23 May 1970. It's a barnstorming performance and its influence on Led Zeppelin's 'Black Dog' released the following year is plain to hear.

'Summertime Blues' 3:22 (Eddie Cochran, Jerry Capehart)

This was a staple of The Who's sets during the '60s and '70s, even when they mostly stopped playing covers. It made its vinyl debut on *Live at Leeds* in May 1970 and is considered to be one of The Who's definitive live recordings. Released as a single on 10 July 1970, it reached 38 in the UK and number 27 in America. It was the first Who single recorded live and was released without their consent while they were away touring in America. A live recording is also available from The Who's appearance at the Monterey Pop Festival in June 1967. Marc Bolan followed The Who's example and regularly played 'Summertime Blues' during the T. Rex shows of the early '70s.

'Shakin' All Over' 4:20 (Johnny Kidd)

The Detours supported Johnny Kidd & the Pirates in the early '60s and they proved to be a big influence. Daltrey, in particular, was impressed by Johnny Kidd's stylised rock and roll vocal mannerisms which is evident on this recording from *Live at Leeds*. 'Shakin' All Over' is Johnny Kidd & the Pirates' best-known song and The Who don't disappoint with their rousing version. They occasionally incorporated lines from the William Dixon blues standard 'Spoonful'. For the Isle of Wight Festival appearance in August 1970, it was performed as a medley with 'Spoonful' and 'Twist and Shout' as featured on the *Live at the Isle of Wight Festival 1970* album.

'Heaven and Hell' 3:31 (John Entwistle)

The B side of the 'Summertime Blues' single, this was recorded for a BBC radio session at IBC Studios on 13 April 1970. It's Entwistle's observation on the obsession and belief in an afterlife. His pummeling bass lines glue the song together with Moon running riot over his kit. Townshend provides the power chords and a rampant solo that dominates the second half of the song. Even before the recording, 'Heaven and Hell' had an illustrious run as a live song. It opened The Who's set during the 1969/'70 *Tommy* tours as well as their performances at Woodstock, the 1970 Isle of Wight Festival and the *Live at Leeds* gig. As such, there are several live versions of this song available on official releases.

Who's Next (1971)

Personnel:
Roger Daltrey: vocals
Pete Townshend: guitar, VCS 3, organ, ARP synthesiser, vocals, piano on 'Baba O'Riley'
John Entwistle: bass, brass, vocals, piano on 'My Wife'
Keith Moon: drums, percussion
Additional personnel:
Dave Arbus: violin on 'Baba O'Riley'
Nicky Hopkins: piano on 'The Song Is Over' and 'Getting in Tune'
Produced by: The Who
Engineered by: Glyn Johns (associate producer)
Recorded at: Olympic, London, England, Stargroves, East Woodhay, England
(Rolling Stones Mobile Studio), April – June 1971
Record label: UK: Track, USA: Decca
Release date: UK: 27 August 1971, USA: 14 August 1971
Highest chart places: UK: 1, USA: 4
Running time: 43:38

After the weighty concept of *Tommy*, there was a general consensus within the band that the next studio album should be a collection of unrelated songs. Pete Townshend had other ideas, however. He set his sights on *Lifehouse* and wrote a script for a proposed multi-media film and album project. Although it would remain unfilled, Townshend would revisit the work over the ensuing years. To draw a comparison with Brian Wilson, if *Tommy* was Townshend's *Pet Sounds* then *Lifehouse* was his *Smile*.

The synopsis of *Lifehouse* is a future England under a strict government regime following an ecological disaster. With the exception of those that work in rural areas as farmers, the majority of the population are forced to stay in their homes wearing 'experiences suits' that cater for their needs. The suits are connected to a 'Grid' controlled by the government, ensuring that unruly elements, such as rock music, are prohibited. Bobby, the hero of the piece, gains access to the 'Grid' and broadcasts songs – performed by The Who – from a disused theatre he renames the 'Lifehouse'. *Lifehouse* proved to be prophetic, pre-empting later technological developments like the internet and virtual reality, not to mention blockbuster sci-fi action in the shape of *The Matrix*. Townshend also channelled environmental issues such as pollution and artificial environments into the songs, influenced by artist Gustav Metzger.

Rehearsals for the *Lifehouse* concerts began at the Young Vic Theatre in south-east London on 4 January 1971. These were intended to be interactive performances involving the audience and captured on camera for the proposed film. The shows continued sporadically from February, and the final performance on 26 April 1971 was recorded using the Rolling Stones' mobile studio. Townshend cancelled the rest of the concerts when he realised they were not functioning as he intended.

At Kit Lambert's suggestion, in March 1971 The Who encamped for a week at New York's Record Plant Studios for the initial recording of the album. When they returned to London at the end of the month, Glyn Johns was given the task of mixing the New York tracks but he felt he could improve on the recordings. At his suggestion, recording began anew in early April with a two-day session at Mick Jagger's Victorian mansion 'Stargroves' utilising the Rolling Stones' sixteen-track mobile studio. The mansion's hallway provided the perfect acoustics for 'Won't Get Fooled Again'. The rest of the album was recorded at Johns' preferred studio, Olympic Sound in south-west London from the 9 April through to June. When they finished, they had recorded a double album's worth of material. In his book *Sound Man*, Johns, an experienced producer and engineer, admitted that Townshend's demos used for reference purposes during the sessions sounded so professional, he felt intimidated by them.

Although Townshend was fully committed to *Lifehouse*, he met resistance from those that were essential to its success. Neither the rest of the band, their management or Johns fully understood or empathised with the story. They also had their doubts about the film. Under mounting pressure, Townshend agreed to abandon the project and Johns was given free rein to filter the tracks into a coherent, single album. The outtakes appeared on subsequent singles and compilations. Ironically 'Pure and Easy', one of the key songs, was relegated to the *Odds & Sods* album, released three years later. Townshend's demos for *Lifehouse* which were recorded in his eight-track home studio in Twickenham were released as part of the six disc *Lifehouse Chronicles* box-set in February 2000. The story would also be mined for later Who works including the 2006 *Endless Wire* album.

Townshend had been experimenting with ARP and VCS3 synthesisers in his home studio and these, along with organ and piano, played a key role in the songs on *Who's Next*. The principal guitars he used on the album were gifted to him by two American guitarists, namely a Les Paul Junior from Mountain's Leslie West and a 1959 Gretsch 6120 from future Eagle Joe Walsh. Although the latter was rarely used on stage because it wouldn't stay in tune, at the time, Townshend said it was the best guitar he ever owned and was used on virtually every track on the album.

Who's Next was released in the USA on 14 August 1971 to coincide with the North American summer tour where they unveiled their new, cutting edge PA system. The album appeared two weeks later in the UK and would be the band's only number one record in their home country. The album received unanimous praise on both sides of the Atlantic and is often cited as The Who's best collection of songs.

The inglorious and infamous cover image features the four band members seemingly having urinated on a large concrete block protruding from a slag heap. Photographer Ethan Russell spotted the location on 3 July 1971 while he and the band were en route from a gig in Sheffield to Leicester. It's an irreverent reference to the monolith sequences in Stanley Kubrick's sci-fi, art classic *2001:A Space Odyssey* released three years earlier. Kubrick had turned down an offer of directing a film version of *Tommy*.

'Baba O'Riley' 5:08 (Pete Townshend)

If *Who's Next* rose Phoenix-like out of the ashes of *Lifehouse*, then this is perhaps its crowning glory. 'Baba O'Riley' – which was originally titled 'Teenage Wasteland' – was similarly intended to be the opening song to *Lifehouse*. It sets the scene where the main character named Ray leaves his farm in Scotland to travel with his wife Sally and their children to London. The song's title is a homage to both Meher Baba and American minimalist composer Terry Riley.

The majority of the song is performed by Daltrey – in stupendous form – with Townshend singing the famous bridge 'Don't cry, don't raise your eye, it's only teenage wasteland'. These lines were inspired by Townshend's experiences at the 1969 Woodstock festival where he witnessed thousands of teenagers strung out on acid. The song opens with a circular instrumental motif from Townshend's demo played on a Lowrey organ manipulated by a synthesiser. He was influenced by modernist classical composers like Philip Glass and Terry Riley, especially the latter's 1969 album *A Rainbow In Curved Air*. Townshend used the ARP 2500 and 2600 synthesisers as he later would on *Quadrophenia*, the *Tommy* film soundtrack and *Who Are You*.

For both 'Baba O'Riley' and 'Won't Get Fooled Again', drums, bass and additional guitar were overdubbed on Townshend's demo recordings, a pattern that would be followed for later Who albums. The demo was much longer than the finished version but was edited down by Glyn Johns to a manageable length, retaining the key parts of the song. Pounding piano chords enter at 0:42, followed by drums at 0:57. Bass enters at the beginning of the first verse and crunching guitar riffs take over at the end of the verse. Dave Arbus, fiddle player with prog-folk group East of Eden and a friend of Moon's plays the vibrant violin solo. When it was subsequently played live, the violin coda was usually performed by Daltrey on harmonica.

'Baba O'Riley' didn't become an immediate stage song due to the inability of The Who quartet to perform the song without the aid of a pre-recorded backing tape. Come the 1971 UK Autumn tour, it was a regular part of the setlist. For both 'Baba O'Riley' and 'Won't Get Fooled Again' a sequencer was utilised on stage for the elaborate keyboard parts. Moon, and later Kenny Jones, played to a click track heard through headphones while the rest of the band took their timings from the drummer. An extract from 'Baba O'Riley' opened The Who's seven minute set that closed the 2012 London Olympic Games. It was released as a single in mainland Europe on 23 October 1971 where it reached number eleven in the Dutch chart. It's been much used in films and on TV, most notably as the title song to the popular American television series *CSI: NY*.

'Bargain' 5:34 (Pete Townsend)

Meher Baba is once again referenced, this time with the opening line 'I'd gladly lose me to find you'. It was inspired by his 1950 saying 'We must lose ourselves in order to find ourselves, thus loss itself is gain' which struck a chord with Townshend. In *Lifehouse*, 'Bargain' relates to the spiritual search derived from the premise that giving up everything in order to be at one with God is a bargain.

The Who were at the peak of their powers in 1971 and 'Bargain' benefits from a strong ensemble performance. Townshend stamps his authority on the song, playing acoustic rhythm, sharp riffs and weeping guitar embellishments. There's also a soft but effective synthesiser arrangement to underline the quieter moments. Daltrey is in strident form, hardly sounding better with Moon's inventive fills and flurries anchored by Entwistle's rock-solid bass lines. The song, along with several others, was premiered during The Who's live dates in April and May 1971 prior to the album's release. Although 'Bargain' was never released as a single, it's occasionally featured on compilations no doubt due to the album's popularity. It's also one of Townshend's favourite songs which he's performed in his solo shows. It featured in the setlist during the 50th anniversary *The Who Hits 50!* tours.

'Love Ain't for Keeping' 2:10 (Pete Townshend)

An acoustic love song but when performed on stage, it was an all-electric affair. It tells of the pastoral, almost idyllic lifestyle of the two principal characters in *Lifehouse*, Ray and Sally, and the unconditional love they share. The song has a bluesy vibe and boasts a soaring melody with superb three-part harmonies. Daltrey's measured vocal shows more restraint than usual while drums and bass maintain a more conventional rhythm. It's the shortest and most laid back song on *Who's Next* and a far cry from the heavy rock version The Who recorded in New York before returning to the UK to work with Glyn Johns. The NY version appears on the reissues of both *Who's Next* and the *Odds & Sods* compilation and features Townshend on vocals and Leslie West from American hard rockers Mountain guesting on lead guitar.

This was another song performed live in the UK in April and May 1971 and on the subsequent summer tour of North America where it occasionally opened the set. In addition to the electric studio version, a live version recorded at the Young Vic Theatre on 26 April 1971 appears on the 2003 deluxe edition of *Who's Next*.

'My Wife' 3:41 (John Entwistle)

A late addition to *Who's Next* and the only song not written for *Lifehouse*. After the project had been abandoned, it was felt that a contribution from Entwistle would help balance Townshend's songs, as they had done on the previous two albums. The bassist had only one song available which he'd been saving for a solo album. Although he had been happily married since June 1967, this is a tongue in cheek tale of a dysfunctional relationship written following an argument. It's sung from the perspective of a man who's been out drinking all weekend and is evading his wife. In the hands of The Who, 'My Wife' didn't swing as much as Entwistle would have liked and he re-recorded the song for his 1973 third solo album *Rigor Mortis Sets In*. Even so, he dominates here providing the lead vocals as well as playing bass, piano and brass. In the absence of a customary guitar solo, stabbing horns provide the lead breaks between the verses.

'My Wife' was performed on the *Who's Next* 1971 North American summer tour and would quickly become another stage favourite from Entwistle. Understandably, when played live, the horns and piano were dispensed with, replaced by Townshend's guitar soloing. The 'Baba O'Riley' single released in mainland Europe in November 1971 featured 'My Wife' as the B side. A live version recorded at the Gaumont State Cinema, Kilburn, London on 15 December 1977 featured as the B side on The Who's 1979 single 'Long Live Rock'.

'The Song Is Over' 6:14 (Pete Townshend)

Another key song from *Lifehouse*, it would have appeared at the end of the proposed film and album. After the final 'Note' had been played, everyone would disappear, signifying in Townshend's words 'the end of lifetime, the end of experience'. Together with 'Getting in Tune' which opens side two of the original LP, 'The Song Is Over' reflects that music is the key to the story of *Lifehouse*. The closing lines 'Searchin' for a note, pure and easy, laying so free, like a breath rippling by' are adapted from the song 'Pure and Easy' which was recorded for *Lifehouse* but omitted from the album. Although initially satisfied with the selections for *Who's Next*, Townshend later said that 'Pure and Easy' should have been on the album.

Townshend and Daltrey share lead vocals with their contrasting styles conveying a sense of both sadness (Townshend) and optimism (Daltrey). Nicky Hopkins' plaintive piano beautifully underscores Townshend's melancholic singing and the full band kick in for Daltrey's uplifting vocal, emphasised by upward key changes and the guitar and synth embellishments. Moon and Entwistle are at their absolute best here, displaying control, precision and when need be, attack. The rising coda that begins at 5:19 with Moon accelerating with controlled dexterity is stunning. It's one of The Who's best moments on record, and probably my favourite on the album. Because of its complex structure and synthesized arrangement, 'The Song Is Over' did not lend itself to live performances.

'Getting in Tune' 4:50 (Pete Townshend)

Like 'Pure and Easy', this song borrows from the writing of Sufi teacher and musician Inayat Khan and his philosophy of the mysticism of sound. More specifically, it is about how individuals can connect through the power of music. In the song, Townshend is also questioning his relevance as a rock star, a topic that would haunt him throughout his career. Like 'The Song Is Over', it features contrasting sections. This time it's Daltrey who begins the song in a subdued mood before the band enters to lift his spirits. The verses have a poppy zest although the call and response chorus and bluesy 'Getting in tune to the straight and narrow' section are a tad too drawn out in my opinion. That said, Hopkins' jazzy piano fills are superb and Entwistle's articulate bass lines are worth the price of admission alone. This song's best moment for me is the delicate 'I'm singing this note 'cause it fits in well' bridge at 2:12 with Daltrey and Townshend harmonising beautifully. Hopkins and Moon lock horns for the energetic finale. This is another song that was performed live in April and May 1971. Although it's very rarely been played since, it was revived briefly in 1999.

'Going Mobile' 3:42 (Pete Townshend)

Townshend's Dodge motorhome which he bought in 1970 and christened 'Maxine' was the inspiration for this song. It was parked backstage during The Who's weekend residency at the Isle of Wight Festival in August that year. Using the motorhome as a metaphor and driving across America as a theme, the song is about freedom and escaping from one's duties and responsibilities. Within the context of *Lifehouse*, the song reflects the character's necessity to travel, regardless of the consequences of pollution. It's one of the project's lighter songs in terms of subject and treatment.

Like 'My Wife', 'Going Mobile' was recorded without Daltrey's participation. Townshend is responsible for the lead vocals, acoustic rhythm guitar and synthesizer effects. In keeping with the subject, the song moves along at a lively pace with Townshend's singing having an uncharacteristically buoyant spring in its step. In the extended coda, Moon goes into overdrive and the processed solo – filtered through the ARP synthesiser – gives the guitar a gritty, wah-wah sound. In November 1971, 'Going Mobile' was the B side to the 'Behind Blue Eyes' single release in Europe. As a stage number, however, it never made it beyond the rehearsals.

'Behind Blue Eyes' 3:42 (Pete Townshend)

A song originally written for the villain of *Lifehouse* who believes his motives are well intended. Containing themes of isolation, anger and being misunderstood, Townshend later reflected that it could be interpreted as an autobiographical song although that wasn't his intention. Daltrey felt this song was very un-Who like at first but developed a strong affinity for it. He was often portrayed as The Who's bad boy although he believed he was always acting in the group's best interest. As written and demoed by Townshend, it's a sad, reflective song, but when recorded by the band, it gained a passion and urgency. Daltrey's masterful vocal is perfectly controlled and it remains his favourite Who song. The words reflect his situation back in October 1965 when he was temporarily thrown out of the band for his aggressive behaviour. On his return, he became a more tolerant person, 'Peaceful Perce' as he dubbed himself. The song's most telling line in that respect is 'When my fist clenches, crack it open' during the bridge although Townshend had originally written it as a prayer to Meher Baba. It followed Townshend's encounter with a groupie after a Who concert in Denver on 9 June 1970.

'Behind Blue Eyes' is a masterclass in tension and release. It begins as a sympathetic ballad with rippling acoustic guitar before exploding at 2:18 into a full-blown anthem of seismic proportions. The harmonies behind the choral hook are sublime and Daltrey's shift from melancholia to aggression is the ultimate statement in his maturity as a rock singer. The guitar riff at 3:05 is reprised as the instrumental bridge in 'Won't Get Fooled Again'. It was released as a single A-side in the USA on 6 November 1971 after being passed over by Decca as the B side for the 'Won't Get Fooled Again' single. It reached 34 on the Billboard chart. Although Townshend didn't think 'Behind Blue Eyes' was suitable for the UK singles market, it did appear in that format in parts of mainland Europe.

Along with 'Baba O'Riley' and 'Won't Get Fooled Again', 'Behind Blue Eyes' is one of The Who's most popular songs and was regularly performed live, including the 50th anniversary *The Who Hits 50!* 2014-2016 tours. The song has also been widely covered including an international hit for American rappers Limp Bizkit in 2003 and 2004. The original, unused version of the song, recorded at the Record Plant, New York in March 1971 with Al Kooper on Hammond organ surfaced as a bonus track on the 1995 CD reissue of *Who's Next*. An 'Alternate Version' from the same sessions is included on the 2003 deluxe edition.

'Won't Get Fooled Again' 8:32 (Pete Townshend)

If there is such a thing as a definitive Who song, 'Won't Get Fooled Again' is a strong contender for the title. A firm favourite, it has all the requisite elements including power, tension, release, light and shade, superb musicianship, sonic experimentation and cut glass production. With the exception of the six-part 'A Quick One, While He's Away' and *Tommy* instrumental 'Underture', it's the band's longest studio recorded song. By 1971, long songs were commonplace for the likes of Pink Floyd and Yes but remained a rare indulgence for The Who, even with a rock opera under their belt.

In 1971 when Che Guevara's visage adorned T-shirts and posters on student bedsit walls, the anti-revolution lyrics appeared decidedly unhip. They question the disruptive nature and negative effects of revolutions and causes for cause sake. Townshend, however, wasn't jumping on anyone's political bandwagon, left or right. It's a critique of power, corruption and the hollow promises of politicians. He later stated that he didn't believe in wars or revolution and that the latter was the ultimate betrayal. In a 1987 interview for *Rolling Stone*, he backtracked on his earlier comments, saying that 'It was an irresponsible song'. That didn't prevent The Who from performing it whenever they took to the stage. In 1999, Townshend continued to defend his opposition to revolution.

Compared with his original demo, The Who version is more aggressive, thanks to Daltrey's emotive vocal – and scream – which turned the song into a rock anthem. It's a defiant song, exemplified by power chords and a watertight rhythm. Despite Moon's reputation for excess, his drum volleys are controlled and articulate, especially during the build-up to Daltrey's famous scream. The synth background beat is a pulse modulated frequency taken from sound experiments conducted by Townshend. He used an EMS VCS3 synthesiser, to modify the block chords he played on the Lowrey organ. It would swiftly become a stage favourite and an obvious show finale. During the 1970s, when The Who performed without a keyboardist, 'Won't Get Fooled Again' would feature a pre-recorded synth track. It was the last song Keith Moon played live with The Who, filmed at Shepperton Studios on 25 May 1978. It closes The *Kids Are Alright* documentary and soundtrack. For the 2019 *Moving On!* tour, it was pared down to a duet with Daltrey backed by Townshend on acoustic guitar.

Prior to the release of *Who's Next*, a three minute 36-second edit of 'Won't Get Fooled Again' was released as a single. This appeared in the UK on 25 June 1971 and in America on 17 July, reaching number nine and fifteen respectively. It did even better in Canada, peaking at number seven.

'Won't Get Fooled Again' has been covered numerous times, most notably by Eddie Van Halen. Like 'Baba O'Riley', it's also cropped up on the soundtrack of several films and American TV shows. The 2003 deluxe edition of *Who's Next* includes two alternate versions of the song as bonus tracks. The first is the original, unused recording at the Record Plant, New York in March 1971 with Leslie West on guitar. The second is a live version from London's Young Vic theatre recorded on 26 April 1971.

Related Tracks

This section includes non-album songs, singles and B sides released during this period and tracks from the 1995 and 2003 CD reissues of *Who's Next* not discussed elsewhere in the book.

'I Don't Even Know Myself' 4:56 (Pete Townshend)

The B side to the 'Won't Get Fooled Again' single. It was recorded in 1970 at Eel Pie Sound for a proposed EP that never materialised. The subject is identity, or rather a lack of it, and finding one's path to spiritual enlightenment. Like so many of Townshend's songs, it has a personal, almost autobiographical feel. Daltrey's lead vocal is strong, driven by acoustic guitar and piano, although the country and western style theme for the chorus seems a tad out of place. That aside, Townshend's vigorous slide guitar playing is a joy although Entwistle's stunning basslines take top honours. It featured in the band's 1971 setlist following the release of *Who's Next*. It's included as a bonus track on the 1995 CD reissue and an extended live version from April 1971 on the 2003 deluxe edition.

'Let's See Action' 3:57 (Pete Townshend)

The Who's twenty-second single, released on 15 October 1971. Recorded during the *Who's Next* sessions, it was the first of three, non-album singles featuring leftover songs from *Lifehouse*; the other two being 'Join Together' and 'Relay'. It was released in the UK and mainland Europe only, reaching number sixteen in the UK, its highest chart placing in any region. Like 'Won't Get Fooled Again', 'Let's See Action' appears to be about revolution but it has a more positive, spiritual message. For Townshend, it expressed his feelings for Meher Baba, who's referenced in the line 'Avatar has warmed my feet'. He also preferred his demo to The Who's version.

Although one of my least favourite Who singles, it has its merits with Daltrey's delayed, double-tracked vocals perfectly conveying the song's rhythmic thrust. Townshend's acoustic rhythm and electric lead guitar fills add to the song's potency as does Nicky Hopkins' ever-present piano. The verses and chorus blend into one and, as is often the case, it's those small moments that stand out. Here, it's the mellow bridge at 1:51 sung by Townshend. The uplifting coda is also a highpoint, although as I recall when it was played on the radio, this provided an excuse for DJ's to talk over the ending. Originally titled 'Nothing Is Everything', Townshend's *Lifehouse* demos of this song, 'Pure and Easy' and 'Time Is Passing' appeared on his debut solo album *Who Came First*, released in October 1972.

'When I Was a Boy' 3:31 (John Entwistle)

The B side of the 'Let's See Action' single finds a despondent Entwistle trying to come to terms with adult life. His mournful horns provide the intro and superb accompaniment to the verses. The up-tempo chorus, lifted by Hopkins' piano and Townshend's guitar fills, is surprisingly upbeat. Moon's busy drumming is exceptional for what is possibly one of Entwistle's most underrated songs.

'Join Together' 4:20 (Pete Townshend)

The Who's twenty-fifth single A-side was released on 16 June 1972 in the UK and three weeks later in the USA. It reached number nine and seventeen respectively and was one of The Who's highest UK charting songs of the 1970s. It was their last release on Decca in the States before the label was taken over by MCA. Intended for the aborted follow-up album to *Who's Next*, 'Join Together' was recorded at Olympic Sound Studios, London in May 1972 with Glyn Johns producing. A memorable promo video for the single was directed by Michael Lindsay-Hogg on 25 June 1972. It features the band miming with instruments played on the record by Townshend.

Structurally, it's an unusual song with Daltrey's strident lead vocal providing the obvious Who factor. It opens with a Jew's harp and harmonica arrangement that provides a rhythmic undercurrent throughout the song. The overall effect is quite hypnotic and Entwistle and Moon make their presence felt with a solid, and not overly fussy, accompaniment. The song effectively restarts around the halfway mark with Townshend's jagged guitar fills and synthesizer embellishments leading the final assault. Unsurprisingly, 'Join Together' has remained a popular stage song. It was regularly performed in the '70s and '80s and maintained a constant presence throughout *The Who Hits 50!* world tour. It was also played during the 2019 *Moving On!* tour.

'Baby Don't You Do It' 6:09 (Brian Holland, Lamont Dozier, Eddie Holland)

A song with a long history. The Motown original was a hit in America for Marvin Gaye in 1964. The Who first recorded it in March 1965 with Shel Talmy and this 2:30 version appeared on the 1998 *Odds & Sods* remaster. The first released version, however, was a live recording from San Francisco's Civic Auditorium in December 1971 which was the B side to the 'Join Together' single. It was re-recorded on 16 March 1971 during the initial *Who's Next* sessions at The Record Plant in New York and a 5:13 edit appeared on the 1995 reissue of the album. Leslie West guests on lead guitar. The full 8:21 recording was made available on the 2003 deluxe edition of *Who's Next*. It was regularly performed live in 1964 and '65 and was dusted down for the 1973 *Quadrophenia* tour where it provided a showcase for Moon's energetic drumming.

'Time Is Passing' 3:59 (Pete Townshend)

Another *Lifehouse* outtake, this was recorded live on 26 April 1971 at London's Young Vic Theatre. It's featured on disc two of the 2003 edition of *Who's Next*. Daltrey affects a southern American drawl which suits this mid-tempo country rocker. Townshend and Entwistle play rhythm, for the most part, allowing Moon to venture into lead territory although the harmonica solo is courtesy of Daltrey. A 3:30 studio version is included on the 1998 CD reissue of *Odds & Sods*. Recorded at Olympic Studio on 12 April 1971 with Glyn Johns producing, it's a fine version with keys replacing the harmonica and deft acoustic guitar picking from Townshend.

'Road Runner' 3:14 (Ellas McDaniel)

The original version of this twelve-bar blues rocker was a minor American hit for Bo Diddley in 1960. Like 'Time Is Passing', The Who recorded it live at the Young Vic in 1971. Townshend's Duane Eddy style incessant riff and Daltrey's howling vocals take the band back to their R&B roots. It surfaced as a bonus track on the 2003 deluxe edition of *Who's Next*.

'Bony Moronie' 3:18 (Larry Williams)

Another live performance at London's Young Vic theatre in April 1971. It was included on the 'Won't Get Fooled Again' UK EP released in August 1988 and the 1994 *Thirty Years of Maximum R&B* box-set. Like 'Road Runner', this

R&B rocker allowed The Who to let their hair down in between the songs they were trialling for *Lifehouse*. Entwistle's running bass line is superb. Larry Williams' 1957 original was a top twenty hit single in both America and Australia.

'Going Down' 3:41 (Don Nix)

Another live song, this was included on the 1987 *Two's Missing* compilation. It was recorded at San Francisco's Civic Auditorium on 13 December 1971 during the second American leg of the *Who's Next* tour. Don Nix's rock and roll standard has been covered by numerous artists and The Who give it a hard rock treatment thanks to Townshend's jagged guitar chords. This was one of only three performances of the song on the tour.

Quadrophenia (1973)

Personnel:
Roger Daltrey: lead vocals
Pete Townshend: guitars, keyboards, banjo, cello, vocals, sound effects
John Entwistle: Bass guitar, horns, vocals
Keith Moon: drums, percussion, vocals
Additional personnel:
Jon Curle: newsreader voice on 'Cut My Hair'
Chris Stainton: Piano on 'The Dirty Jobs', '5:15' and 'Drowned'
Produced by: The Who
Associate producer: Glyn Johns on 'Is It in My Head?' and 'Love Reign o'er Me'
Engineered by: Ron Nevison
Recorded at: Olympic Sound Studios, London, May – June 1972,
Ramport Studios, Battersea, London with Ronnie Lane's Mobile Studio, May –
September 1973
Record label: UK: Track Records, USA: MCA Records
Release date: USA: 27 October 1973, UK: 2 November 1973
Highest chart places: UK: 2, USA: 2
Running time: 81:42

In 1972, The Who recorded the obligatory singles and in May and June, tracks
for the autobiographical *Rock Is Dead – Long Live Rock!*, the aborted follow-
up to *Who's Next*. Work began afresh on their sixth studio album on 21 May
1973. The sessions were conducted at their own Ramport Studio in Battersea,
London, which was under conversion from an old church hall. Without a
functioning control room, they brought in Ronnie Lane's mobile studio which
had been upgraded to sixteen-track by its designer Ron Nevison who also
engineered *Quadrophenia*. The initial sessions were recorded in quadraphonic
sound, but this was abandoned during the mixing stage for technical and
practical reasons.

Although Kit Lambert was involved in the very early stages, it was produced
by the band themselves with Pete Townshend having more control than he had
on any previous album. He began work on the songs in 1972 following the
Rock Is Dead sessions. Sound effects, synthesizer and piano from his original
demos ended up on the finished album. They were assembled at Townshend's
Eel Pie Sound Studio in Goring-on-Thames and he travelled to several outdoor
locations including Cornwall to record the natural sounds of rain, thunder
and crashing waves. These were converted from eight-track to sixteen-track
at Olympic Studios. At Rampart, each band member separately recorded their
parts which were then overdubbed onto the demos. Mixing was carried out
back at El Pie Sound by Townshend and Nevison during August and September
1973. Mastering was overseen by Townshend at The Mastering Lab, Los Angeles
in September.

Although there are no songs from John Entwistle, his contributions to the album are immense. In addition to his fluid bass lines, he recorded several horn parts which, along with Townshend's synth orchestrations, give the music an extra depth. Entwistle felt his bass was too low in the mix however and Roger Daltrey had similar concerns regarding his vocals. During rehearsals at Shepperton Studios in October for the subsequent tour, an escalating argument between Daltrey and Townshend left the guitarist flat out on the stage floor, followed by a trip to the hospital. Entwistle had the final word when he remixed the songs for the 1979 *Quadrophenia* film soundtrack.

Like *Tommy*, *Quadrophenia* occupied four sides of vinyl, but unlike the sensory impaired Tommy, the story of Jimmy has a gritty realism, even though his fate is equally ambiguous. Although the album, and Jimmy's split personality, is based on the four individual personalities within the band – thus explaining the title – the protagonist was inspired by The Who's London based fans during the mid-'60s. Jimmy is a diehard Mod and his trail of partying, pills, violence, romance, rejection, disillusionment, paranoia and redemption takes him from London to Brighton. Born during the latter part of World War two, Jimmy is also roughly the same age as The Who. Compared with *Lifehouse*, this was a more successful attempt to keep The Who musically relevant for the times, even though the story was reaching back to their past.

Complications arose when The Who took *Quadrophenia* on the road. It was a complex and difficult work to perform live, especially by a four-piece band. The 1973 tour began in the UK on the 28 October to coincide with the album's release. They used a quadraphonic sound system and an assortment of backing tapes for the *Quadrophenia* songs. During the shows, especially later in America, Daltrey felt compelled to explain the ongoing story in between each song which disrupted The Who's normally vigorous performance. As a result, at least five songs from *Quadrophenia* were dropped from the setlist partway into the tour. Another concern was the pre-recorded backing tapes of keyboard parts and sound effects, essential ingredients on the album. Things came to a head at the Odeon in Newcastle, UK on 5 November. When the tapes failed to operate in sync, Townshend vent his anger on road manager Bob Pridden and, after ripping out the tapes, he stormed off the stage. During the opening night of the North American leg in San Francisco on 20 November, Keith Moon collapsed on stage and nineteen-year-old audience member Scott Halpin bravely took his place to conclude the show.

Following its release, *Quadrophenia* rapidly scaled the album charts and stalled one place below the top spot on both sides of the Atlantic. By that point, however, it was already a resounding success; in America, it went gold as soon as it hit the shops and platinum two days later. Perhaps inevitably, reviews in the music press compared the album with *Tommy*, sometimes favourably – *Melody Maker* and the *NME* in the UK – and sometimes less so – *Rolling Stone* in America. Townshend would later say that as an artistic achievement, *Quadrophenia* was The Who album he was most proud of. It also remains the author's favourite.

By the following summer, a handful of songs from the album remained in the setlist with 'Drowned', 'Bell Boy', 'Doctor Jimmy', '5:15' and 'The Punk and the Godfather' occasionally played. It would be 22 years before The Who revisited *Quadrophenia* in its entirety.

The elaborate packaging for the original double LP incorporates a 44-page booklet. The evocative black and white photos perfectly capture the mid-60s and provide a visual accompaniment as Jimmy's story unfolds. Photographer Ethan Russell also supplied the cover for the previous album *Who's Next*. The cover depicting Jimmy – played by Terry Kennett – on his beloved scooter with the faces of The Who reflected in the rearview mirrors is inspired.

'I Am the Sea' 2:09 (Pete Townshend)

The album opens with Jimmy stranded on a rock in the sea to the sound of crashing waves, rain, thunder and rippling piano. The story then unfolds to explain how he came to be there. Water is a recurring theme throughout the album and 'I Am the Sea' is almost a mini-overture. A French horn fanfare introduces the principal themes, a leitmotif for each band member and the four sides of Jimmy's personality. Sung by Daltrey, they are 'Helpless Dancer', 'Is It Me?', 'Bell Boy' and 'Love, Reign O'er Me'.

'The Real Me' 3:21 (Pete Townshend)

The album's first song proper. Although the story is told in flashback, like *Tommy*, Jimmy's story unfolds in a linear fashion. The defiant young mod is suffering from an identity crisis and attempts to make sense of his mood swings with little help from his psychiatrist, mother and a preacher. Like several of Townshend's demos, the original was more laid back than The Who's version. Townshend plays electric rhythm, allowing Entwistle's prominent – and quite stunning – bass lines and horns to drive the song at a breakneck pace. As Jimmy, Daltrey is in majestic, defiant form.

This is one of a handful of songs on the album that was regularly performed live outside the *Quadrophenia* shows, including the 2019 *Moving On!* Tour. In certain regions outside the UK and USA, It was released as a single on 12 January 1974 with 'Doctor Jimmy' as the B side. It was backed with 'I'm One' in America, but it barely scraped into the Billboard top 100. The song segues into...

'Quadrophenia' 6:14 (Pete Townshend)

The title track is an instrumental and, like 'I Am the Sea', could be loosely described as an overture. It contains themes that would be expanded in the later songs. It was recorded at Townshend's El Pie Sound Studio he'd established at his home in Goring-on-Thames. Using an ARP 2500 synthesiser as a starting point, the track was built up in layers in the studio. With keyboards to the fore, lead guitar is less evident in the mix although Townshend provides some superb soloing. Each tune, especially the bridge from 'Doctor Jimmy', benefits from a sweeping, symphonic treatment. Soaring synths, horns and piano are underpinned by tastefully deployed bass, drums and electric guitar embellishments. Back in 1973, this was, and probably still is, my favourite track on the album. Live performance was restricted to the UK leg of the 1973 tour before the piece was revived when The Who reformed in 1996. The sound of rain leads into...

'Cut My Hair' 3:45 (Pete Townshend)

Jimmy has an argument with his dad over his nocturnal lifestyle and his mother finds pills and porno mags in his bedroom. He reflects on the expectations of his parents and the lifestyle of being a mod which involves pills, styling his hair and wearing the latest fashion to fit in. Townshend adapted the lines 'Zoot suit, white jacket with side vents, five inches long' from the High Numbers song 'Zoot Suit' released nine years earlier.

'Cut My Hair' alternates between two distinct parts. A Townshend sung melodic sequence with a sparse arrangement of weeping guitar, cymbals and hi-hat gives way to a strident, full-band arrangement voiced by Daltrey. Honours, however, go to the soaring middle-eight at 2:29 with Townshend accompanied by Entwistle's brass and thundering bass. Part of the song's musical theme used in the chorus was taken from an unfinished song titled – appropriately – 'Unused Piano'. Like many of the album's songs, this was dropped from the live set in 1973 before being resurrected in 1996.

'The Punk and the Godfather' 5:11 (Pete Townshend)

A popular Who song that has enjoyed a regular stage life outside the *Quadrophenia* shows. For some unknown reason, it was retitled 'The Punk Meets the Godfather' for the American album release. It's described in the sleeve note as 'a mini-opera'. Jimmy – the Punk in the title – goes to a rock concert and is disappointed to find that the group and their singer – the Godfather – are no different from the mod audience despite their aloof attitude. The song parallels Townshend's self-doubt regarding his own rock star persona and The Who's relevance to a young audience. This is underlined by a line in the song that references 'My Generation'. Although they're not specifically mentioned in the song, Townshend's sleeve notes confirm that the group is The Who. The booklet also shows Jimmy looking on as The Who walk from the Hammersmith Odeon to a waiting limousine with their arms around a group of Mod girls. Appropriately, given the subject, the song is pure Who, opening with frantic strummed, acoustic chords. Daltrey spans the full gamut of his vocal range and once again, the listener is continually drawn to Entwistle's majestic bass runs.

'I'm One' 2:38 (Pete Townshend)

The opening track on side two was recorded sans Daltrey with Townshend providing the lead vocal. Jimmy is having a crisis of confidence and although he considers himself to be something of a loser, at least he's still a Mod. This song was born from Townshend's own insecurities as a boy and an inability to fit in. A pastoral acoustic guitar opening finds Townshend in reflective mood before his electric rhythm ushers the band in. Fittingly, it ends on a positive, defiant note. Although this remains a popular song from the album, its rarely been performed outside the *Quadrophenia* shows.

'The Dirty Jobs' 4:30 (Pete Townshend)

One of three songs on the album featuring Chris Stainton of the Grease Band on piano. Townshend had wanted Stainton to tour with the band, but Daltrey insisted they remain a quartet. It's another personal favourite with a majestic synth line announcing a buoyant rhythm and a beautifully measured vocal from Daltrey. Moon's busy drumming fills every available nook and cranny in the song.

   Jimmy has left school and taken a job as a dustman – or garbageman if you're reading this book Stateside. In the sleeve notes, this song is labelled 'A complaining mini-opera' for good reason. Jimmy is frustrated with his elder workmates who complain about poor conditions and wages but won't stand up for their rights despite being war veterans. The booklet includes a superb photo of Jimmy almost lost – *Where's Wally?* style – in the middle of a huge rubbish tip. The sampled march at the end of the track is John Philip Sousa's 'The Thunderer' performed by a genuine brass band, secretly recorded in London's Kensington Gardens.

'Helpless Dancer' 2:34 (Pete Townshend)

(Roger's theme)

Daltrey represents the tough and violent side of Jimmy's character and here, dancing is a metaphor for tackling the hardships that life throws at you. Frustrated with the injustices in the world, Jimmy's anger turns to violence and in a photo montage in the album booklet, he and his Mod friends wreck a parked car. Rumbling piano and horns open another defiant song. Appropriately, Daltrey sings both sides of the venomous call and response verses – there's no chorus – against a marching piano rhythm. Townshend utilised a Bosendorfer grand piano for writing and recording the album's demos which he had recently installed in his home studio.

'Is It in My Head?' 3:44 (Pete Townshend)

The opening refrain from The Who's 'The Kids Are Alright' and the 'Is it me, for a moment' line from 'Doctor Jimmy' provide a link between 'Helpless Dancer' and this song. Full of self-doubt and a growing sense of despair, Jimmy begins to question his own sanity. Piano, bass and serene guitar underpin Daltrey's plaintiff introduction. Entwistle's lead vocal takes the song down a familiar Who path with power chords, rousing guitar, drums and piano fills. Given the subject, Daltrey's vocal bridge is surprisingly jubilant but works well within the context of the song's treatment. It was originally recorded in May 1972 at Olympic Studios with producer Glyn Johns for the abandoned *Rock Is Dead – Long Live Rock!* album.

'I've Had Enough' 6:15 (Pete Townshend)

Jimmy has walked out on his parents and is sleeping rough. The girl he fancies ignores him and is more interested in his friend Dave. The final straw comes, when, in a moment of anger and frustration, he crashes his beloved GS scooter. He decides to return to Brighton, where he has happier memories of being part of a Mod gang in the 'land of dreams'.

Entwistle's pounding bassline and Moon's rampant drumming is the heart and soul of this song. Daltrey conveys Jimmy's tortured soul with convincing venom and Townshend deploys acoustic guitar, electric guitar and banjo for rhythm, riffs and fills. This is the halfway point of *Quadrophenia* and appropriately the 'Love, Reign O'er Me' theme appears briefly, supported by piano and a spiralling synth motif. The track and side two of the original LP conclude with the sound of a speeding train to underline Jimmy's resolve.

'5:15' 5:01 (Pete Townshend)

If 'Pinball Wizard' was the obvious single from *Tommy*, then '5:15' is its counterpart on *Quadrophenia*. The many hours Entwistle spent overdubbing the brass parts really pays off here with his rousing horn arrangement driving '5:15' at an exhilarating pace. The song tells of Jimmy's train journey from London to Brighton, surrounded by commuters on their way home from work. The song is not only a metaphor for Jimmy's despondent, pill addled state but also the speeding train and its assorted passengers. The sound of train doors closing and whistle at the beginning were recorded at London's Waterloo Station – immortalised by the Kinks' 'Waterloo Sunset'. Although the lyrics are firmly grounded in the early '70s, the song still packs a punch. Entwistle's brass stabs and bass riff are matched by Stainton's lively piano. Townshend delivers one of his best guitar solos and Daltrey can hardly contain his exuberance.

'5:15' was released as a single in Europe on 5 October 1973, four weeks before the album, peaking at number twenty in the UK. In his review at the time, legendary Radio One DJ John Peel gave '5:15' a thumbs-up while having a sly dig at the Rolling Stones' ballad 'Angie' released a few weeks before. When '5:15' was re-released in September 1979 to promote the *Quadrophenia* film and soundtrack album, it reached 45 in the Billboard chart. Often played with horns and piano accompaniment, it's another firm stage favourite and a highlight of The Who's *Quadrophenia* shows. As a tribute to Entwistle, when it was performed in 2012, ten years after his death, footage of him playing the bass solo at the Royal Albert Hall in 2000 was inserted into the band's live performance.

'Sea and Sand' 5:02 (Pete Townshend)

Jimmy wanders the Brighton beaches, reminiscing about happier times with his Mod friends and making love to his girl on the beach. He reflects on the failings in his love life and the strained relations with his parents and friends. Opening with the sound of surf and seagulls, 'Sea and Sand' is for the most part standard Who fare. Although it rocks with convincing aggression, it's perhaps one of the album's least memorable songs. The guitar riff and drum pattern at 3:30 following the false ending sounds like a rehash of 'Won't Get Fooled Again' although Daltrey's wistful 'The girl I love' bridge at 1:03 is a welcome interlude. The lyrics describing Jimmy's Mod regalia sung by Townshend are reprised from 'I've Had Enough' and there's a brief reference to the High Numbers' 'I'm The Face' as the song fades.

'Drowned' 5:28 (Pete Townshend)

'Drowned' explores Jimmy's spiritual search, although Townshend describes it as 'desperate and nihilistic'. Jimmy has been searching without success for the 'Ace Face' Mod who he remembers from the previous trip to Brighton. Based on a Meher Baba quote, he contemplates immersing himself and becoming one with the water 'Let me flow into the ocean, let me get back to the sea'. It's one of the oldest songs on *Quadrophenia* which Townsend wrote in 1970 as a tribute to Baba.

Announced by crashing power chords, 'Drowned' is one of the hardest rocking songs on the album, harking back to The Who's R&B roots. Moon's drumming is phenomenal, filling every inch of the track. Stainton's bluesy piano motif that accompanies the verses was borrowed from 'Hitchcock Railway', a song on Joe Cocker's 1969 self-titled second album. According to director Ken Russell, who visited Ramport in 1973 to discuss the *Tommy* film, the studio flooded during the recording of Stainton's piano part. Entwistle reprises the horns arrangement from '5:15' and at the end of the track, Townshend recorded himself walking along a beach to the sounds of seagulls and surf singing a verse from 'Sea and Sand'. A blues-based song with room for improvisation, 'Drowned' became a live staple. In the '80s onwards, Townshend replaced Daltrey as the song's lead singer and occasionally performed it solo on acoustic guitar.

'Bell Boy' 4:56 (Pete Townshend)

(Keith's theme)

Unsurprisingly, Moon is the irresponsible, reckless side of Jimmy's character. Daltrey introduces the song as Jimmy. He sings the first two verses accompanied by pounding drums and bass, piano and synth trills. Introduced by heavy guitar chords, Moon sings the part of the 'Ace Face' in an over the top cockney accent. A disillusioned Jimmy discovers that the Mod leader he admired is now working as a porter in a Brighton hotel. The encounter is the final straw for Jimmy, for him, being let down as a Mod is the ultimate betrayal.

The 'Some nights I still sleep on the beach' bridge at 2:00 sung by Moon – without the accent – provides a tranquil respite.

Although this song was only performed during the *Quadrophenia* tours, given Moon's comical turn, it was much requested. He can be heard on the 1979 film soundtrack even though Sting plays the part of the 'Ace Face'. During later shows following the drummer's death, it was often performed by guest vocalists. On the original double LP, it adds a welcome note of levity to close side three before the deadly serious finale.

'Doctor Jimmy' 8:37 (Pete Townshend)
(Including John's theme 'Is It Me?')
Jimmy's schizophrenia is made evident in the album's most potent song. It's also the longest track by some distance. Inspired by Robert Louis Stevenson's nineteenth-century classic *Strange Case of Dr Jekyll and Mr Hyde*, 'Doctor Jimmy' emphasises the contrast between the romantic and violent sides of Jimmy's character. When he's not keeping himself in check with pills, the latter is brought on by gin. It contains Townshend's most hard-hitting words committed to song, delivered with appropriate venom by Daltrey.

The track opens with the ominous sounds of wind, rain and thunder before the band explodes into action. It's the most ambitious song on *Quadrophenia*, with contrasting sections, imaginative arrangements and rich instrumentation. Synth provides a rhythmic undercurrent and the powerful chorus is emphasised by majestic horns and organ. Entwistle is the romantic side of Jimmy's character, represented by the delicate 'Is It Me, for a moment' middle-eight at 3:18. It's sung by Daltrey however, accompanied by Townshend's shimmering cello and piano. Rippling piano and the hum of a boat's engine lead into...

'The Rock' 6:38 (Pete Townshend)
High on pills and armed with a bottle of gin, Jimmy steals a boat and heads out to sea to a jagged rock. In his mind, the drone of the boat's engine becomes the sound of heavenly music and choirs. Townshend is drawing from his boyhood past here and a bizarre incident he experienced as an eleven-year-old Sea Scout. During a boat journey, the rhythmic sound of the boat's engine had lured him into a trance where he imagined he could hear angelic voices. This same experience would be revisited and amplified in his later work *The Boy Who Heard Music*.

Like the title track, this instrumental was recorded at Townshend's Eel Pie Sound studio. Lead guitar is prominent with superb soloing powered by Moon's explosive fills. Several themes are reprised including 'Is It Me?' at 1:12 with piano, horns and synth providing the accompaniment. The two-minute mid-section beginning at 2:46 is for want of a better description, a lively piano and guitar-led Russian dance arrangement. It's a dazzling sequence.

'Love, Reign O'er Me' 5:49 (Pete Townshend)
(Pete's theme)

Although Townshend's theme is the album's most triumphant, as a typically self-debasing gesture, he also represents the beggar and hypocrite in Jimmy's personality. The boat has drifted away, leaving Jimmy stranded on the rock in the pouring rain. This song again borrows from the philosophy of Meher Baba who taught that rain was a blessing from God and for Townshend, the sound of thunder is his voice. Jimmy contemplates suicide, but instead, he discovers an inner strength, maturity and finally, redemption. Here the falling rain, which can be heard at the beginning of the track becomes a metaphor for love. The song opens with a gorgeous piano solo with Daltrey entering at the one minute mark. He's supported by the rhythmic synth motif first heard in the title track. As the song builds to its grandiose finale, the synth is used to replicate the sound of cascading strings. The mellow guitar solo at 3:58 has more than a hint of David Gilmour about it.

Like 'Is It in My Head?', this was another song leftover from the aborted 1972 project *Rock Is Dead – Long Live Rock!*. It was also offered to producer Lou Reizner following a request for additional material for the 1972 orchestral version of *Tommy*. Townshend envisaged Maggie Bell who played Tommy's mother singing it. Given that *Tommy* already had an uplifting finale in the shape of 'Listening to You', he wisely withdrew it. 'Love, Reign O'er Me' was performed in the 1973 and '74 *Quadrophenia* tours and was one of four songs played at *Live Aid* in 1985. A drastically edited version was released as a single in America on 27 October 1973, reaching a disappointing 76 in the Billboard chart. Pearl Jam frontman Eddie Vedder is a devoted Who fan and the Seattle rockers recorded a memorable cover in 2006 complete with piano and strings.

Related Tracks

'Relay' 3:49 (Pete Townshend)
A non-album single A side released in the USA on 25 November 1972 and the UK on 22 December. It was retitled 'The Relay' for the American market, The Who's first release on MCA. It was recorded during the same sessions as the previous single 'Join Together' in May 1972. It failed to reach the same heights chart wise however, stalling at 21 in the UK and 39 in America. Like 'Join Together', it's a remnant of *Lifehouse* and would have been included on the proposed *Rock Is Dead—Long Live Rock!* album had it gone ahead in 1972.

As part of the *Lifehouse* concept, the song alludes to 'the relay', Townshend's imagined forerunner of the internet. The unnatural, stop-start sound that opens the song and provides a rhythmic undercurrent throughout was produced by processing a guitar through an ARP synthesiser. The song is very rhythmic and as such, a close cousin to 'Magic Bus'. Daltrey certainly liked the song which is evident in his gutsy delivery. Townshend was less enthusiastic which is perhaps why subsequent performances were sporadic despite it being a marginal hit.

It was performed during The Who's 1972 European tour and made occasional stage appearances before and after the band reformed in 1996.

'Waspman' 3:09 (Keith Moon)

The B-side of the 'Relay' single, recorded at Olympic Studios on 7 August 1972. The song was so-called because one of Moon's antics was to dress in a wasp costume to entertain – and distract – the rest of the band during recording sessions. It was dedicated to Link Wray who Townshend and Moon had met and befriended at New York's Record Plant in March 1971. In the bizarre stakes, the song matches the title. It's based around a repetitive, see-sawing rhythm with nonsensical lyrics and little in the way of musical development. Although Moon's authorship of the song has been disputed, it's the kind of ditty one can readily associate with his warped sense of humour.

'Water' 4:39 (Pete Townshend)

'Water' has the distinction of being the B side to both the UK '5:15' single and the USA 'Love, Reign O'er Me' single. The latter was also released in Belgium and the Netherlands. Recorded at Eel Pie Studios, Twickenham in May 1970, it was another outtake from the *Lifehouse* sessions. It was also intended for an aborted EP/maxi-single and is included as a bonus track on the 1998 remaster of *Odds & Sods*.

'Water' was inspired by an incident on the Cuyahoga River, Cleveland, Ohio on 22 June 1969 when a fire raged as a result of the river's excessive pollution. The song's treatment is simple but effective. Daltrey digs deep for a raunchy, blues delivery backed by acoustic rhythm and electric lead guitars. Although a Townshend original, the song sounds like a throwback to the Detours in their R&B heyday. The Who regularly performed 'Water' live in 1970 and '71 where it often took on epic proportions. A live recording from London's Young Vic Theatre on 26 April 1971 was included as a 6:30 edit on the 1995 CD reissue of *Who's Next*. The full, 8:20 live version features on the 2003 deluxe edition.

'We Close Tonight' 2:56 (Pete Townshend)

Dropped from *Quadrophenia* at the mixing stage, this surfaced on the 1998 expanded CD of *Odds & Sods*. Like 'Four Faces', 'Get Out and Stay Out' and 'Joker James', Townshend's original demo of this song appears on the 2011 five-disc 'Director's Cut' of *Quadrophenia*. Townshend's demos, including songs that didn't make it onto the finished album, occupy discs three and four of this set. Following the drum solo entry, it rolls along at a lively, piano-driven pace. It's a rare instance of Entwistle singing a Townshend composed song. There is no chorus as such and he exchanges the verses with a manic sounding Moon.

'Four Faces' 3:20 (Pete Townshend)

Like 'We Close Tonight', this is another *Quadrophenia* outtake. It was remixed by Entwistle for the 1979 film soundtrack. Here as Jimmy, Townshend sings about his split personality. With its jaunty, piano-led melody, it sounds like nothing else on *Quadrophenia* which is perhaps why it was excluded from the original album. It has an agreeable vibrancy, however, with engaging acoustic guitar picking.

'Get Out and Stay Out' 2:26 (Pete Townshend)

Along with 'Joker James', this was recorded for the 1979 *Quadrophenia* film soundtrack. They are the first Who recordings with Kenney Jones on drums. Together with 'Four Faces', they were added to advance the narrative and here the title is self-explanatory. Fed up with his behaviour and nocturnal activities, Jimmy's frustrated parents throw him out. Given the subject, it has a surprisingly upbeat melody with Townshend once again supplying the vocals. In the film, the song accompanies Jimmy and his Mod friends riding their scooters towards Brighton.

'Joker James' 3:13 (Pete Townshend)

Here, a restrained Daltrey – backed by a harmonious Townshend and Entwistle – sings about the relationships with various girls in Jimmy's love life which seem to end in tears every time. Unlike 'Get Out and Stay Out' where Jones' drumming is clipped and precise, here his busy fills that punctuate the verses and chorus bring to mind Moon's playing on 'Substitute'.

Right: The debut album *My Generation* is one of the quintessential rock albums of the 1960s and the title song became an anthem for the Mod generation. *(Brunswick)*

Left: Inspired by the popular TV pop show *Ready Steady Go!*, The Who's first EP *Ready Steady Who* was a UK-only release. *(Reaction)*

Right: The 1966 *A Quick One* album concludes with The Who's first 'mini-opera', the near ten minute 'A Quick One, While He's Away'. *(Reaction)*

Left: An early example of the promotional film with the Who miming to the 1966 single 'The Kids Are Alright'. It was shot in London's Hyde Park in the Summer of 1966. *(Polydor)*

Right: Pete Townshend and Keith Moon strutting their stuff in 'The Kids Are Alright' promo. *(Polydor)*

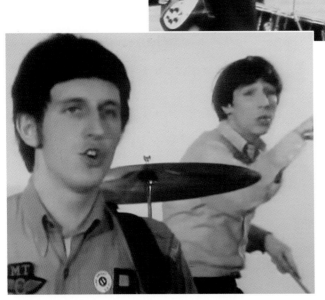

Left: A fresh-faced John Entwistle and Keith Moon in the 1966 promo for the 'Substitute' single. It was one of the band's most popular tunes of the 1960s. *(Polydor)*

Right: A debonair Roger Daltrey in polo neck jumper and check jacket from the promo video for the highly successful 1965 debut 'I Can't Explain' single. *(Polydor)*

Left: John Entwistle opts for the Beatles look in the same video. *(Polydor)*

Right: The 'Ace Face' – Pete Townshend, once again from the 'I Can't Explain' promo video. *(Polydor)*

Left: *The Who Sell Out* includes the author's favourite Who single 'I Can See for Miles'. Disappointingly, it failed to reach its deserved position at the top of the charts. *(Track)*

Right: Often cited as the best live album ever by a rock band, *Live at Leeds* is The Who in their prime. It was greatly expanded on subsequent CD reissues. *(Decca)*

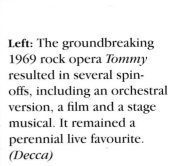

Left: The groundbreaking 1969 rock opera *Tommy* resulted in several spin-offs, including an orchestral version, a film and a stage musical. It remained a perennial live favourite. *(Decca)*

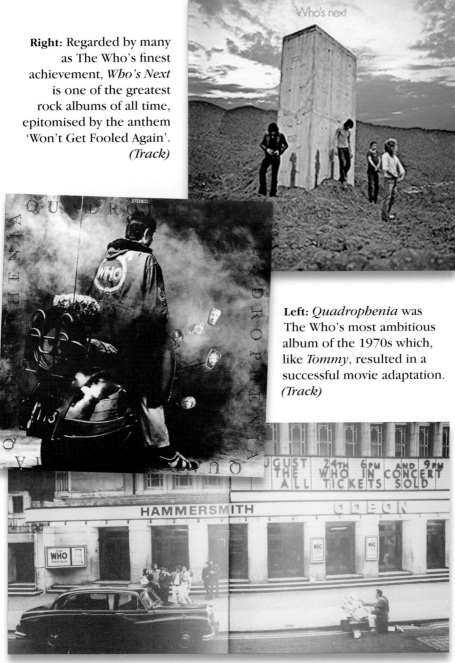

Right: Regarded by many as The Who's finest achievement, *Who's Next* is one of the greatest rock albums of all time, epitomised by the anthem 'Won't Get Fooled Again'. *(Track)*

Left: *Quadrophenia* was The Who's most ambitious album of the 1970s which, like *Tommy*, resulted in a successful movie adaptation. *(Track)*

Above: From the booklet with the 1973 double LP release of *Quadrophenia*, the band emerge from London's Hammersmith Odeon to a waiting limousine while Jimmy looks on. *(Geoffrey Feakes)*

SUNDOWN
SILVER ST. 463

Sundown

SILVER STREET
EDMONTON, N.18.

Evening 7-30
SATURDAY
DECEMBER 22
THE WHO

Circle
£2·20
Incl. VAT

EVENING 7-30 p.m.   Doors open 6-45
SATURDAY, 22nd DECEMBER, 1973

JOHN & TONY SMITH in association with Track International present
THE WHO

CIRCLE
£2·20
Incl. VAT

021

021

Cameras & Tape Recorders
are not allowed in the
Auditorium.
_____

For conditions of sale see over

Above: The Who's performance at the Edmonton Sundown, London in
December 1973 is rated by Pete Townshend as one of the band's finest.
(Geoffrey Feakes)

Right: The author was
fortunate enough to be
in the audience at The
Granby Halls, Leicester in
October 1975, when The
Who's state of the art lasers
made their debut.
(Geoffrey Feakes)

John Smith Entertainments in association with Trinifold
presents

THE WHO
plus
THE STEVE GIBBONS BAND
SATURDAY 18th OCTOBER 1975
at 8 pm Doors open 7.15 pm Tickets £2.20 inc. VAT
The Granby Halls
Welford Road, Leicester

No re-admission
For conditions see reverse
To be retained and produced
on demand.
Scot. Auto. Edin.

N° · 5974

C30

C30

ODEON
QUEEN ST.
LEICESTER

THE BIG
SCREEN
SCENE

Screen 1

Front Circle
11
ODEON
WEDNESDAY
OCTOBER 22
Final
Eve. Perf.

Screen 1

Front Circle
WEDNESDAY

OCTOBER 22

FOR TIME SEE
DAILY PRESS

Final
Eve. Perf.

TOMMY
(AA)

Ticket cannot be exchanged or money refunded

Left: The
screening of
the *Tommy*
film in 1975
was so popular
that this ticket
had to be
purchased
in advance.
*(Geoffrey
Feakes)*

Left: The front cover of the 1975 UK tour programme. *(Geoffrey Feakes)*

Below: Inner pages of the 1975 UK tour programme – the 'Greatest Show on Earth'. *(Geoffrey Feakes)*

Above: Filmed at Shepperton Studios on 25 May 1978, this was Keith Moon's final performance with The Who before his untimely death less than four months later. *(Universal Music)*

Below: A hyper Pete Townshend during The Who's performance of 'Won't Get Fooled Again' at Shepperton Studios. It was filmed for the closing sequence of *The Kids Are Alright* documentary. *(Universal Music)*

Above: The peerless and stolid John Entwistle during 'Won't Get Fooled Again' at Shepperton Studios on 25 May 1978. *(Universal Music)*

Below: 'Rock God' Roger Daltrey bathed in blue lasers at Shepperton Studios. This sequence was filmed separately and inserted into the 'Won't Get Fooled Again' footage. *(Universal Music)*

Above: Keith Moon in full flight during the 'Who Are You' promo video. It was filmed at London's Ramport Studios on 4 May 1978 for *The Kids Are Alright* documentary.

Below: A relaxed John Entwistle records his backing vocals for the 'Who Are You' promo.

Above: An animated Keith Moon entertains John Entwistle and Pete Townshend during the 'Who Are You' promo.

Below: The 'Who Are You' promo again and Roger Daltrey is not amused.

Left: The aptly titled 1974 album *Odds & Sods* demonstrated that even the Who's outtakes were worthy of release. *(Track)*

Right: Compared with *Quadrophenia, The Who by Numbers,* released in 1975, is a back to basics Who album that drew mixed reviews. *(Polydor)*

Left: The 1978 album *Who Are You* was the last to feature drummer Keith Moon, who sadly died just three weeks after its release. *(Polydor)*

Right: The *Face Dances* album demonstrated that The Who could hold their own in the 1980s. It contains the international hit 'You Better You Bet'. *(Polydor)*

Left: The tenth studio album *It's Hard* was The Who's last before disbanding in 1983. It was also the last to feature bassist John Entwistle. *(Polydor)*

Right: The 1979 documentary *The Kids Are Alright* and the companion soundtrack album, is a fine showcase of The Who in their prime and a fitting testimony to Keith Moon.

Left: A thoughtful Kenney Jones tries to remember where he left his drumsticks during the promo video for 'Eminence Front' filmed during the band's 1982 US tour.

Right: A stately John Entwistle and a boyish Pete Townshend in the 'Eminence Front' promo, rehearsing for the evening's show at Landover, Maryland.

Left: Roger Daltrey, Pete Townshend and three empty beer bottles interviewed on BBC2's *Later... with Jools Holland* in November 2007. *(BBC)*

Above: The Who in full-throttle on a huge stage performing a rousing 'Baba O'Riley/Listening to You/My Generation' medley at the Olympics closing ceremony in 2012.

Right: Pete Townshend chooses the yachting look with a striped t-shirt and a white jacket at the Olympics.

Left: Roger Daltrey, the ultimate frontman looking dapper in his grey suit, is again pictured during the 2021 Olympics performance.

Left: *Endless Wire,* released in 2006, is The Who's penultimate album with Roger Daltrey and Pete Townshend backed by their touring musicians. *(Polydor)*

Right: Released in 2019, *Who* almost – but not quite – put the band back at the top of the UK and US album charts. *(Polydor)*

Above: The Who band and orchestra having fun at the Amalie Arena in Tampa, Florida on 22 September 2019 during the Moving On! Tour.

Odds & Sods (1974)

Personnel:
Roger Daltrey: lead vocals, backing vocals, harmonica
Pete Townshend: guitar, piano, synthesizer, backing and lead vocals
John Entwistle: bass, brass, backing and lead vocals
Keith Moon: drums, occasional vocals
Original production by Glyn Johns, Kit Lambert, Peter Meaden, Chris Parmeinter, Shel Talmy and The Who
Compiled and remixed by John Entwistle, John Alcock
Recorded at: Various studios, 1964 – 1973
Record label: UK: Track Records/Polydor, USA: MCA
Release date: UK: 4 October 1974, USA: 12 October 1974
Highest chart places: UK: 10, USA: 15
Running time: 40:23

In addition to his involvement with the *Tommy* film soundtrack and solo activities, John Entwistle spent a good deal of 1974 revisiting The Who's past. This involved several visits to the tape archives located at Track Records in Soho. Here, he sifted through an ever-growing assortment of unused recordings from the previous ten years. He was motivated by the poor quality bootlegs of unreleased Who material prevalent at the time. It would provide a stopgap to fill the two-year void between *Quadrophenia* and *The Who by Numbers*. He began work the previous summer when he mixed several tracks recorded in 1970 at Eel Pie Studios, Twickenham. Earlier mono recordings from the '60s were upgraded to stereo. The majority of the production and mixing was carried out at Ramport and Nova Sound Studios, London and completed in July '74. Entwistle was assisted by John Alcock who also co-produced his fourth solo album, *Mad Dog*. Although a double LP's worth of material had been amassed, for budgetary reasons it was restricted to the one vinyl disc. The leftover tracks appeared on an expanded and remastered CD version in 1998. A 2011 reissue included the 1998 tracks, reassembled to reflect the running order of the original LP.

Strictly speaking, *Odds & Sods* is a compilation album, but given the wealth of high quality, previously unreleased material it warrants its own chapter. It also boasts one of The Who's most familiar covers. The photo of the band wearing American football helmets was taken backstage at Chicago's International Amphitheatre on 29 November 1973 during the *Quadrophenia* tour. Photographer Graham Hughes tore it into pieces and then stuck it back together to achieve the desired, discarded effect in keeping with the album and title.

'Postcard' 3:27 (John Entwistle)
Entwistle opens the collection with one of his own tunes. It was recorded in May 1970 at Townshend's Eel Pie Studio in Twickenham and was originally

intended for an aborted Who EP/maxi-single that year. For this version, Entwistle recorded a new bass part and overdubbed horns at Ramport Studios in 1974. 'Postcard' is literally that, a memento in song of the various countries visited by The Who during their tours. Naturally, Entwistle provides the lead vocals and both his bass and brass arrangement are suitably upfront. It was released as a single in America on 23 November 1974 to promote *Odds & Sods*. It was a rare instance of an Entwistle A side although it failed to crack the Billboard chart.

'Now I'm A Farmer' 3:59 (Pete Townshend)

Although written by Townshend, Daltrey relates the joys of being a man of the land. In 1970, the singer had purchased his own country mansion complete with farmland. Some of the lyrical rhyming couplets would do Entwistle proud, and it also contains veiled drug references. The melody in the verses is very similar to 'Christmas' on *Tommy* and Townshend takes over for the mock country and western bridge. Moon's flays his tom-toms for all their worth. The Who at their most tongue in cheek and another song from the abandoned 1970 EP recorded during the same sessions as 'Postcard'.

'Put the Money Down' 4:14 (Pete Townshend)

A song originally intended for *Lifehouse* and an outtake from the *Who's Next* sessions. It was originally recorded with Glyn Johns in June 1972, and Entwistle re-recorded Daltrey's lead vocal at Ramport Studios in 1974. It was the B side to the 'Postcard' single. The verses bring to mind 'Join Together' and both Daltrey's tough vocals and Townshend's edgy guitar fills are pleasingly robust. The lyrics recall a Who gig in Columbus, Ohio on 1 November 1969 and the line 'there are bands killing chickens' is a reference to Alice Cooper, one of the support acts on the North American tour.

'Little Billy' 2:15 (Pete Townshend)

This was recorded on 11 February 1968 for an advertising campaign by the American Cancer Society but was rejected on the grounds that it was too long. There may have been other reasons because it's hard to imagine this jaunty little number as an advertising jingle despite the lyrical content. Daltrey sings almost falsetto style against a restrained instrumental arrangement. The playful backing harmonies are a delight.

'Too Much of Anything' 4:26 (Pete Townshend)

Originally titled 'Bit Too Much', this is another quality leftover from the *Who's Next* sessions. The song is about excess, vices and living life to the extreme. It was recorded with Glyn Johns at Olympic Studios, Barnes on 12 April 1971. The original studio version appears as a bonus track on the 1995 CD reissue of *Who's Next* and a live version on the 2003 deluxe edition. Daltrey is in a reflective mood for this laidback song with acoustic guitar and Nicky Hopkins' articulate piano providing sympathetic support. It kicks up its heels for the rousing bridge. The song's tone and Moon's tasteful drumming is reminiscent of The Band's 1968 ballad 'The Weight', immortalised by the film *Easy Rider*.

'Glow Girl' 2:20 (Pete Townshend)

Recorded in January and February 1968, a song about a couple who are reincarnated after dying in a plane crash. It was inspired by The Who's jaunts across America by air during their 1967 tour with Herman's Hermits. The chartered plane was an old DC-8 and Townshend was in constant fear that it might crash. Another inspiration was early '60s songs by the Shangri-Las, John Leyton and Jan and Dean that often included death as a theme. Daltrey and Townshend share unison lead vocals to harmonious effect and the coda 'It's a girl, Mrs Walker, It's a girl' was reworked for 'It's a Boy' on *Tommy*. 'Glow Girl' was originally considered for single release in early 1968 and the lead track for an aborted album titled Who's For Tennis? It was included as a bonus track on the 1995 *The Who Sell Out* CD reissue.

'Pure and Easy' 5:23 (Pete Townshend)

A surprise omission from the *Who's Next* album and a pivotal song in the abandoned *Lifehouse* project. Originally titled 'The Note', it would have closed the album. Townshend described it as 'the 'Amazing Journey' of *Lifehouse* and essential to the story. It was performed live in April and May 1971 prior to the release of the album. It's certainly ambitious in its subject matter, intended to reflect creation musically. The opening line 'There once was a note, pure and easy' was inspired by the writing of Sufi teacher and musician Inayat Khan. His philosophy reflected Townshend's and the spiritual search for the one musical note that suits us all.

A drum solo intro finds Daltrey in a thoughtful mood. Townshend alternates between acoustic rhythm and electric lead with aggressive soloing, setting the scene for the rousing coda. This version was produced by The Who and Glyn Johns at Olympic Studios in May 1971. The original March 1971 recording is a bonus track on the 1995 CD reissue of *Who's Next*. A six-minute live recording from London's Young Vic Theatre on 26 April 1971 is included on the 2003 deluxe edition.

'Faith In Something Bigger' 3:03 (Pete Townshend)

Like 'Glow Girl' on side one, this is another unreleased song from 1968, recorded in January that year with Kit Lambert producing. Townshend discovered Meher Baba the previous year which may well have influenced the song's spiritual message. Musically, It's more down to earth and reminiscent of the lightweight pop ballads of the '60s by Merseybeat acts like the Searchers and the Hollies. It boasts a gorgeous melody with Daltrey crooning over sweet counterpoint harmonies. An utter – and at the time unexpected – delight.

'I'm the Face' 2:32 (Peter Meaden)
See 'Related Tracks' in the *My Generation* chapter.

'Naked Eye' 5:10 (Pete Townshend)
Although this song was omitted from *Who's Next*, it was performed during the band's 1971 tour following the album's release. During the '70s, it was occasionally played alongside 'Magic Bus' as part of a closing medley. This version was initially recorded at Townshend's Eel Pie Studio in May 1970 for an EP/maxi-single that went unreleased. The recording was revived at Olympic Studios on 7 June 1971 as a possible contender for *Lifehouse*. Following Daltrey's reflective intro, the song swings in a different, more strident direction. Townshend provides alternate lead vocals, but it's his aggressive guitar soloing that dominates. A live version was recorded at the Young Vic theatre in 1971 and a 5:30 edit is included on the 1995 CD reissue of *Who's Next*. The full live version features on the 2003 deluxe edition.

'Long Live Rock' 3:54 (Pete Townshend)
This was recorded in May 1972 at Olympic Studios with Glyn Johns. It was intended for the shelved *Rock Is Dead – Long Live Rock!* album, a planned history of The Who. It's pure rock and roll modelled on Chuck Berry's 'Johnny B. Goode' and was performed during The Who's 1972 European tour. Following its inclusion in the 1979 documentary *The Kids Are Alright*, it was released as a single in the UK and USA, charting at 48 and 54 respectively.

'Long Live Rock' was re-recorded for the 1973 film *That'll Be The Day* with Billy Fury on lead vocals. The film stars David Essex and Ringo Starr along with a typecast cameo from Keith Moon as drummer J. D. Clover. In a memorable scene, Essex's character Jim MacLaine is asked by singer Stormy Tempest – played by Fury – if he can play the drums. J. D. intervenes with the line 'What Mr. Tempest is trying to say is that he would like to get rid of me, but you can't, can you Stormy!' followed by a ferocious drum solo to underline the point.

Related Tracks
With the exception of 'My Way', the twelve additional songs on the CD reissue of *Odds & Sods* have all been discussed in previous chapters.

'My Way' 2:26 (Eddie Cochran, Jerry Capehart)
This is not to be confused with the Paul Anka ballad immortalised by Frank Sinatra. The Who remain faithful to Eddie Cochran's original, right down to the solo guitar intro and Daltrey's raunchy vocal. It has a typical rock and roll,

good time feel with a loose arrangement and handclap rhythm. Following the recording on 10 October 1967, The Who performed 'My Way' during the North America spring tour the following year. The original was a posthumous 1963 UK hit single following Cochran's fatal road accident three years earlier. He was just 21 years old.

The Who by Numbers (1975)

Personnel:

Roger Daltrey: lead vocals

Pete Townshend: guitar, banjo, ukulele, backing vocals, lead vocals on 'However Much I Booze' and 'Blue, Red And Grey'

John Entwistle: bass, French horn, trumpet, backing vocals, 2nd lead vocal on 'Success Story'

Keith Moon: drums

Additional personnel:

Nicky Hopkins: piano

Produced and engineered by Glyn Johns

Recorded at: Shepperton Studios, Surrey, England using Ronnie Lane's Mobile Studio, April – June 1975

Record label: UK: Polydor, USA: MCA

Release date: UK: 3 October 1975, USA: 25 October 1975

Highest chart places: UK: 7, USA: 8

Running time: 37:19

The Who – minus Roger Daltrey to begin with – convened at Shepperton Film Studios on 30 April 1975 to begin rehearsals and sessions for the next album using a mobile studio. The singer was temporarily engaged filming his starring role in *Lisztomania*, Ken Russell's follow-up to *Tommy*. Glyn Johns returned and received a full production credit. At the beginning of April, Pete Townshend had begun recording the demos at his studio in Goring. Mentally, he was going through a particularly bad period and the songs and demos he presented to the rest of the band were very personal in nature. As such, *The Who by Numbers* is regarded as The Who's most introspective offering. On 19 May, partway through the recording, Townshend hit his 30th birthday and as a maturing rock star, he was suffering a crisis of confidence.

The recording was complete by the end of May and overdubs were added in June. The album was mixed in July and August at Island's Basing Street Studios, west London. On 16 September, Johns mastered the final mixes at IBC Studios. The album was released on 3 October in the UK on Polydor rather than Track Records due to litigation between The Who and their management. It followed three weeks later in the USA and peaked at seventh and eighth positions respectively. They were The Who's lowest chart placings on both sides of the Atlantic since *The Who Sell Out* almost eight years earlier. In several regions of Europe and in Scandinavia, it failed to chart. Following consistent sales, it achieved platinum figures in the USA and gold in the UK and Canada. Given the self-loathing and despair in the songs, UK music weekly *NME* described the album as 'Pete Townshend's suicide note'. For some commentators, it was more akin to a solo effort than a true Who album.

The Who commenced a year-long sell-out tour on the 3 October, coinciding with the UK album release. They were billed as the 'Greatest rock and roll band in the world', reflecting the well-publicised rivalry between The Who and the Rolling Stones in 1975. On Saturday 18 October, lighting engineer John Wolff unveiled The Who's customised lasers for the first time on stage at Leicester's Granby Halls. Lasers would become commonplace in rock concerts, but in 1975, they were groundbreaking. I was fortunate enough to be there and I have to say it was quite spectacular, especially during the finale. The lasers were banned from the following three gigs at the Empire Pool, Wembley for fear of endangering the audience. The GLC's safety officer had clearly been watching too many Bond movies!

The Who by Numbers tours continued well into 1976 with dates in the UK, Europe and North America although only a handful of songs from the album featured in the setlist. When they returned to London's Charlton Athletic Football Ground on 31 May, it earned them the title of the 'World's Loudest Pop Group' in the *Guinness Book of Records*. The final show at Toronto's Maple Leaf Gardens on 21 October 1976 was Keith Moon's last Who gig in front of a paying audience.

In addition to his talents as a musician and songwriter, John Entwistle displays his artistic abilities with his playful cover artwork for *The Who by Numbers*. His monochrome caricatures of the band members is a literal interpretation of the album title in the style of a children's dot-to-dot puzzle.

'Slip Kid' 4:29 (Pete Townshend)

The opening song finds a disillusioned Townshend imparting his wisdom to would-be rock and rollers, warning them of the dangers of the music business. It's yet another leftover song from *Lifehouse* and musically, unlike most anything The Who had recorded before. Like 'Magic Bus', it's the percussive effects that provide the song's momentum. Moon and Entwistle's infectious shuffle groove provides a solid base for Nicky Hopkins' robust piano chords and Daltrey's strident singing. In addition to supporting Daltrey vocally, Townshend lays down a simple but effective guitar break. Given the absence of synthesiser, Hopkins' piano playing on the album contributes significantly to its artistic success.

An edited take of 'Slip Kid' was belatedly released as a single in North America on 7 August 1976, ten months after the album. It failed to chart either side of the border. It was also released in parts of mainland Europe and is generally considered to be one of The Who's most underrated songs. Although dropped from the repertoire soon after the 1976 tours, it was resurrected briefly for the 50th anniversary *The Who Hits 50!* tour and is included on the companion compilation album.

'However Much I Booze' 5:03 (Pete Townshend)

An introspective Townshend lays bare his soul and alcohol dependency. The song suggests that his excessive drinking is a result of the weight of responsibility he carries within the band. It's such a personal song, Daltrey understandably refused to sing it. Lines like 'It's clear to all my friends that I habitually lie, I just bring them down' couldn't be more self-deprecating. His longer demo version titled 'No Way Out' was released on the 2001 2CD *Scoop 3*. It's another song with a compelling rhythmic drive, for the chorus at least which brings Paul Simon to mind. Given the subject, it's surprisingly upbeat with Townshend's vocal bursting with energy and confidence. Moon attacks his kit with his usual vigour although, for me, the drumming on this song at least lacks the finesse he brought to *Who's Next* and *Quadrophenia*. It was played on the subsequent 1975 tour but was dropped soon after.

'Squeeze Box' 2:41 (Pete Townshend)

Townshend developed a reputation for being able to play almost any instrument he laid his hands on and in the case of 'Squeeze Box', it was the accordion. With the instrument, he produced a polka-esque rhythm around which the song was constructed. The acoustic guitar shuffle, banjo and electric guitar picking also give it a distinct, country and western vibe. It's a light-hearted song, but the blatant sexual innuendo has dated it somewhat. In 2000, Townshend stated that this is a song he wished he hadn't written. He loved his demo but was less enthusiastic about the band's treatment. In the cringe-worthy stakes, he likened it to Paul McCartney and Stevie Wonder's 'Ebony and Ivory'.

Although I agree with Townshend, it struck a chord with the times when it was released as a single in North America on 22 November 1975 and in the UK on 16 January 1976. It was the only single released in 1975; Townshend exhausted virtually every song he had at the time for the album. It peaked at number sixteen on the Billboard chart and ten in the UK. Canada was especially smitten, placing it at number one. Canada is one of the few regions where a Who single has topped the charts with 'Happy Jack' doing the same in 1967. Not surprisingly given its popularity, 'Squeeze Box' was regularly performed during the 1970s and made the occasional appearance in later years.

'Dreaming from the Waist' 4:08 (Pete Townshend)

Like 'However Much I Booze', this is another song where Townshend questions his irrepressible urges, although this time, it's his libido that's the issue. The subject clearly struck a chord with Daltrey because he provides the lead vocal and it's his most self-assured on the album. Following a melodic acoustic and electric guitar intro – beautifully played by Townshend – it rocks along at a breezy pace. Entwistle's fluid bass is high in the mix and when performed live, the song provided a showcase for his dexterity as a soloist. It was MCA's choice as the B side for the 1976 'Slip Kid' single in America. Like 'Squeeze Box', it's another of the album's songs that featured in *The Who by Numbers* tours and occasionally appeared thereafter. With a prominent bass solo, unsurprisingly this was one of Entwistle's favourite stage songs.

'Imagine a Man' 4:00 (Pete Townshend)

In 1975, with his 30th birthday fast approaching, Townshend voiced his concerns that he was too old to rock and roll and The Who were losing their relevance. 'Imagine a Man' is as autobiographical as any song on the album. It contemplates the ravages of time as one grows older and touches on marital disharmony. Daltrey's wistful vocals accompanied by acoustic guitar and a hint of piano is one of the band's most sublime moments on record. Thankfully, the hostility between Townshend and Daltrey in the 1975 press did not blight their working relationship. The occasional burst of drums and lush harmonies add to, rather than distract from, the mood. The album's finest hour – or four minutes at least – in my view and a fitting way to close side one of the original LP. With the exception of the 1994 *Daltrey Sings Townshend* shows, 'Imagine a Man' was never a stage song until 2019 when it made a surprise but welcome appearance during *The Who Moving On!* tour.

'Success Story' 3:20 (John Entwistle)

Like Townshend's 'Squeeze Box', Entwistle's sole writing contribution to the album attempts to lighten the mood, although even here, there is a caustic sting in the tail. It's a sardonic and thinly veiled account of The Who's rise to stardom and the pitfalls encountered along the way as only Entwistle could tell it. It's also one of the album's hardest-rocking songs with a memorable riff and a suitably muscular lead vocal from the bassist, sounding not too dissimilar to Daltrey. He drops into his 'Boris the Spider' guttural voice for the lines 'I'm your fairy manager, you shall play the Carnegie Hall', an obvious reference to The Who's ex-manager fired the previous year. As the flipside to the 'Squeeze Box' single, 'Success Story' was yet another Entwistle B side.

'They Are All in Love' 3:00 (Pete Townshend)

With a hint of sarcasm, this is Townshend's take on the pressures of fame and fortune. It opens with Hopkins' elegant piano setting the scene and continues at a lyrical pace with gorgeous harmonies and subtle rhythm playing from Moon and Entwistle. Townshend's presence is surprisingly low key and Daltrey's occasionally aggressive singing is the only concession to the song's caustic subtext. As many fans have commented online, this is undoubtedly one of The Who's most underrated – and mature – songs. On the original LP, this song and 'Blue, Red and Grey' are separate tracks. On Jon Astley's remix for the 1996 CD reissue, one fades into the other, reflecting the sombre tone shared by the two songs.

'Blue, Red and Grey' 2:47 (Pete Townshend)

This is virtually a solo effort from Townshend, recorded at his home studio. He provides the lead vocals, accompanied by ukulele. On the surface, it's an optimistic song about the enjoyment of life, epitomised by the chorus 'I like every minute of the day'. The song's melancholic tone tells a different story.

When Glyn Johns suggested that it go on the album, Townshend was aghast saying, 'Here's me wanting to commit suicide, and you're going to put that thing on the record!'. The producer had his way and this version was included in preference to a full band arrangement recorded at Shepperton. The exquisite brass band arrangement performed by Entwistle was later added at Ramport Studios.

'How Many Friends' 4:06 (Pete Townshend)

A song about corruption in the music business and how fame attracts money-driven hangers-on. It's a tribute of sorts to Townshend's friends that had been badly affected by the rock business including Kit Lambert, Keith Moon and Eric Clapton. In 2006, he put a different spin on the song saying that it was about fans who impose unrealistic expectations that are difficult to live up to. Despite the subject, it's a fairly upbeat offering with Townshend's ringing Clapton like guitar fills and another prominent bass line from Entwistle. Daltrey rises to the occasion, sounding plaintive during the verses and positively triumphant for the memorable choral hook. This was one of Moon's favourite songs on the album and his masterclass drumming veers from tasteful restraint to explosive fills.

'In a Hand or a Face' 3:25 (Pete Townshend)

The closing song was originally titled 'Round and Round', which is sung in the chorus. 'In a hand or a face' is a line in the second verse. According to Townshend, it's a cynical observation on his growing dependency on mysticism and psychic phenomena. He didn't forsake his spiritual devotion, however, which remained as strong as ever. Shortly after completing the album, he visited the Meher Baba centre in Myrtle Beach, South Carolina and the Sufi family of Murshida Duce in California.

Musically, the album ends on a strident note with Townshend's jagged power chords and Entwistle's fluid bass runs complementing Daltrey's hard as nails vocal. There's a killer bass solo at 1:57 and the wall to wall drumming is Moon at his best. The rising choral section 'I am going round and round' that provides the song's coda harks back to 'I Can See for Miles'.

Related Tracks

None. The bonus tracks on the 1996 CD reissue of *The Who by Numbers* are live versions of 'Squeeze Box', 'Behind Blue Eyes' and 'Dreaming from the Waist'. All three were recorded at the Vetch Field football stadium in Swansea, on 12 June 1976.

Who Are You (1978)

Personnel:
Roger Daltrey: lead vocals, percussion
Pete Townshend: guitars, backing vocals, piano, synthesizer, lead vocals on 'Sister Disco' (bridge), 'No Road Romance' and 'Empty Glass'
John Entwistle: bass guitar, backing vocals, synthesiser, brass on 'Had Enough' and 'Music Must Change', lead vocals on '905'
Keith Moon: drums, percussion
Additional personnel:
Rod Argent: synthesiser on 'Had Enough', piano on 'Who Are You', keyboards on 'Guitar and Pen' and (uncredited) 'Love is Coming Down'
Edwin Astley: string arrangement
Andy Fairweather-Low: backing vocals on 'New Song', 'Had Enough', 'Guitar and Pen', 'Love Is Coming Down', and 'Who Are You'
Billy Nicholls: backing vocals on 'New Song' and 'Had Enough'
Michael Nicholls: backing vocals on 'Had Enough'
Produced by: Glyn Johns, Jon Astley
Engineered by: Glyn Johns
Recorded at: Ramport Studios, Battersea; Olympic Studios; RAK Studios, St John's Wood and Pete Townshend's El Pie Studio, Goring-on-Thames, September 1977 – April 1978
Record label: UK: Polydor, USA: MCA
Release date: UK: 18 August 1978, USA: 21 August 1978
Highest chart places: UK: 6, USA: 2
Running time: 42:13

Pete Townshend dedicated a good deal of 1977 to home life which included writing and demoing songs for the next Who album. On 12 September, in preparation for the recording, Keith Moon and girlfriend Annette Walter-Lax returned to London from Los Angeles where he had been living since August 1974. The band commenced rehearsals for *Who Are You* at Ramport Studios on 19 September. Producer Glyn Johns was again at the helm, for the initial sessions at least. With extended intervals, the recording process dragged on and he had to withdraw in the new year due to prior commitments. Assistant engineer Jon Astley took over and additional sessions took place at Townshend's El Pie Studio in Goring. Astley was Townshend's brother-in-law at the time and maintaining the family connection, his father Edwin Astley was responsible for arranging the strings which were added in December. In February 1978, Townshend injured his hand during an argument at his parents' house and was unable to play guitar, which further delayed the album. Following additional recording at RAK Studios, north-west London in March, overdubbing and final mixing of the album took place at Ramport Studio in April and May 1978.

Keith Moon was not in the best of shape and found the sessions mentally and physically taxing. Roger Daltrey recorded his vocals in the evenings when he felt his voice had warmed up. With Townshend working during the daytime due to family commitments, the pair saw very little of each other during the sessions. Townshend and John Entwistle provided the layering of instruments to create a glossy, radio-friendly sound clearly aimed at the commercial end of the American market. Disco fever was at its height in 1978, some of which rubbed off on this album. Several songs have a musical reference and Townshend originally envisaged the album as a concept along the lines of *Lifehouse*. Entwistle contributes three songs, his best showing thus far on a Who album.

To promote *Who Are You*, elaborate launch events were mounted in America by MCA Records. The 18 August release date in the UK was followed three days later in the USA. It peaked one position below the top spot in both the American and Canadian charts, equalling *Quadrophenia*. Sales figures, however, were higher, achieving double platinum on both sides of the border. As a result, it's one of The Who's best-selling albums in North America, alongside *Tommy* and *Who's Next*.

On 6 September, after attending a party and film premiere to launch 'Buddy Holly Week', Keith and Annette returned to their flat in Mayfair. During the morning of the 7 September 1978, Keith consumed a total of 32 Clomethiazole tablets which had been prescribed to aid his alcohol withdrawal. He was discovered by Annette in the afternoon and rushed to hospital, but it was too late, the overdose was fatal. The band and their management held a hastily-convened meeting the following day and announced that The Who would carry on while acknowledging that Moon was irreplaceable. The cover photograph for *Who Are You* taken in May 1978 shows the band surrounded by their stage equipment in the car park at Shepperton Studios. The wording on the back of Keith Moon's chair 'Not to be taken away', coupled with his defiant expression, provides a fitting epitaph.

'New Song' 4:12 (Pete Townshend)

The opening track finds Townshend decrying the pressure placed on popular bands by fans and radio to keep repeating the formula of their previous hits. It's also a cynical critique of artists who fall into the trap, including himself. The line in the first verse 'there's a danger that I'll plagiarize something old' is a theme Townshend would return to 41 years later for the song 'All This Music Must Fade' on the 2019 *Who* album. Given that the song is atypical Who for the most part, the title is very apt. While *The Who by Numbers* was a synth free zone, here they are an integral part of the song. Townshend's ARP embellishments feature throughout with bubbling washes adding substance to the melodic bridge. Lead guitar fills match the synth for presence, and Daltrey sings with his customary zeal. Moon and Entwistle lay down a solid rhythm and the memorable riff that follows each chorus is perhaps the song's best part. 'New Song' remains an anomaly however and, perhaps, as a result, it was never attempted live.

'Had Enough' 4:30 (John Entwistle)

This is not to be confused with 'I've Had Enough' on *Quadrophenia* even though it was written for a concept album where the protagonist, like Jimmy, has reached the end of his tether. It's the first of two back-to-back compositions from Entwistle. Not only does it feature Daltrey on lead vocals, uncommon for an Entwistle song, but it's also the first Who track to include orchestral strings. Allowing Daltrey to sing was Entwistle's ploy to get more of his songs on the album. Daltrey's vocal is even more surprising given that he hated what he considered to be a 'slushy' arrangement. The man responsible, Townshend's father-in-law Edwin Astley, previously orchestrated the strings for Townshend's song 'Street in the City' on the 1977 *Rough Mix* album.

'Had Enough' boasts a stomping, typically Who riff with prominent piano. Although strings are present throughout, they only come into their own for the triumphant instrumental bridge, supported by Entwistle's brass stabs. The synth – too low in the mix in my view – is courtesy of Rod Argent. As a double A-sided single c/w 'Who Are You', it preceded the album by a matter of weeks in the summer of 1978. As far as UK radio playlists were concerned, however, 'Had Enough' was strictly a B side.

'905' 4:02 (John Entwistle)

Both 'Had Enough' and '905' were taken from Entwistle's planned sci-fi opera, which, like some of Townshend's ambitious concepts of the '60s and '70s, remained unfulfilled. Here, following an artificial birth and childhood spent in suspended animation, the main character 905 makes his entrance. The Polymoog synth introduction that continues rhythmically throughout the song was recorded at Entwistle's studio to suggest the futuristic setting. Despite this, the song to my ears has a folk-rock vibe thanks to the compelling riff. Entwistle provides his only lead vocals here and his singing seems to improve with every album. '905' was another Entwistle single B side, although, on this occasion, the A-side 'Trick of the Light' was also one of his compositions. Like 'New Song', '905' was never played on stage by The Who although Entwistle performed it with his own band.

'Sister Disco' 4:21 (Pete Townshend)

Townshend was justifiably proud of his synthesised string arrangement for 'Sister Disco' which was recorded using an ARP 2500 at his Eel Pie Studio in Goring with Jon Astley assisting. Daltrey was less than happy, however, complaining that it had been over-produced. Glyn Johns overruled and despite an altercation between the pair, it made it intact onto the finished recording. It's melodic, rhythmic thrust brings *Quadrophenia* to mind. The lyrics have confounded many, not least the lead singer. In 1978, the Bee Gees were at the height of their fame and Townshend stated that this was a defiant declaration that The Who would not jump onto the blue-eyed soul and disco bandwagon. Daltrey declined to sing the bridge 'Goodbye Sister Disco, I go where the music fits my soul' which he felt sounded pompous. Townshend does the honours instead, his only lead vocal on the album.

When The Who visited America in 1979 for their first Stateside tour in three years, 'Sister Disco' and 'Who Are You' were the only two songs from the album performed. For both songs, a sequencer was utilised on stage for the elaborate keyboard parts. During these sections, Kenney Jones drummed to a click track played through his headphones and the rest of the band took their cues from him.

'Music Must Change' 4:37 (Pete Townshend)

Townshend was unhappy with the state of popular music at the time which is apparent in several songs on the album, particularly this one. He also had concerns over The Who's current relevance in popular music culture where disco and new wave ruled the airwaves. The song successfully combines elements of The Who's roots with the contemporary sounds of the late '70s. Mellow blues guitar introduces a walking bass line and Daltrey's moody vocal. This is offset by crashing synth effects and rich organ crescendos. When it was performed during the 1979 to 1981 tours, it became an extended jam, showcasing Townshend and John Bundrick's guitar and keyboard histrionics.

'Music Must Change' almost didn't make the album. During the recording with Glyn Johns, the below-par Keith Moon struggled with the 6/8 time and after the fourth take, he vented his frustration with the classic statement 'I'm the best Keith Moon type drummer in the world!'. The track was later completed by Townshend and Astley at Eel Pie Studio. Townshend used the sound of his footsteps from his original demo to provide the rhythm. He retained Daltrey's vocal and Moon's cymbals from Johns' recording.

'Trick of the Light' 4:48 (John Entwistle)

To open side two of the original LP, the album's heaviest track. What sounds like a lead guitar riff is played by Entwistle on eight-string Alembic bass. The result is suitably monumental, enforced by Moon's John Bonham style rhythmic stomp. Although it lent itself to live performance, the song featured only briefly in The Who's repertoire. In the lyrics, Entwistle alludes to an evening spent with a prostitute where the protagonist questions his own sexual adequacy and a desire for the relationship to be more than carnal lust. Although Daltrey provides the lead vocals, this was not one of his favourite Who songs. He sang it during the 1979 / 1980 *Who Are You* tours but Entwistle took over for the 1989 25th anniversary tour. Released as an edited single in the USA on 2 December 1978 b/w '905', it's a rare example of Entwistle providing both the A-side and B-side. Although it failed to chart in any region, 'Trick of the Light' was included on the 2014 *The Who Hits 50!* two-disc compilation.

'Guitar and Pen' 5:58 (Pete Townshend)

'Guitar and Pen' is a song about writing songs. With lines like 'You pick up your guitar, you can suddenly play, when your fingers are bleeding and the knuckles are white' and 'Get off of the floor tonight, you have something to write' it's Townshend's most personal contribution to the album. Even so, Daltrey sings lead and Townshend provides backing for the chorus. It's a lively, upbeat song driven by a staccato riff, energetic guitar and vibrant organ and piano fills. Both Townshend and Rod Argent play keyboards on this song which remains a likeable curio in The Who's cannon. An alternate 'Olympic '78 Mix' is included as a bonus track on the 1996 remastered edition of *Who Are You*. Recorded after the LP version, guitar and keys have more presence in the mix.

'Love Is Coming Down' 4:06 (Pete Townshend)

Like 'Had Enough', this song benefits from a glossy string arrangement by Edwin Astley. Although the song's protagonist is unlucky in love, in the final line, he asserts that 'I'm looking forward to doing it all again'. The song has a melodramatic, show tune feel with a surging melody, soaring strings and dramatic backing vocals that punctuate Daltrey's verses. Entwistle's articulate bass harmonics that accentuate the melody are stunning and Moon's playing demonstrates that he can play with subtlety and restraint when need be. Only the ponderous chorus lets the side down. A 'Work-in-Progress Mix' with only a guide vocal is included as a bonus track on the 1996 CD reissue of *Who Are You*.

'Who Are You' 6:21 (Pete Townshend)

An earlier version of the title song had been performed on stage in late 1976, Keith Moon's final American tour. When performed with Kenney Jones in the band, it was dependent upon a pre-recorded synthesised backing track. It's remained a live staple ever since. The original demo was longer than the finished version and, with Townshend's consent, was edited by Jon Astley for the finished track. The recorded version was inspired by two divergent events that occurred on the same day in January 1977. Following a lengthy business meeting involving American businessman Allen Klein, a very bitter Townshend went to London's Speakeasy club. The worse for alcohol, he ran into Sex Pistols' Steve Jones and Paul Cook, mistaking the latter for Johnny Rotten. After leaving the club, Townshend was woken in the early hours by a policeman to find himself in a shop doorway in Soho.

Townshend later described the song as a plea to God – 'who are you?' – a kind of prayer, although he felt this was lost in Daltrey's aggressive performance. Although some listeners and radio stations missed it, the song became infamous for the use of 'fuck' in the chorus. It's the most successful song on the album and remains one of The Who's best known. The choral hook is a real earworm, and it rocks along at a lively pace. The low-key bridge featuring Rod Argent on piano allows the band to come crashing back in a similar style to 'Won't Get Fooled Again'.

A single edit of 'Who Are You' was released in the UK on 14 July 1978 and an even shorter version in the USA on 5 August 1978. It reached number eighteen in the UK and four places higher on the Billboard chart. The 1996 CD reissue of *Who Are You* includes as a bonus track a 'Lost Verse Mix' with a different second verse. In the original, the verse refers to the mundane activity of returning home after a working day whereas the bonus track verse alludes to Townshend's rock star persona. The song achieved a wider audience when in 2001 it was adopted as the theme song for the popular American TV drama *CSI: Crime Scene Investigation*.

Related Tracks

'No Road Romance' 5:05 (Pete Townshend)

The first of two original songs to feature as bonus tracks on the 1996 remastered CD of *Who Are You*. It's essentially a Townshend demo, cut at his Goring studios in April 1978. He brought it to the album sessions, but it was not recorded by the band. He plays piano, organ, fretless bass and drums. The song is a meditation on the love interests of a touring rock star, concluding that 'There's never really any romance on the road'. His vocal has an engaging vulnerability and the song has a more than decent melody. A band version would have been well worth hearing.

'Empty Glass (Demo)' 6:23 (Pete Townshend)

Originally titled 'Choirboy', 'Empty Glass' would eventually find a home as the title song on Townshend's 1980 solo album. This version was recorded at The Who's Ramport Studios in April 1978 with Entwistle's bass and Moon's drums overdubbed onto Townshend's demo. Despite being a rough mix and Townshend's thin guide vocal, it has a compelling urgency with bass front and centre.

'Dancing in the Street' 3:43 (William Stevenson, Marvin Gaye)

A Motown standard, The Who recorded 'Dancing in the Street' live at Philadelphia's Spectrum arena on 11 December 1979 during the *Who Are You* tour. It's one of four tracks on the 'Won't Get Fooled Again' EP released in August 1988 in the UK only. It's a rousing version that benefits from the four-piece horn section backing The Who during the tour. 'Dancing in the Street' was a top-five hit for Martha and the Vandellas in 1964 on both sides of the Atlantic. It had a new lease of life when David Bowie and Mick Jagger recorded it for a video appearance on *Live Aid* in July 1985. The subsequent single topped the UK chart.

Face Dances (1981)

Personnel:

Roger Daltrey: lead vocals

Pete Townshend: guitar, keyboards, backing vocals, lead vocals on 'I Like Nightmares', 'Somebody Saved Me' and 'How Can You Do It Alone'

John Entwistle: bass, backing vocals, lead vocals on 'The Quiet One'

Kenney Jones: drums

Additional personnel:

John 'Rabbit' Bundrick: keyboards

Produced by: Bill Szymczyk

Engineered by: Bill Szymczyk and Allen Blazek

Recorded at: Odyssey Recording Studios, London, July – December 1980

Record label: UK: Polydor, USA: Warner Bros. Records

Release date: 16 March 1981

Highest chart places: UK: 2, USA: 4

Running time: 40:57

Following the tragic loss of Keith Moon, Pete Townshend recruited ex-Faces drummer Kenney Jones in November 1978, turning down Phil Collins in the process. On 3 December 1979 during a tour of America, The Who were struck by another tragic event. When the doors opened at Cincinnati's Riverfront Coliseum, a sudden rush towards the stage resulted in eleven fans being crushed to death. Unaware of the tragedy, the band performed that night and although understandably shocked by the incident, they played the remaining dates of the tour.

At the beginning of 1980, a deal was negotiated with the American Warner Brothers label for five albums over the next five years. Outside of the USA and Canada, The Who's albums would still be released on the Polydor label. Townshend was now based in Soho in the heart of London where he wrote and produced the demos for *Face Dances*. He retained Eel Pie Studios in Twickenham which he renamed Oceanic. Before the sessions, he spent two weeks in AIR Studios, London assembling the demos.

American Bill Szymczyk was hired as producer and he came with a strong track record, including a succession of hit albums with The Eagles in the 1970s. He chose Odyssey Studios in London as it was equipped with an American MCI console. Following a test session in March 1980, recording began in earnest in June. Townshend enjoyed the sessions thanks to Szymczyk's methodical approach, which involved recording three takes of each song and, if necessary, cutting the best parts together. In addition to keyboards, John Bundrick played a Bösendorfer grand piano which Townshend had shipped in from his own studio. He later sold it to Rick Wright of Pink Floyd fame when he closed his studio. The album was mixed at Szymczyk's own Bayshore Recording Studios in Florida with Townshend's assistance.

In January 1981, The Who began rehearsals for the *Face Dances* 26 date UK tour. Songs from the album included in the setlist were John Entwistle's 'The Quiet One' and Townshend's 'Don't Let Go the Coat', 'How Can You Do It Alone', 'Another Tricky Day' and 'You Better You Bet'. There was also a decent representation from the previous two albums, *The Who by Numbers* and *Who Are You*. Both Townshend and Entwistle enjoyed performing with Jones with his disciplined drumming giving them more room to manoeuvre while Bundrick provided inventive keyboard solos. The addition of brass on stage was also a bonus. Roger Daltrey, however, blamed Jones for the lack of fire on *Face Dances* and issued an ultimatum that if Jones did not leave the band, then he would. The situation was resolved, but it resulted in an uneasy alliance.

The reviews for *Face Dances* were lukewarm at best, although sales were healthy. The album peaked at number two in the UK chart, higher than the previous two albums. It didn't have the same staying power however, and overall sales were lower. It did well in most other regions, especially Canada where it topped the chart and in America where it climbed to number four in the *Billboard* chart.

Face Dances was Peter Blake's first album cover since the iconic *Sgt. Pepper's Lonely Hearts Club Band* sleeve. He invited twelve other artists to each provide a portrait of a band member. Among those involved were David Hockney and American artist Ronald Kitaj who had been one of Townshend's lecturers at Ealing art college in the '60s. A possible inspiration for the album title is 'Face Dancers' from Frank Herbert's *Dune* sci-fi novels. According to Townshend however, it was a friend of his who's party piece was to grip a match between her teeth and move it and her eyes to the rhythm of a song.

'You Better You Bet' 5:36 (Pete Townshend)

Although Townshend said this was a spontaneous pop song, it was written for a female friend, Jackie Vickers. He was still married to Karen Astley at the time although they were estranged. The protagonist has an overwhelming fixation for the girl in the song and in a drunken state, he listens to Marc Bolan's T. Rex. Bolan's earlier band, John's Children, supported The Who in 1967. Like several songs on the album, it makes ample use of keyboards. Townshend was concerned that his guitar playing had become predictable, reliant on the same three or four chords, so he made liberal use of synths to add colour. It's certainly one of The Who's most infectious songs with Daltrey's tough vocal backed by Townshend and Entwistle's tuneful harmonies. Atypical for a Who song, it opens with the choral hook, backed by Townshend's jangly Rickenbacker twelve-string and keys. Bundrick's piano flourishes are superb, harking back to Nicky Hopkins' playing on previous albums. Jones' drumming combines adventurous fills with impeccable timing.

'You Better You Bet' was released as a single on 27 February 1981 and reached number eighteen on the Billboard chart. In the UK, it peaked at nine, initiating The Who's first appearance on *Top Of The Pops* – where they regularly appeared in the '60s – in several years. It was the last Who single to breach the top twenty in the UK and USA although Canadian record buyers would remain loyal. Despite the deteriorating relationship between Daltrey and Jones, all appears harmonious in the promotional video, even sharing the same hairstyles. A popular stage song, it remained a prominent fixture in The Who's repertoire and was performed as recently as the 2017 North American tour.

'Don't Let Go the Coat' 3:44 (Pete Townshend)

The title comes from a Meher Baba saying 'Hold fast to the hems of my robe'. The song's message is simple and heartfelt; through life's changes, for better or worse, always hang onto the love and affection you share with those around you. Like 'You Better You Bet', it features a jangly guitar riff and a sprinkling of keys, although this is a more lightweight offering. Daltrey's uncharacteristically smooth, soulful singing recalls vocal acts like the Drifters and Smokey Robinson. Once again, he's backed by engaging harmonies for the choral hook. The hesitant, Spanish flavoured acoustic guitar solo at 1:17 sounds a tad out of place. It was the second single from *Face Dances*, released on 5 May 1981. It failed to match the success of 'You Better You Bet' with 47 in the UK being its highest chart placing. That was good enough to warrant its inclusion on the compilations *The Ultimate Collection* in 2002 and *The Who Hits 50!* in 2014. It was played regularly throughout the 1981 *Face Dances* tour before being shelved.

'Cache Cache' 3:57 (Pete Townshend)

This is not one of the band's strongest efforts although Daltrey does his best to inject the requisite energy and spirit. The best parts, however, are instrumental, namely Entwistle's melodic bass lines and Townshend's twangy guitar solo at 2:36. Unsurprisingly, it wasn't performed live by The Who. This song relates to a bizarre period in Switzerland in March 1980. During a break in The Who tour, Townshend spent two days wandering the hills around the town of Berne armed with a bottle of brandy, living like a hermit. Mentally, he was in a bad state during the European tour and he felt the rest of the band and management didn't appreciate what he was going through. 'Cache Cache' was his response, and sensing this, Daltrey reluctantly sang it on the album.

'The Quiet One' 3:10 (John Entwistle)

Entwistle wrote this song to replace 'Boris the Spider' and 'My Wife' in The Who's repertoire. He was getting tired of playing the same live staples. He achieved his aim when it was played during the 1981 and 1982 tours, but when The Who reformed, his more popular tunes returned to the setlist. A live version recorded at New York's Shea Stadium on 13 October 1982 during The Who's farewell tour is included as a bonus track on the 1997 CD reissue of *Face Dances*. This studio take was the B side to the successful 'You Better You Bet' single released a couple of weeks before the album.

'The Quiet One' is a reference to Entwistle's perceived persona. The point made in the song is that it's a myth and he isn't normally a quiet person. To prove the point, he stretches his vocal chords to shredding point for this hard rocker, although it rocked harder and better on stage. He's well supported by staccato guitar riffs, fluid piano runs and thunderous drumming. Jones' drum pattern provided the inspiration for the song.

'Did You Steal My Money' 4:11 (Pete Townshend)

Daltrey liked this song and its Police influences as it displayed a lighter, less agonising side of Townshend's writing. It also provides an upbeat closer to side one of the original LP. It certainly has all the requisite Police hallmarks including a staccato, reggae inspired beat, ringing guitar chords and a pretty convincing Sting impression from Daltrey. Townshend wrote the song as a result of an incident in Tempe, Arizona during the 1980 American tour. He spent the night with a fashion model who he believed took 50,000 dollars of the band's money from his tote bag. It was performed a handful of times during the subsequent *Face Dances* tour before being dropped.

'How Can You Do It Alone' 5:26 (Pete Townshend)

In keeping with the subject, there is a welcome element of humour in this song. The stately intro gives way to a bouncing piano-led melody with Daltrey singing deep down and soulful. He raises several octaves for the uplifting, reverb-drenched chorus although the piano-led rhythm hardly skips a beat. When the original demo was released on the *Scoop 3* album, in the liner notes Townshend commented that although Daltrey sang it really well it perhaps lacked the acidic tone of his own version.

The song relates to a bizarre encounter early one morning on London's Holland Park Road. When Townshend stopped to ask a man coming out of the tube station for a light, he noticed that he was naked beneath his coat. As he walked away, he thought how sad it was for a lone man to get his kicks that way. One can only assume that the flasher had a Scottish accent because at 2:45 a stately march appears, complete with bagpipes style keys and a martial drum pattern. An edited performance of 'How Can You Do It Alone' at Chicago's International Amphitheatre on 8 December 1979 is one of five bonus tracks on the 1997 remastered CD of *Face Dances*.

'Daily Records' 3:27 (Pete Townshend)

Addictions of one kind or another are all too familiar to Townshend. 'Daily Records' is about music and how writing songs and making records had become a drug, he couldn't get enough of. It's left to an exuberant Daltrey to convey the message although Townshend is on hand for the vocally complex chorus. The stuttering rhythm brings out Jones' most accomplished drumming on the album and Entwistle's bass harmonics are as lucid as ever. Piano and organ provide a melodic undercurrent and Townshend's electric guitar picking at 1:51 has a distinct country flavour.

'You' 4:31 (John Entwistle)

This is another Entwistle song featuring Daltrey on lead vocals. It was the B side to the less than successful 'Don't Let Go the Coat' single in May 1981. It's one of the closest songs on the album to the traditional Who sound. It races along at a breathless pace, driven by propulsive bass and explosive drums. The guitar riff and searing power chords hark back to *Who's Next* and Daltrey's vocal is suitably muscular. Surprisingly, it was never played live by The Who, but Entwistle did perform it with his own band. Like 'The Quiet One', 'You' came about through Jones' involvement. The song had been written for Entwistle's 1981 solo album *Too Late the Hero* but he was persuaded to bring it to *Face Dances* instead. It displays the more serious side of his songwriting; he's in a traumatic relationship with a girl, but he's in too deep to save himself.

'Another Tricky Day' 4:55 (Pete Townshend)

Lyrically, this song is similar to the Rolling Stones' 'You Can't Always Get What You Want' from 1969. The resigned message is that life inevitably has its setbacks – 'You can't expect to never cry' – but be patient – 'Gotta get used to waiting' – and do not harbour unrealistic aspirations – 'You can't always get it at all'. Although the song is often cited as pessimistic, for me, it has an optimistic tone, helped by the band's buoyant performance. It eases into its mid-tempo groove from the very start. Keyboardist Bundrick provided the song's inspiration and toured consistently with The Who until 2012. This song was performed during the 1981 UK and European tour. Although it's not one of The Who's strongest tunes, Daltrey's bravado vocal, intersected by Townshend's catchy counterpoint 'Just gotta get used to it' during the chorus, work their charm. It may have been intended as a single at one point because a similar black and white video was recorded at the same time as the 'You Better You Bet' and 'Don't Let Go the Coat' promos.

Related Tracks

'I Like Nightmares' 3:09 (Pete Townshend)

Along with 'It's In You' and 'Somebody Saved Me', this is an outtake from the *Face Dances* sessions. All three are bonus tracks on the 1997 CD reissue. Despite the angry line 'Got to be a fucking fool to blame TV', it's a jaunty song with lively piano. Townshend is clearly having fun with the lead vocal but it's not up to album quality standard.

'It's In You' 4:59 (Pete Townshend)

This song features a rare reference to a band member by name. The second verse opens with the lines 'Your letter came and today is the eighth, this is the day that Moonie earned his wraith'. The song is a pointed critique of the scathing mail received from some of The Who's less benevolent followers.

Daltrey was not a fan of this song, and it was pulled from *Face Dances* at the last minute. It's a mid-tempo – if a little clichéd – rocker that, as Daltrey observed, would have been better suited to the Rolling Stones.

'Somebody Saved Me' 5:31 (Pete Townshend)

A different version of this song appeared on Townshend's 1982 solo album *All the Best Cowboys Have Chinese Eyes*. It was thought to be too un-Who like to be included on *Face Dances* even though there are several tunes on the album that could be similarly cited. The song is based on Townsend's unrequited love for a girl he knew at art college. It's a lovely, slow ballad and easily the best of this trio of previously unreleased songs. The acoustic guitar and Bundrick's piano and oboe-like accompaniment exude charm.

It's Hard (1982)

Personnel:

Roger Daltrey: lead vocals, rhythm guitar, backing vocals on 'Eminence Front' and 'One at a Time'

Pete Townshend: lead guitar, backing vocals, lead vocals on 'Eminence Front', co-lead vocals on 'Athena' and 'Cooks County'

John Entwistle: bass, backing vocals, horns, lead vocals on 'One at a Time'

Kenney Jones: drums

Additional personnel:

Andy Fairweather Low: rhythm guitar on 'It's Your Turn'

Tim Gorman: keyboards

Produced and engineered by: Glyn Johns

Recorded at: Turn Up-Down Studio at Glyn Johns' home in Surrey, England, June 1982

Record label: UK: Polydor, USA: Warner Bros. Records

Release date: 4 September 1982

Highest chart places: UK: 11, USA: 8

Running time: 49:06

In early 1982, while Pete Townshend was in California taking part in a rehabilitation programme, the rest of the band began work on a new album. Andy Fairweather Low deputised on guitar and the sessions took place at producer Glyn Johns' new studio in rural Surrey. With just two demos written, Townshend eventually joined them on the 3 March to discuss song ideas. He found little in the way of creative input from the rest of the band and John Entwistle characteristically concentrated on his own songs. *It's Hard* was an appropriate title for The Who's tenth album given the difficulty Townshend had in providing the songs. He had become accustomed to writing for his solo albums and his third *All the Best Cowboys Have Chinese Eyes* preceded The Who album by less than three months. Entwistle's fifth solo album *Too Late the Hero* was also a recent release.

In Roger Daltrey's view, the songs did not stand up to The Who's earlier work, and he again criticised Kenney Jones' drumming. In his book *Who Am I*, Townshend opinionated in hindsight that it was a very good album whereas Daltrey remained critical. When he heard the final mixes, he felt it sounded unfinished and wanted to delay the release. They were running out of time however and with a tour fast approaching, Townshend convinced him otherwise. As the band's principal songwriter, he was conscious of their commitment to the contract with Warner Brothers.

Although sales were not as high as previous successes, *It's Hard* did respectable business, reaching eighth and eleventh positions respectively in the USA and UK charts. It was the first Who album since *The Who Sell Out* in 1967 not to breach the UK top ten. Canada remained characteristically loyal where it climbed to number three. Critics were divided with *Rolling Stone* magazine describing it as 'their most vital and coherent album since *Who's Next*'.

A 42 date, three-month tour of North America followed, and such was Daltrey's disillusionment, in the September 1982 press launch he announced that it would be their last. As a result, it was billed as The Who's 'Farewell Tour'. After two warm-up nights at Birmingham's National Exhibition Centre, they headed off to America with Tim Gorman on keyboards. Not surprisingly given Daltrey's announcement, the tour proved to be one of the most lucrative in The Who's career and set new records for the fastest-selling tickets. The tour concluded with two nights at Toronto's Maple Leaf Gardens with the final date on 17 December filmed for American pay-to-view television.

In January 1983, Townshend began writing and demoing songs in his studios in Twickenham and Soho. The project, with the working title *Siege*, came to a halt in March when he decided the songs were not suitable for The Who. In May 1983, Townshend drove to Daltrey's country house and informed him that he would be leaving the band. Although this would effectively end The Who, the singer was sympathetic. The decision was announced to the rest of the band at a management meeting that summer and made public in December. Townshend also terminated his contract with Warner Brothers. It would be almost six years before another Who tour and 23 years before the next album.

The cover artwork for *It's Hard* is not one of The Who's most inspired. It shows the four band members who, with the exception of Townshend, are self-consciously avoiding eye contact with the camera. In the background, a small boy is playing the video arcade game 'Space Duel'. Although this is clearly an update of the pinball machine in *Tommy*, the image now looks very dated. On the rear cover, the band and song titles are elements of the video game.

'Athena' 3:46 (Pete Townshend)

After seeing director Nicolas Roeg's latest film *Bad Timing*, Townshend became besotted with lead actress Theresa Russell who was Roeg's girlfriend at the time, becoming his wife in 1982. When Townshend went to Los Angeles in February 1980 to record some demos, he met Russell and in his words, 'totally fell in love with her'. It also marked the beginning of his cocaine habit. When he tried to visit her again on Valentine's Day, she refused to see him. Two days later on 16 February, he demoed the song 'Theresa', eventually changing the title and lyric to 'Athena' to conceal the song's inspiration. It remains a solid and lively album opener however and Jones' frantic 'rat a tat tat' snare sets the song in motion. The stop-start rhythm underpins Daltrey's verses bolstered by horns while Townshend handles the chorus and vocal bridge.

'Athena' featured strongly in the 1982 'Farewell tour' but the band felt it didn't work as a live song. It's been mostly absent from The Who's repertoire ever since. Daltrey resurrected it for a Teenage Cancer Trust concert at London's Royal Albert Hall in March 2018. Released the same day as the album, it was the first of three singles from *It's Hard*. It reached a respectable 28 in the Billboard chart and number three in the rock radio chart. It fared better in Canada, peaking at number five, the song's highest chart placing. In the UK, it was The Who's last top 40 single.

'It's Your Turn' 3:39 (John Entwistle)

The first of three compositions from Entwistle. During the recording of all three, the sessions were so loud, Townshend's hearing problems once again surfaced. The bassist would be similarly affected in the 1990s. The song is about trying to stay ahead in the music business as you get older when there's someone younger eager to replace you. Like 'You' on the previous album, this is another Entwistle song with Daltrey on lead vocals that attempts to recapture the classic Who sound of old. The rasping bass lines and wall to wall drumming certainly fit the bill, as do the meaty guitar chords. Daltrey roars with suitable gusto, and the core riff is memorably epic. It's another contender for 'The Who's most underrated song' list. It was the B side to the 'Athena' single in North America.

'Cooks County' 3:51 (Pete Townshend)

Daltrey remains in strident vocal mode for another memorable, up-tempo rocker. Townshend's pulsating guitar and Tim Gorman's rich keys provide the melodic, circular riff. It goes into overdrive for the rapid-fire chorus where the tough, but melodious counterpoint harmonies are superb. The song was inspired by an American TV documentary Townshend had seen about Chicago's Cook County hospital. It's located in one of the poorer neighbourhoods where violence was rife and, with no government support grants, the hospital was under threat of closure. As a mark of solidarity, The Who performed 'Cooks County' at Chicago's Rosemont Horizon arena on 6 October 1982. It was the only time the song was played during the farewell tour or since. The Who continued to support charities in Chicago. Two performances at the House Of Blues in November 1999 raised money in aid of Chicago's Maryville Academy for neglected and abused children.

'It's Hard' 3:47 (Pete Townshend)

Townshend wrote and recorded the demo for this song partway through the sessions for the previous album *Face Dances*. He was disappointed by the lukewarm reception that this, and several other demos, received from the other band members. The original title was 'Popular' which Townshend changed along with the chorus, thus providing the title track for this album. Although critics dismissed the song for its 'self-pitying' lyrics and unoriginal structure, it was performed in every show on the 1982 tour. It was also an opportunity to see Daltrey playing rhythm guitar with the band.

Despite critics' dismissal, the lyrics are honest and quite simple: long term commitment is much harder than superficial relationships. It's one of the album's mellowest offerings but none the worst for that. The melodic guitar

121

intro is excellent and the song motors along at an upbeat lick, driven by a galloping drum pattern and solid bass riff. The catchy chorus benefits from the high harmonies. It was belatedly released as a single in February 1983, five months after the album. It failed to chart in any region and it would be another 21 years before The Who released another single of original songs.

'Dangerous' 3:36 (John Entwistle)

Like '905' and 'Had Enough' on the *Who Are You* album, this was a leftover from Entwistle's aborted sci-fi concept. The song's message, there is nothing more dangerous than fear, brings to mind the saying 'We have nothing to fear but fear itself'. The line 'Back to the stone age, constitution no solution' refers to a quote by American General Curtis LeMay. In his 1965 autobiography, he warned that if North Vietnam did not cease their aggression, 'we're going to bomb them back into the stone age'. Appropriately, there is a barely suppressed undercurrent of danger throughout the song. Entwistle's monumental bass sound is nicely upfront for the first time on the album with a driving guitar riff against an ominous wash of keys. Daltrey is in superb form, attacking the song with suitable aggression. 'Dangerous' was the B side to 'It's Hard', the third and final single from the album. Deservedly, it was performed during the 1982 'Farewell tour'.

'Eminence Front' 5:39 (Pete Townshend)

The most commercial, radio-friendly track on the album and it was Glyn Johns who suggested that Townshend sang it. The producer insisted on using the first take, although Townshend felt that given time, he could have sung it better. Although it wasn't used, a version featuring Daltrey on lead vocals was recorded. It is for many, the album's crowning glory and an obvious choice when compilation albums roll around. It's a comment on the hypocrisy and shallowness of western materialism amongst the wealthy and the use of recreational drugs as an emotional crutch. Although it opens with a rhythmic organ motif that continues throughout the song in a similar vein to 'Baba O'Riley', stylistically this is a different kettle of blue-eyed funk. In addition to the jazzy guitar break, Townshend's supplies the scat vocals with suitably muscular backing. Oh, and you can dance to it.

Although it remains the album's most durable song, when it was released as the second single in America – and parts of Europe – on 25 December 1982, it stalled at 68 on the Billboard chart. A planned release in the UK was aborted. With the exception of 'Cry If You Want', this was the only song from the album to have any longevity as a stage number. It was played during the 50th anniversary *The Who Hits 50!* tour and as recently as the 2019 *Moving On!* Tour.

'I've Known No War' 5:56 (Pete Townshend)

Opening side two of the original LP is the album's longest song. Prior to release, Townshend referred to 'I've Known No War' as 'the key song' on the album and called it 'violently aggressive'. Like 'Eminence Front', it begins with a pulsating rhythm that stays with the song. It also recalls the 1972 single 'Join Together'. Musically, however, this is tougher in a mid-tempo, rock vein with Daltrey's stirring vocal and the ringing guitar fills giving it an anthemic quality. The sampled orchestral sequence at 4:00 and 5:43 is lifted from the *Quadrophenia* film soundtrack version of 'I've Had Enough'.

This is one of the songs that came about as a result of Townshend's brainstorming session for song ideas with the rest of the band. The theme is war or at least the threat of war that hangs over every generation. The lines 'On the nineteenth day of a spring day in May, Albert Speer was deleted, and as soon as the battle was over, I was born in victorious clover' refers to his own birth at the end of the second world war.

'One Life's Enough' 2:22 (Pete Townshend)
A very un-Who like song written for Townshend's wife Karen, and although their relationship was faltering, he still had a good deal of affection for her. It's a slow ballad about acceptance and the simple pleasure of making love. Townshend described this song as a filler, but given that the album runs to almost 50 minutes, that's hardly likely. He assumed that he would sing the song, but Daltrey willingly took it on. In Townshend's view, he sings it tenderly and beautifully and it's one of his favourite vocal performances from Daltrey. There is certainly a fragility and tenderness not often found in his singing. He's accompanied by a beautiful piano and orchestral keys arrangement.

'One at a Time' 3:20 (John Entwistle)
Another song intended for Entwistle's '905' rock opera, abandoned in 1978. It was the B side to the American single 'Eminence Front'. Lyrically, it's typical Entwistle with a potent subject delivered with humorously pointed lines, e.g. 'You can pick her up in your clapped out Humber'. The protagonist's partner is cheating on him, but he hardly cares because there's someone else waiting in line. It opens with a looped horn arrangement and motors along in a vintage, rock and roll fashion. Entwistle's vocal and the arrangement has a loose, thrown together feel about it but everyone seems to be enjoying themselves.

'Why Did I Fall for That' 3:56 (Pete Townshend)
This song, along with 'A Man Is a Man', was producer Johns' attempt to recapture the commercial, radio-friendly sound of the *Who Are You* album. Subject wise, it relates to the 1960s cold war between America and Russia where society, in general, was seemingly apathetic to the real threat of a nuclear war. As such, thematically it relates closely to 'I've Known No War'. Political tensions in 1981 – the year before the album was released – caused similar concerns. A solid bass riff and ringing guitar usher in the mid-tempo melody with energetic bursts of drumming. Daltrey's vocal during the verses is low and moody, offset by bright harmonies for the poppy, and quite memorable choral hook. Not The Who's finest four minutes, but a decent album track all the same.

'A Man Is a Man' 3:56 (Pete Townshend)

The majority of the album's songs hover just below the radio-friendly four-minute mark although it's hard to imagine this low-key offering receiving much airplay even though it was the B side to the UK 'Athena' single. Daltrey almost sleepwalks his way through the vocal melody although Jones and Entwistle try their best to inject a semblance of drive. The message in the lyrics is that real men don't need to act tough – much like the song itself. The theme would resurface in Townshend's short story 'Fish Shop' which is included in the *Horse's Neck* book published in 1985. It was given a live airing during the 1982 tour but unsurprisingly was dropped part-way through to make way for more familiar material.

'Cry If You Want' 5:18 (Pete Townshend)

To close the album, a song with a good deal more spirit. Like 'One Life's Enough', this is another song that Townshend expected to sing himself as he didn't think it suited Daltrey. He intended it for his *All the Best Cowboys Have Chinese Eyes* solo album but wasn't able to master the vocal. Daltrey took a shine to the song. He learnt the 'torrential stream' of words by heart and then sang it through perfectly without a pause. The twangy bass riff and martial drum pattern establish an air of tension; aided by sharp power chords, rippling piano and powerful vocals. The song's only failing is that although it builds the tension in dramatic fashion, unlike say 'Won't Get Fooled Again', there is no release. After 'Eminence Front', this was the album's most durable stage song and it was certainly more effective when performed live. It was played throughout the 1982 farewell tour and enjoyed a brief outing during the 2014 50th anniversary tour.

Related Tracks

The four bonus tracks on the 1997 CD reissue of *It's Hard* are live versions of the title song, 'Eminence Front', 'Dangerous' and 'Cry If You Want'. They were all recorded at Toronto's Maple Leaf Gardens on 17 December 1982, the last date of the 'Farewell tour'. Additionally, the original album tracks were remixed and remastered with several changes to the original recordings.

'I Saw Her Standing There' 2:59 (Paul McCartney, John Lennon)

Filmed at New York's Shea Stadium on 13 October 1982, Entwistle sounds a tad strained singing this early Beatles classic, but his bass playing and Jones' drumming keeps things moving at a nimble pace. It's included on the 2015 *Live at Shea Stadium 1982* DVD and Blu-ray.

'Twist and Shout' 3:56 (Phil Medley, Bert Berns)

A rare live Who single and a cover to boot. It was released in November 1984 with 'I Can't Explain' as the B side to promote the live album *Who's Last*.

Unsurprisingly, it stalled at a meagre 87 in the UK chart. It's another recording from the 17 December 1982 Maple Leaf Gardens show. In previous years, Daltrey had sung the song, but Entwistle did the honours throughout the 1982 tour where it usually closed the set. Live recordings of the song from 1982 also appear on *Live From Toronto* and the *Thirty Years of Maximum R&B* box-set. Entwistle's throat-shredding delivery is clearly influenced by John Lennon's singing on the Beatles version which closed their 1963 debut album *Please Please Me*. It's been recorded by numerous artists, most notably the Isley Brothers, giving them an American hit in 1962.

'Saturday Night's Alright for Fighting' 4:33 (Elton John, Bernie Taupin)

A 1991 single to promote the *Two Rooms: Celebrating the Songs of Elton John & Bernie Taupin* tribute album. It's also the final track on *Thirty Years of Maximum R&B*. An obvious song to cover by The Who, the original was a 1973 hit single for Elton John and featured on the excellent *Goodbye Yellow Brick Road* double LP. The song as written and performed by Elton and his band was a clear homage to The Who and as such, the aggressive vocal stance and staccato power chords were tailor-made for Daltrey and Townshend. Wisely, they adhere closely to the original, complete with rousing piano. At 3:06, it morphs into Elton's 1970 song 'Take Me to the Pilot' before a barnstorming finale.

'Dig' 4:07 (Pete Townshend)

One of two songs performed by The Who on *The Iron Man: The Musical by Pete Townshend* album released in 1989. It's a melodic, upbeat song with a spirited vocal from Daltrey and colourful counterpoint harmonies. Townshend's guitar solo at 2:36 is supremely executed and Entwistle keeps things motoring at a lively pace. 'Dig' was played during the 1989 25th anniversary reunion tour and a live version is included on the 1990 *Join Together* album.

'Fire' 3:47 (Arthur Brown, Vincent Crane, Mike Finesilver, Peter Ker)

Another song from *The Iron Man* performed by the band. Although it doesn't match the sheer bravado of Arthur Brown's 1968 original – and I can't imagine Daltrey wearing a flaming helmet on stage – it's a worthy version nonetheless. It rocks hard with Simon Phillips' seismic drumming standing out.

'Rough Boys' 4:44 (Pete Townshend)

The Who were not averse to including solo songs in their repertoire, especially those by Townshend. This is a rousing performance featuring a majestic keyboards intro. It was recorded at the Tampa Stadium in Florida on 29 July

1989 and is included on the 1990 *Join Together* live album. A recording from Los Angeles' Universal Amphitheatre on the same tour is included on the 2005 *Tommy and Quadrophenia Live* DVD box-set. Townshend's original was released as a single and is the lead track on his 1980 solo album *Empty Glass*.

'Face the Face' 6:15 (Pete Townshend)
Another live recording of a Townshend song from the *Join Together* album. It was recorded on the 22 August 1989 at the Jack Murphy Stadium, San Diego. Like 'Rough Boys', a video recording from the Universal Amphitheatre is included on *Tommy and Quadrophenia Live*. It's a storming, soulful take that benefits from the three backing singers. The original was another Townshend single and is included on his 1985 *White City: A Novel* concept album.

'A Little Is Enough' 5:05 (Pete Townshend)
Another 1989 video recording from *Tommy and Quadrophenia Live*, this time filmed at the Giants Stadium, New Jersey. Following a synth fanfare, it rocks along at a lively pace with Townshend in strong vocal form. The original was another 1980 single lifted from *Empty Glass*.

'After the Fire' 4:49 (Pete Townshend)
Yet another live recording of a solo song, this time one of Daltrey's, although it was penned by Townshend. The original was released as a single and featured on the 1985 *Under a Raging Moon* solo album. This version was recorded during The Who's 1999 winter tour and is included on the *Blues to the Bush* 2CD released in 2000. Daltrey gives a moving performance of this memorable mid-tempo ballad backed by Townshend's acoustic guitar and Bundrick's organ.

'Heart to Hang Onto' 4:41 (Pete Townshend)
Recorded live at London's Royal Albert Hall on 27 November 2000, this engaging, guitar-led ballad is included on the 2003 *Live at the Royal Albert Hall* 3CD and *The Who & Special Guests: Live at the Royal Albert Hall* DVD. The original was included on the 1977 *Rough Mix* album Townshend recorded with Ronnie Lane.

Endless Wire (2006)

Personnel:
Roger Daltrey: lead vocals
Pete Townshend: guitars, vocals, bass guitar, drums, piano, keyboards, violin, banjo, mandolin, drum machine
Additional personnel:
Lawrence Ball: Electronic music on 'Fragments'
Ellen Blair: viola on 'Trilby's Piano'
John 'Rabbit' Bundrick: Hammond organ, backing vocals
Jolyon Dixon: acoustic guitar on 'It's Not Enough'
Rachel Fuller: keyboards on 'It's Not Enough', orchestration supervisor on 'Trilby's Piano'
Peter Huntington: drums
Gill Morley: violin on 'Trilby's Piano'
Vicky Matthews: cello on 'Trilby's Piano'
Billy Nicholls: backing vocals
Pino Palladino: bass guitar
Stuart Ross: bass guitar on 'It's Not Enough'
Zak Starkey: drums on 'Black Widow's Eyes'
Simon Townshend: backing vocals
Brian Wright: violin on 'Trilby's Piano'
Produced: Pete Townshend, Bob Pridden and Billy Nicholls (Roger Daltrey's vocals only)
Engineered by: Myles Clarke
Recorded at: Pete Townshend's home studio and Eel Pie Oceanic Studios, Twickenham, December 2004 – May 2006
Record label: UK: Polydor, USA: Republic Records
Release date: 30 October 2006
Highest chart places: UK: 9, USA: 7
Running time: 52:35

A new album with the working title 'Who2' was originally slated by Pete Townshend for release in 2005. He didn't have sufficient songs ready however, and drummer Zak Starkey had touring commitments with Oasis until January 2006. Some pre-production work did begin in 2005 by Bob Pridden, Billy Nicholls and Myles Clarke. Following the initial work at Townsend's home studio using a vintage mixing desk and 8-track tape machine, recording began at Oceanic Studios on 28 February 2006. Townshend produced and The Who's regular touring musicians provided instrumentation. In Starkey's absence, Peter Huntington from the band led by Townshend's partner Rachel Fuller provided the majority of the drums. In addition to guitar, Townshend filled in with a variety of instruments and divided the lead vocals equally between Roger Daltrey and himself. Daltrey's vocals were added separately at the end of the sessions.

In early June 2006, The Who rehearsed for what would be one of the longest tours of their career. Townshend continued working on the album during the tour including the mixing using a mobile studio. As a result, he had complete control although Daltrey had wanted the album to be recorded as a band. Townshend was able to take chances with several songs which may have otherwise appeared on a solo project.

As the album would not be released before the 2006 tour, a condensed, six-song version of 'Wire & Glass' was released in the UK on 10 July in Maxi-CD and 12" single format. Following two warm-up events at Knebworth and Leeds University in June, the tour continued through the UK, into Europe and in September, North America. Arenas and outdoor festivals were favoured and during the European leg, the shows were streamed across the internet, a first for The Who.

When the album was released in October, it was their best received since *Who Are You* in 1978. *Rolling Stone* magazine was positive, although perhaps inevitably, some writers missed John Entwistle. *Endless Wire* entered the American *Billboard* chart at number seven, its peak position. It also did well in most other regions and reached nine and ten respectively in the UK and Canada. In his autobiography *Who I Am*, Townshend said that he really enjoyed making the album and much to his relief, Daltrey was also satisfied with the end results.

The cover artwork for *Endless Wire* takes its inspiration from 'Wire & Glass' and the song 'Mirror Door'. It features a series of random shapes spilling through a doorway and over a stairway. Designer Richard Evans also incorporates a flight of birds. During his time with Hipgnosis in the 1970s, Evans had a hand in some of the most iconic album covers of that era. He had worked for The Who since 1976 and provided the artwork for many of their compilations and live albums.

'Fragments' 3:58 (Pete Townshend, Lawrence Ball)
'Fragments' was a rare songwriting collaboration for Townshend. Lawrence Ball is a musician, composer and mathematician and along with Townshend and Dave Snowdon, he set up *The Lifehouse Method* interactive website which was launched on 1 May 2007 and discontinued in July 2008. The song is based on the 'Method' way of creating individual pieces of music taken from the parameters and information from individuals who accessed the website. Townshend stated that it was a homage to 'Baba O'Riley' and there is certainly a ring of familiarity in the hypnotic keys motif that introduces the song. The counterpoint harmonies are lush and Pino Palladino establishes his debut on a Who studio album with articulate bass harmonics. This is a more mellow Who although the spoken part is an unnecessary distraction. 'Fragments' was played on the 2006/2007 *Endless Wire* tour.

'A Man in a Purple Dress' 4:14 (Pete Townshend)
This finds Townshend in a reflective, folky mood although the gutsy vocal

is courtesy of Daltrey. It recalls early '60's Bob Dylan with acoustic guitar providing the only accompaniment. The words are a scathing comment on the robes worn by priests and those in the legal profession when passing judgement on their peers. Townshend wrote this song after watching Mel Gibson's controversial film *The Passion of the Christ*. He was also reflecting on the humiliation he suffered following his arrest in January 2003. This was another song performed during the 2006/2007 tour, providing a welcome, unplugged respite in the middle part of the set.

'Mike Post Theme' 4:28 (Pete Townshend)

Mike Post is an American composer best known for his work on television. His prolific output includes the theme tunes for *NYPD Blue*, *The Rockford Files*, *Magnum P.I.*, *Hill Street Blues* and *The A-Team*. Townshend reflects on the timeless nature of these shows through endless repeats while we, the viewer, grow older. The message here is that while a person can be moved to tears watching a favourite TV programme or movie, men, in particular, can find it difficult to express their feelings for the one they love. In 2001, The Who had their own taste of American TV success when the song 'Who Are You' was adopted as the theme song for the popular drama *CSI: Crime Scene Investigation*.

Following a crashing intro, the song exchanges laidback verses for a surging choral hook. The electric rhythm guitar chords contrast nicely with the Dobro like acoustic strumming. Townshend also plays drums on this track. It was occasionally played during the subsequent *Endless Wire* world tour including the return visit to Leeds University on 17 June 2006.

'In the Ether' 3:35 (Pete Townshend)

A very un-Who like song and, possibly as a result, Townshend's favourite. In his autobiography *Who I Am*, he said that it was 'a song for the voice of an old man, a ghost, singing from beyond reality'. It expresses how it feels to grow older which Townshend accentuates with a deliberately raspy vocal in the style of Tom Waits. Together with 'Black Widow's Eyes', Townshend wrote this song back in early 2002. At the time he had anticipated Entwistle and Daltrey to make song contributions to the next album and therefore tried to produce songs that were darker and more extreme to balance their contributions. He wrote a number of other songs around this time for potential inclusion but were shelved. After Townshend played the demo to Daltrey and asked his opinion, the singer said it was too music theatre and suggested he remove the piano leaving only guitar, much to Townshend's annoyance. Fortunately, the piano remained intact for one the most melancholic songs on a Who album.

'Black Widow's Eyes' 3:07 (Pete Townshend)

This is more standard Who fare although the harmonies give it a distinctly American vibe. Again, there's an engaging combination of acoustic and electric guitars and the song counters measured verses with a brisk, mid-tempo chorus. This is the only song to feature drummer Starkey and here he favours cymbals and hi-hat. It made its stage debut in Philadelphia on 12 September 2006 and was played on the subsequent tour. It was also released as a CD single in Europe backed with 'It's Not Enough'. Townshend stated that the televised events of the Beslan massacre in North Ossetia on 1 September 2004 were the inspiration for this song. A man, who's holding a dead child, describes the female terrorist responsible as 'having the most penetrating and beautiful eyes'. Townshend describes it as a song about falling in love in circumstances where we least expect, or want to.

'Two Thousand Years' 2:50 (Pete Townshend)

Another song inspired by *The Passion of the Christ*. It expounds the theory that 2,000 years ago, rather than betraying Jesus as it says in the gospels, Judas was actually following his instructions. Townshend also reflects that 2,000 years on, believers are still waiting for the return of Christ. Daltrey and Townshend's combined vocals are deliberately loose here with the latter also playing banjo, violin and viola. The slowly rising orchestral keys arrangement that enters at 1:09 is the song's best element.

'God Speaks of Marty Robbins' 3:26 (Pete Townshend)

Townshend returns to the Bible for this next song only this time, it's the old testament. It started out as simply 'Marty Robbins' and appeared on the 2001 compilation album of demos, *Scoop 3*. Here, Townshend muses that when God contemplated the creation of mankind, he was encouraged to do so simply to hear music by artists like Marty Robbins. A country and western singer and musician, Robbins was a particular favourite of Townshend, who so loved the sound of his name, he wrote a song around it. A slow ballad, Townshend sings with solo acoustic guitar, and despite the subject, there's scarcely a hint of country in his performance.

'It's Not Enough' 4:02 (Pete Townshend, Rachel Fuller)

Another rare co-composition from Townshend, this time with his partner Rachel Fuller who along with her band, was responsible for the backing track. It was born out of Rachel's attempt to write a radio hit using Townshend's formula; a rhythmic electronic loop, simple but heavy chords and earnest lyrics. The result was a song called 'Magic Flute' which she was unable to finish, so Townshend co-opted the backing track for this song. He changed the words, added an aggressive guitar part and Daltrey's anthemic choral hook. Townshend clearly had faith in his formula because it was released as a single in October 2006.

The lyrics were again inspired by a film, in this case, Jean Luc Godard's 1963 French drama *Le Mépris* starring Brigitte Bardot. In the film, which translates into English as *Contempt*, Bardot asks her husband if he likes the various parts of her anatomy. After he's replied yes each time, she says 'It's Not Enough'. This left Townshend to ponder why it was that some people choose partners that are clearly not right for them.

'You Stand by Me' 1:36 (Pete Townshend)

A self-explanatory song that was written just before Townshend appeared with Rachel on one of her *In The Attic* live webcast shows transmitted from his London studio. It's an acknowledgement of her belief and support, and that of his family, friends and fans who have stood by him over the years. More specifically, it's for Daltrey and his stolid faith and support following Townshend's arrest in January 2003. It's another sparsely arranged acoustic solo offering, and if it wasn't for Townshend's distinct vocal, it would have sat comfortably on Simon & Garfunkel's 1964 *Wednesday Morning, 3 A.M* debut album.

Wire & Glass: A Mini-Opera

Despite having demos that dated back to 2002, Townshend was still short of material for the album. It was Townshend's friend and business manager Nick Goderson who suggested he incorporate a mini-opera based on the on-going solo project *The Boy Who Heard Music* novella. This was later adapted into a full-length rock musical. He also returned to the 1971 *Lifehouse* project for story ideas, which are incorporated in the opening songs 'Sound Round' and 'Pick Up the Peace'. By the end of February 2006, Townshend had ten songs ready which varied in style and length although at that point it was going to be called 'The Glass Household'. 'Wire & Glass' made its stage debut at Leeds University on 17 June 2006 and was often played in its entirety on the subsequent tour.

'Sound Round' 1:21 (Pete Townshend)

The story opens with the narrator, a young man named Ray High, driving a camper bus around an estuary close to a large power station. It's a throwback to the early '70s when Townshend owned his own motorhome which he called 'Maxine'. Ray has a vision of a future society being strangled by wires and communication technology. It's a suitably up-tempo song to open the opera. In fact, it's the album's most typically Who song thus far with Huntington's relentless drumming driving Daltrey's tough vocal.

'Pick Up the Peace' 1:28 (Pete Townshend)

The story fast forwards to a sanatorium cell where the elderly Ray, through meditation, has visions of three teenagers, Gabriel, Josh and Leila who form a band called The Glass Household. He also sees his own childhood in the same neighbourhood with bombed out buildings and old soldiers. The story here contains elements from Townshend's own childhood experiences in post-war

London. Another strong, Who-like song with edgy guitar and razor-sharp vocals recalling 'Doctor Jimmy' on *Quadrophenia*. Its only fault is that it's way too short.

'Unholy Trinity' 2:07 (Pete Townshend)

'Unholy Trinity' focuses on the three members of The Glass Household. Gabriel is from a showbiz family of lapsed Christians, Josh is from a devout Jewish family and has suffered the loss of his father while Leila's family is Muslim and her mother died when she was very young. Despite their different backgrounds and religions, the trio become committed friends and share their secrets; Gabriel hears music, Josh hears voices and Leila can fly. Daltrey sings against banjo and a lilting keys rhythm which gives the song an infectious charm.

'Trilby's Piano' 2:04 (Pete Townshend)

Gabriel's Aunt Trilby, who has nurtured his musical talent since he was young, attracts the attention of Josh's uncle Hymie. The teenagers perform this song at Leila's father's studio and it's sung by Gabriel. The most un-Who like song on *Endless Wire*, it sounds like a Stephen Sondheim style show tune in the style of 'Send In The Clowns'. It features a wistful Townshend backed by a haunting string arrangement. Townshend orchestrated the string quartet which was a first for him although he acknowledged Rachel Fuller's support and supervision.

'Trilby's Piano' grew out of a piece called 'Stella'. It was inspired by Townshend's real-life Aunt Trilby, his 'creative angel' as he called her. She was one of the first people to encourage his musical aspirations. She had a piano in her flat which Townshend played as a young boy whenever he visited. When she heard him play, she said 'You are a real musician'.

'Endless Wire' 1:51 (Pete Townshend)

The three teenagers find documents that belonged to Ray High, Leila's father's old studio partner. They detail a scheme to use the global wire network that Ray had seen in his vision to spread unifying music to all. Studying Ray's plans, the trio believes it's something that they can make a reality. This part of the story again links back to *Lifehouse* and *The Lifehouse Method* website. Townshend later dedicated this song to American Internet pioneer Vint Cert. Another song with a folksy, American country vibe, this time sung by Townshend. The arrangement is simple but effective. A 3:03 'Extended version' was included as a bonus track on the *Endless Wire* CD release in America and Europe. It has an additional middle section and a repeated verse at the end.

'Fragments of Fragments' 2:23 (Pete Townshend, Lawrence Ball)

'Fragments' is the title of The Glass Household's hit record. This part instrumental track reprises the rhythmic, electronic loop from the album's opening song 'Fragments'. The electronically treated vocals create a lush effect reminiscent of the band Yes circa their *90125* album.

'We Got a Hit' 1:18 (Pete Townshend)

This song charts the success of The Glass Household and their hit record on TV, radio and stage. It's a lively, up-tempo song performed by Daltrey with gravelly-voiced gusto. Rhythm guitar, bass and drums provide a rock-solid base for the intricate counterpoint harmonies. Like the song 'Endless Wire', a 3:03 'Extended version' featured on the American and European release. It has a new middle and a new verse at the end. Both bonus tracks were mixed by Townshend in September 2006 during the American leg of the world tour.

'They Made My Dream Come True' 1:13 (Pete Townshend)

As the narrator, the Ray High character sings this song. While still in his cell, during meditation, he observes the teenagers rise to fame. He foresees the death of someone during The Glass Household's final concert. He's unsure however if the concert is a dream or takes place in reality. The song itself is certainly grounded in reality. The opening line 'People died where I performed' recalls the tragic incident on 3 December 1979 when eleven Who fans died before a show in Cincinnati. It features a subdued melody and a pensive vocal from Townshend with fine bass and drums support.

'Mirror Door' 4:14 (Pete Townshend)

The Glass Household perform an elaborate show which expands on their play-acting as children in New York's Central Park. It's webcast to the entire world, thus demonstrating Ray High's original scheme. The stage includes a large stairway and at the top, famous singers, now deceased, appear. Josh, who has stopped taking his medication for paranoid schizophrenia, grabs a pistol and shoots Gabriel dead. Gabriel ascends the stairway and joins the other dead singers. It brings to mind a superb sequence in the 1946 Powell and Pressburger classic *A Matter of Life and Death*. In America, the film was retitled *Stairway to Heaven* which in turn inspired a song by a certain heavy rock quartet in 1971.

The longest song in 'Wire & Glass', it recreates a concert atmosphere with crowd cheers, Who-like staccato power chords and Daltrey's edgy vocal. Bundrick adds inspired Hammond organ fills, and the fiery rhythm partnership of Palladino and Huntington is a throwback to The Who of old. Embarrassingly, the lyrics name Doris Day amongst the presumed dead singers. She didn't pass away until 13 May 2019 at the grand old age of 97. 'Mirror Door' was released as a promo single in the UK, Australia and several other regions.

'Tea & Theatre' 3:24 (Pete Townshend)

The epilogue finds the now elderly Josh and Leila taking tea together. Josh is in a sanatorium cell next to Ray's and he and Leila re-enact their childhood play for the benefit of the inmates. The opera leaves open the possibility that Ray, the narrator here, has confused the play he has just witnessed with the vision in his meditations. During the 2006/2007 *Endless Wire* world tour, 'Tea & Theatre' closed each show on an intimate note. On stage, Josh and Leila's reminisces on their career and lives together draws parallels with the two surviving members of The Who. Daltrey believed the song summed up their feelings for each other and their audience. He performs it with a Van Morrison style sensitivity – and a touch of reverb – backed by acoustic guitar and a metronome-like drum machine beat. Townshend stated that the simple arrangement 'focuses the attention where it should really be, which is on the song'. It remained in the band's setlist and was performed on the 2019 *Moving On! Tour*.

Related Tracks

Greyhound Girl 3:04 (Pete Townshend)
Yet another *Lifehouse* remnant dating back to 1971. It's one of *The Who Live at Lyon* bonus tracks issued with *Endless Wire* in Europe, Asia, and Best Buy stores in America. It was recorded at the Vienne Amphitheatre in France on 17 July 2006. It's a touching song performed solo by Townshend with an uncharacteristically gutsy vocal and strummed acoustic guitar.

'Real Good Looking Boy' 5:42 (Pete Townshend, Luigi Creatore, Hugo Peretti, George David Weiss)
Recorded for the 2004 compilation *Then and Now*, this was also released as an edited single on 26 April 2004. The first new Who song in 22 years, it's a piano ballad based on 'Can't Help Falling in Love', a 1962 hit for Elvis Presley. The song is about two men based on younger versions of Townshend and Daltrey. Both are concerned about their looks; the Townshend character wants to look like his handsome friend who in turn wants to be Elvis Presley. It's one of The Who's strongest, post-Entwistle offerings with a razor-sharp vocal from Daltrey. It even manages a sly nod to 'The Magnificent Seven' theme at 3:23. It was recorded in 2003 at Townshend's Eel Pie Oceanic Studios in Twickenham. In the same sessions, they recorded Daltrey's country and western-style song 'Certified Rose'. In addition to Bundrick, Starkey and Townshend's brother Simon playing on the song, ex-ELP bassist Greg Lake filled in for Palladino who was on touring duties with a reunited Simon & Garfunkel. Simon Townshend was credited as producer for both this song and the B side.

'Old Red Wine' 3:43 (John Entwistle)
The B side to 'Real Good Looking Boy' was also included on the *Then and Now* compilation. It was written in New York as a homage to Entwistle and

his love of expensive claret, even when it was past its prime. Elements of the song had been around since the year 2000 and parts of it were played on subsequent tours throughout the noughties. For the recording session in early 2004, Palladino had returned on bass. Otherwise, personnel remain the same as 'Real Good Looking Boy'. Like the wine in question, the song has a vintage quality. It boasts another strong melody and vocal from Daltrey and the rousing, guitar-led coda that begins at 2:41 is stunning.

'Be Lucky' 3:16 (Pete Townshend)

This was recorded for the 2014 anniversary compilation *The Who Hits 50!* and released as a single on 7 October 2014. It was the first new Who song in eight years. With its upbeat melody, catchy choral hook and Daltrey's commanding vocal it was certainly worth the wait. In addition to the Palladino and Starkey rhythm partnership who are in excellent form, Mick Talbot plays keyboards. It was produced and mixed by Dave Eringa who would work on the next Who album.

Who (2019)

Personnel:
Roger Daltrey: lead vocals
Pete Townshend: guitars, vocals, bass guitar, tamarind shaker, bass harmonica
Additional personnel:
Carla Azar: drums
Gordon Giltrap: guitar
Pino Palladino: bass guitar
Gus Seyffert: bass guitar
Zak Starkey: drums
Benmont Tench: keyboards
Simon Townshend: guitar
Joey Waronker: drums
Produced by: Pete Townshend, Dave Sardy and Dave Eringa (Roger Daltrey's vocals only)
Engineered by: Myles Clarke, Jim Monti and Bob Pridden
Recorded at: British Grove and Metropolis Studios, London, Los Angeles, 3 February 2019 – August 2019
Record label: Polydor Records
Release date: 6 December 2019
Highest chart places: UK: 3, USA: 2
Running time: 46:45

54 years after 'My Generation' hit the shops in December 1965, The Who returned with their first new studio album in thirteen years. Pete Townshend recorded his demos in the summer of 2018. The subjects were diverse, even by his standards, including plagiarism, incarceration, personal tragedy and freedom of speech. In September, he sent around fifteen demos to Roger Daltrey, but the singer was slow to commit. It was a familiar scenario where he felt the lyrics were too personal for him to sing and were better suited to a solo album. To appease the singer, some of the more politically biased aspects were toned down.

Preparation for the album took place on 31 January 2019 at Townshend's Grand Cru barge studio, assisted by engineer Myles Clarke. Recording sessions began at British Grove Studios in Chiswick on 3 February with American producer Dave Sardy and engineer Jim Monti. In the first few days, Zak Starkey's drums and Pino Palladino's bass, together with additional guitar parts, were overdubbed onto Townshend's demo recordings. After working on seven tracks, Palladino had to take his leave to return to Los Angeles for a prior engagement. On the 5 March, the sessions reconvened at the more spacious Metropolis Studio A. Rather than working with Townshend and the other musicians, Daltrey elected to record his vocals separately at a studio closer to his home in East Sussex with producer Dave Eringa and engineer Bob Pridden. Daltrey believed Eringa brought the best out in his voice and he produced his most recent solo album. Sessions were interrupted by the first leg of *The Who Moving On!* tour of America which ran throughout May. Recording continued on and off into August which included the orchestral arrangements. Sessions also took place in Los Angeles which was closer to home for producer Sardy.

During the Autumn tour at Houston's Toyota Centre on the 25 September, Daltrey's failing voice caused the abandonment of the show and postponement of the following dates in Dallas and Denver.

Daltrey rated the album as The Who's best work since *Quadrophenia* in 1973. The music press including the *NME* and newspaper critics, were similarly impressed with a five-star review in *The Times*. Several noted that despite Daltrey and Townshend being in their mid-70s, these elder statesmen of rock could still produce powerful, uncompromising music. There was a general consensus that this was the best Who album since the 1970s. The release date came almost 55 years after The Who's first record 'I Can't Explain' hit the shops. It entered the UK album chart at number three and the Billboard chart at two, their best showing Stateside since *Who Are You* in 1978.

Renowned artist Peter Blake is responsible for the striking cover design having last worked with The Who on the 1981 album *Face Dances*. A pioneer of pop art, it's a collage effect that provides thinly veiled references to The Who's past. There's a similarity between The Who cover and Blake's artwork for the tenth anniversary edition of Paul Weller's *Stanley Road* album.

'All This Music Must Fade' 3:20 (Pete Townshend)

The defiant opening line 'I don't care, I know you're gonna hate this song' is a clear indication that The Who have not lost their edge. Townshend had read that most people only listen to the first few seconds of a track online before moving on. As a result, with every song on *Who* he was keen to grab the listener's attention from the start. The intro features processed voices and a slow organ fade-in before rolling back the years and hitting its Who-like stride. Daltrey's vocal has lost none of its power, the driving riffs and acoustic strumming are in place and Starkey and Palladino play with precision and weight. It's as if they've never been away.

Daltrey admitted that he hated this song the first time he heard it. The main concern was Townshend's rapping on the demo which he wisely refused to attempt. Ironically, when *Who* entered the 'Billboard 200' chart at number two in the third week of December 2019, it was kept off the top spot by American rapper Roddy Ricch. Townshend dedicated the song 'to every artist who has ever been accused of ripping off someone else's song'. On 3 October, it was the second song from the album to be released as a single.

'Ball and Chain' 4:29 (Pete Townshend)

Another song that packs a welcome punch. The rhythmic piano intro and underscoring is a throwback to 'Baba O'Riley'. This is a more ballsy and bluesy offering however with chunky acoustic guitar chords. Daltrey sounds suitably mean and moody, offset by sweet wordless harmonies in the chorus. At 3:45, Townshend's guitar and Benmont Tench's organ lock horns for the scorching coda.

It's a reworking of a Townshend song called 'Guantanamo' that originally appeared on his 2015 compilation *Truancy: The Very Best of Pete Townshend*. It's a critique of America's Guantanamo Bay detention camp in Cuba which president Barack Obama promised to close. Due to opposition, it didn't happen, although the number of inmates was significantly reduced. 'Ball and Chain' made its debut on 6 July 2019 at London's Wembley Stadium. It was also the lead single from the album, released on 13 September.

'I Don't Wanna Get Wise' 3:54 (Pete Townshend)
They ease off the throttle a little for this catchy, mid-tempo song. It benefits from a memorable melody and a superb, rhythmic arrangement that allows Benmont Tench's organ and mellotron washes to shine through. He's probably best known as keyboardist with Tom Petty and the Heartbreakers, a role he occupied from 1976 to 2017. As a download only, this was the third song from the album to be released as a single in November 2019. Subject wise, Townshend and Daltrey are looking back at their mid-1960's younger selves. At the singer's insistence, the lyrics were changed to sound less personal.

'Detour' 3:46 (Pete Townshend)
Townshend's message here is that we need to find different ways in dealing with the various aspects of our lives, including relationships. Some have interpreted the title as a reference to the pre-Who group the Detours, and certainly, the tone of the song fits the bill. With a Bo Diddley jive beat, hand-clamp rhythm, call and response choral hook and cooing harmonies, it's firmly entrenched in the early '60s. Palladino lays down a bouncing bass riff and at 1:51, Starkey all but lays waste to his kit in dexterous Moon fashion. Townshend is responsible for a variety of instruments on the album and here he adds bass harmonica and tamarind shaker.

'Beads on One String' 3:40 (Pete Townshend, Josh Hunsaker)
Rippling keyboard strings usher a change of mood and pace. Townshend discovered musician Josh Hunsaker's original composition on the internet and offered to write lyrics for it. It boasts a haunting melody and a memorable choral hook and to my ears, it would make a fine single. Daltrey's stately vocal is beautifully judged, demonstrating that he has lost none of his touch. The layered backing vocals are sumptuous. Judging by the reviews, this is one of the album's most underrated songs and probably my favourite. The subject is as old as rock music itself. It's an anti-war statement and a call for people of different races and religions to learn to live in harmony. The title and theme come from a Meher Baba saying 'I want to bring the religions of the world together like beads on one string'.

'Hero Ground Zero' 4:52 (Pete Townshend)

The title of this song comes from a fictional band in Townshend's novel *The Age of Anxiety*. The lyrics recount the story of the band's singer, Nik. After experiencing a vision, he disappears from the top of Skiddaw mountain located in the Lake District National Park, where he lives in a cave for several years. Benefitting from a rich orchestral arrangement with soaring strings, the song hits the ground running. Like the view from Skiddaw itself, the melody has a majestic, panoramic quality that avoids falling into orchestrated rock bombast. Along with 'Ball and Chain', 'Hero Ground Zero' premiered at London's Wembley Stadium on 6 July 2019 backed by a 40-piece orchestra.

'Street Song' 4:47 (Pete Townshend)

Many music critics cited this as the album's best song. Townshend was moved to write it following the Grenfell Tower fire in North Kensington, west London on 14 June 2017 which claimed the lives of 72 residents. He was particularly inspired by the story of a man who was trapped inside the tower block and phones his wife to say goodbye. Daltrey refused to sing the original lyrics which had a political, finger-pointing bias. Fortunately, he was satisfied with the finished words, giving a suitably heartfelt, moving performance. Despite the subject, it has an uplifting melody introduced by rippling keys and a skipping rhythm. The backing harmonies are vibrant, but honours go to Palladino's warm bass lines and Starkey's busy drum fills.

'I'll Be Back' 5:01 (Pete Townshend)

And now for something completely different. A relaxed Townshend croons his way through this laidback song, caressed by a lush string arrangement. While the vocoder treated vocal bridge at 2:04 is an unnecessary distraction, overall the song provides a welcome mellow interlude. The tasteful harmonica solos are an added bonus. Despite the title, this song wasn't inspired by a certain Austrian actor and ex-bodybuilder. Instead, it's about reincarnation which forms the basis of many religions. It's also a partly autobiographical song that references specific events in Townshend's life during the 1960s.

'Break the News' 4:30 (Simon Townshend)

A song written by his younger brother Simon, it's the first Who song in 37 years not involving Townshend as a writer. Although Simon had performed with the band since 1996 and appeared on *Endless Wire*, this is his first compositional credit. He was inspired to write it following a visit to the doctor and contemplated what it would be like to break bad news to his partner. It rocks along with an upbeat, folk-rock groove. Daltrey's warm, evocative vocal is complemented by acoustic guitar, piano and a lively shuffle rhythm. The uplifting bridge at 2:54 is the song's highpoint. Many critics rightly compared the song to UK folk-rockers Mumford & Sons.

'Rockin' In Rage' 4:04 (Pete Townshend)

A defiant, 75-year-old Daltrey proclaims that he can rock with the best of them and still has something valuable to say. In his interpretation, the song is a sideswipe at political correctness which he feels is stifling freedom of speech. It also demonstrates that even though his range may not be quite what it was, his voice remains as expressive as ever. The intro featuring piano, acoustic guitar, cymbals and orchestral keys gives no forewarning of the song's aggressive tone. When it gets into its stride, it rocks hard with staccato riffs and a strident instrumental hook that in the old days would have been graced with Entwistle's horn stabs. The riff at 1:12 owes a good deal to the Rolling Stones' 'Jumpin' Jack Flash', taken at a slightly slower tempo.

'She Rocked My World' 3:22 (Pete Townshend)

The album bows out with a laidback offering with a distinct Latin flavour. The words look to the past and Townshend's relationship with a 'fabulous' girl who clearly left a lasting impression. Daltrey probably also had someone in mind when he recorded the song because he embraces the words with a sensual intimacy. The sympathetic backdrop includes gentle piano, Spanish guitar picking – courtesy of virtuoso Gordon Giltrap – and an airy, bossa nova rhythm. Only the strident choral bridge at 2:19 seems out of place.

Related Tracks

'This Gun Will Misfire' 3:36 (Pete Townshend)

This, and the following two songs, are bonus tracks on the 'Deluxe' CD of *Who*. Essentially, they are Townshend's demos with instrumental overdubs and he provides the lead vocals on all three. As far as Daltrey was concerned, they didn't belong on a Who record, feeling they spoilt an otherwise perfect album. Personally, I like all three and find them a welcome addition. This is a lively, acoustic guitar-driven song that's anti-guns and anti-wars. Despite the subject and Townshend's barely controlled angst ridden vocals, it features a crisp melody and a compelling rhythmic groove.

'Got Nothing to Prove' 3:38 (Pete Townshend)

Townshend wrote and demoed this song back in the summer of 1966, but it was rejected by producer Kit Lambert. Townshend's nasal vocal and twangy Hank Marvin style guitar clearly did not strike a chord. In 1967, it was offered to soul act Jimmy James and the Vagabonds. They had previously supported The Who at London's Marquee club, but they also turned it down. Producer Dave Sardy added a new backing track to Townshend's original vocal and a swinging '60s style big band arrangement. The strident horns could have been lifted from a John Barry scored James Bond film soundtrack.

'Danny and My Ponies' 4:02 (Pete Townshend)

Townshend's ode to the tramps and vagrants who trudge the streets of England. In recent years, he has clearly developed a penchant for acoustic folk ballads and this delightful song fits that bill. The double-tracked vocals are some of his best and the colourful violin arrangement is a sheer delight.

'Sand (Demo)' 4:27 (Pete Townshend)

An additional bonus track on the Japanese CD of *Who* and the triple vinyl version in other regions. Like 'Got Nothing to Prove', it was written and originally recorded in the summer of 1966 for possible inclusion on the *A Quick One* album. It certainly shows its '60's roots with a poppy melody, reverb-heavy vocals, percussive claves – similar to 'Magic Bus' – and an acoustic guitar riff in the style of The Kinks.

Live Albums and Videos

Given their reputation as a formidable stage act, The Who understandably
have released numerous live albums. The majority are 2CD and often
include the full, unedited concert. Many are also available on DVD, and
more recently, Blu-ray. Although not covered here, live recordings of
The Who also feature in various artist compilations such as the *Monterey
International Pop Festival* box-set and the 40th Anniversary edition of
Woodstock. There is also a proliferation of bootleg material out there, often
masquerading as bonafide releases.

In addition to those discussed here, a raft of live CDs were issued between
2002 and 2007 in the Encore Series. They are official soundboard recordings
released through TheMusic.com and designed to beat bootleggers at their
own game. From the 2002 North American tour alone, there were 25 separate
releases, one from each concert.

Live at Leeds (LP: 22 May 1970)

Sound engineer Bob Pridden recorded 35 dates of the 1969 *Tommy* tour for a
potential live album. When Pete Townshend couldn't face the prospect of sifting
through 240 hours of material, the recordings were abandoned. At his insistence,
the tapes were allegedly burnt to prevent pirating, but some are known to have
survived, such as a performance at Ottawa's Capitol Theatre on 15 October 1969
included with the 2013 reissue of *Tommy*. Instead, in February 1970, The Who
took Pye's eight-track mobile recording studio to Yorkshire to record their only
two shows that month. The first, at Leeds University on Valentine's Day Saturday
14 was an incendiary performance to a capacity audience of 1,500. The following
night's gig at Hull's City Hall would remain unreleased until 2010. The setlist
was structured to showcase The Who at their live best. Opening with Entwistle's
'Heaven and Hell' and 'I Can't Explain'. It featured *Tommy* in its entirety and the
fifteen-minute 'My Generation' medley as an encore.

Townshend mixed *Live at Leeds* at his home studio but was unable to
correct the crackling noises. He omitted the *Tommy* section and 'A Quick
One, While He's Away' from the original LP release in order to showcase
The Who's harder-edged sound, more typical of their live performances. The
album received unanimous praise on its release and is still regarded as one
of the best, if not the best, live recordings by a rock band and an inspiration
for heavy metal. It peaked at number three in the UK, four in America and
breached the top ten in several regions.

The plain brown, functional cover was inspired by the sleeve for the Rolling
Stones' 1969 bootleg *Live'r Than You'll Ever Be* released just five months earlier.
Inside the original LP sleeve was assorted Who memorabilia dating back to 1964.
In February 1995, a 25th anniversary expanded CD was released. In September
2001, a 2CD 'Deluxe edition' produced by Jon Astley included almost the
complete concert. In November 2010, a 40th anniversary 4CD included both the
Leeds and Hull shows in their entirety.

Who's Last (2LP: USA: November 1984, UK: December 1984)

A low point in The Who's catalogue. When the band called it a day in 1983, they intended to mark the occasion with an album that would do justice to their longevity and reputation as a premier stage act. Following the 1982 'Farewell tour', engineer Cy Langston was tasked with compiling a triple album's worth of live material spanning The Who's entire career. The end result was, according to those that heard it, very special. It would never see the light of day; MCA insisted that only recordings from the 'Farewell tour' would be used. When it was finally released in 1984, it had been pared down to a double LP. Even then, the performances were below par by The Who's standards. It reached 48 in the UK chart and 81 in America. With the exception of The Who faithful in Canada who placed it at 56, in most other regions, it failed to chart. Critics gave it a general thumbs down with a review in *Rolling Stone* being particularly scathing.

Join Together (2CD/ 3LP: March 1990)

Compiled from several dates between 27 June and 24 August during the 1989 North American summer tour. The Who had recently reunited and it was part of their 25th anniversary *The Kids Are Alright* tour. Daltrey, Townshend and Entwistle are backed by Simon Phillips on drums, John Bundrick on keyboards, Steve Bolton as second guitarist plus a horn section and backing singers. Disc one is devoted to *Tommy* in its entirety while disc two mixes hits with a few rarities and a couple of Townshend's solo songs. It's an excellent package and they go out with a bang with a near ten minute 'Won't Get Fooled Again'.

Thirty Years of Maximum R&B Live (VHS: 6 July 1994)

A companion video to the *Thirty Years of Maximum R&B* 4CD box-set, released the same week. The songs are presented in chronological order, from 'Anyway, Anyhow, Anywhere' at Richmond Athletic Grounds in 1965 to 'See Me, Feel Me' at Giants Stadium in 1989. It was reissued on DVD in 2001. A 2009 expanded edition includes additional tracks and a second disc recorded live for the German TV show *Rockpalast* on 28 March 1981. Three songs on the original release were also replaced with better quality recordings from other concerts.

The Who's Tommy: The Amazing Journey (VHS/Laserdisc: 27 July 1994)

Released to commemorate the 25th anniversary of the original *Tommy* album. It's a 60-minute compilation of live performances, backstage footage and scenes from the film and theatre production that puts The Who's most famous work in sharp focus.

Live at the Isle of Wight Festival 1970 (2CD/VHS: 29 October 1996)

The Who's legendary performance at the Isle of Wight Festival on 29 August

1970 in its near two-hour entirety. *Tommy*, naturally, provides the centrepiece, bookended by the sixties hits, live staples and a smattering of new songs including 'Water', 'I Don't Even Know Myself' and 'Naked Eye'. The 1996 video release does not include the full concert and the tracks are in a different sequence. When it was re-released on DVD on 3 November 1998 in America and 26 June 2000 in the UK, a couple of songs were restored and a 40-minute interview with Pete Townshend added. Given the vintage recording, sound – and on the DVD – picture quality is pretty decent.

BBC Sessions (CD: 15 February 2000)
This is exactly what it says on the tin. It comprises 26 tracks recorded for the BBC in London between May 1965 and January 1973. The sound quality is as you would expect from the BBC: mostly good although the occasional performance is a tad too close to the original so methinks backing tracks and overdubs were utilised.

Blues to the Bush (2CD: 19 March 2000)
So-called because it was recorded at the Chicago House of Blues on 12 and 13 November 1999 and the Empire Theatre, Shepherd's Bush on 22 and 23 December 1999. The three Who members are joined by 'Rabbit' Bundrick on keyboards and Zak Starkey on drums for a rousing romp through live evergreens bookended of course by 'I Can't Explain' and 'My Generation'. The *Who's Next* album is favoured with five selections including the scarcely played 'Getting in Tune'. This is hard to track down these days.

The Who Special Edition EP (DVD: 25 March 2003)
A 70 minute video released by Classic Pictures which includes just four songs recorded for the German television show *Beat Club*. The band are miming to pre-recorded tracks and the songs, 'See Me Feel Me', 'I'm a Boy', 'Pinball Wizard' and 'I'm Free' last a total of eleven minutes.

Live at the Royal Albert Hall (3CD: June 2003)
The Who & Special Guests: Live at the Royal Albert Hall (DVD: USA: 25 September 2001, UK: 28 July 2003)
Recorded at the end of a UK tour on 27 November 2000 in aid of the Teenage Cancer Trust. Daltrey, Townshend, Entwistle, Starkey and Bundrick are joined by a host of guests including Bryan Adams, Noel Gallagher, Eddie Vedder, Paul Weller and classical violinist Nigel Kennedy. The third bonus CD was of particular interest to fans featuring four songs from Entwistle's final Who concert at the Royal Albert Hall on 8 February 2002. These are not included on the DVD version which also omits 'Mary Anne with the Shaky Hand' and 'Getting in Tune' from the November 2000 show sung by Eddie Vedder.

Live in Boston (DVD: 13 September 2003)

Filmed on 27 September 2002 at the Tweeter Centre in Mansfield, Massachusetts, this was the penultimate show of a North America tour. On the 27 June, the eve of the tour, John Entwistle died from a heart attack and Pino Palladino stepped in as a last-minute replacement. He does a fine job as the band storm their way through two hours of their most popular songs. DVD extras include interviews with Roger Daltrey and Pete Townshend plus a gallery of images dedicated to the departed bassist.

Tangled Up In Who (DVD: 2005)

One of the earliest live recordings of *Tommy* and the last time it was performed in its entirety in the USA before being revived for the 1989 25th anniversary tour. Only 'Underture', 'Cousin Kevin' and 'Welcome' are missing, which was common practice on the 1969/1970 tours. It was filmed at the Tanglewood Performing Arts Centre, Massachusetts on 7 July 1970. They open with a few hits and following the centrepiece, they let their hair down with 'My Generation' to close. Picture and sound are flawed, but it's a unique souvenir of The Who in their prime.

Tommy and Quadrophenia Live (3DVD: 7 November 2005)

As it says on the box, this combines live performances of The Who's two grandest works. The disc one performance of *Tommy* was filmed at Los Angeles' Universal Amphitheatre on 24 August 1989. It had originally been released on VHS and Laserdisc in October 1989 under the title *The Who Live: Featuring The Rock Opera Tommy*. A 90-minute recording of *Quadrophenia* from the Nutter Centre, Dayton, Ohio on 4 November 1996 occupies disc two. The third disc is titled 'Live Hits' and comprises the encores from both concerts plus three songs recorded during a four-day residency at the Giants Stadium, New Jersey in the summer of 1989. In addition to an expanded backing band, both shows feature guest singers. Footage of Gary Glitter performing at Dayton was removed following his conviction for sex offences. On 5 June 2006, the two shows were released separately as *Tommy Live* and *Quadrophenia Live* on single disc including the 'Live Hits'.

Live from Toronto (2CD/DVD: 21 April 2006)

This dates back to the final concert of the *It's Hard* tour at Toronto's Maple Leaf Gardens on 17 December 1982. It was The Who's 'Farewell tour' before disbanding in 1983 so its belated release is of particular interest to fans. Kenney Jones' drumming demonstrates what an asset he was to the band at the time and Tim Gorman fills in on keyboards for an unavailable Bundrick. It was originally released on VHS and Laserdisc in 1983 under the title *The Who Rocks America*. The sound was cleaned up and overdubs recorded for the 2006 release.

The Vegas Job (DVD: 7 November 2006)

The clue is in the title. It was shot at the MGM Grand Garden Arena in Las Vegas on 29 October 1999. Also performing that night were Kiss and the Dixie Chicks. The show marked the return of 'Anyway, Anyhow, Anywhere' to the setlist. Also, 'Pinball Wizard', 'See Me, Feel Me", and 'Baba O'Riley' were played for the first time in ten years.

View from a Backstage Pass (2CD: 5 November 2007)

This was only available to members of The Who fan club to commemorate the launch of the band's new website. Now deleted, it's a compilation of live recordings from 12 October 1969 to 12 June 1976. The 26 tracks are in chronological order and concentrate on hits and live favourites from this period compiled by Jon Astley and produced by Bob Pridden. It's an excellent live document of Moon's latter period tenure with the band.

Live at Glastonbury 2007 (DVD: 6 June 2008)

Recorded on the 24 June 2007 in the rain, Daltrey, Townshend and company negotiate some of their best-known tunes with the occasional surprise to glowing reviews from the UK press. Highlight is the four-song *Tommy* medley before concluding with an acoustic 'Tea & Theatre'.

The Who at Kilburn: 1977 (2DVD: 17 November 2008)

Despite the title, this includes two separate performances. Disc one was filmed at Kilburn's Gaumont State Cinema on 15 December 1977 for *The Kids Are Alright* documentary but wasn't used. The second disc is a performance at the London Coliseum on 14 December 1969. The Kilburn show is the more professionally filmed of the two, but they both have their merits. Disc one features a rare live performance of 'Who Are You' with Keith Moon on drums. Disc two includes 'A Quick One, While He's Away' and an almost complete run-through of *Tommy*. It failed to breach the UK chart but made the top twenty in several European countries.

Greatest Hits Live (2CD: 23 March 2010)

The title says it all. It's another compilation of popular tunes and live standards recorded between 14 February 1970 at Leeds University and 24 March 2009 in Brisbane, Australia. Some of the recordings have been previously available, but it's a superb overview that traverses several stage line-ups of the band. Although the recordings are not chronologically sequenced, disc one at least reflects The Who's regular setlist.

Live In Texas '75 (DVD: 8 October 2012)

Another archive show, filmed at The Summit in Houston, Texas on 20 November 1975 during *The Who By Numbers* tour. It features several songs from the album, along with an eight-song *Tommy* medley prompted by the success of the film version released that year. Shot with just two cameras, the footage has its limitations, but it's recommended viewing nonetheless. Sound quality is pretty good and the band's in top form. The same concert was released on a 2007 DVD called *In Houston 1975* which has a different cover.

Live at Hull 1970 (2CD: 19 November 2012)
The entire, near two-hour performance at Hull's City Hall on 15 February 1970. It was recorded as a backup in case there were any sound or performance issues with the *Live at Leeds* recording the day before. Since then, the tapes have been gathering dust in The Who's archives. Due to a technical fault on the night, part of the bass track was missing from the recording and the bass part from Leeds was overdubbed. Although fans often discuss the merits between this and the Leeds gig, they both feature The Who in stunning form. The bootleg style cover artwork emulates the original sleeve for *Live at Leeds*.

Quadrophenia Live in London (2CD/DVD/Blu-ray/Deluxe box set: 9 June 2014)
The *Quadrophenia and More* tour that started out in 2012 was a stunning extravaganza and this, the final date recorded at London's Wembley Arena on 8 July 2013 does it full justice. It was released in various formats and DVD, or better still, Blu-ray viewing is essential. A good proportion of the two-hour-plus set is devoted to the album in question and video footage was used to add the late Entwistle and Moon to the performance. Otherwise, Townshend and Daltrey are backed by Pino Palladino (bass), Scott Devours (drums), Simon Townshend (guitars), three keyboard players and a horn section. The projected newsreel footage that forms the backdrop documents the changing times and events during The Who's career.

Live at Shea Stadium 1982 (DVD/Blu-ray: 29 June 2015)
Like *Live from Toronto*, this was filmed during The Who's 'Farewell Tour' on the second of two nights at New York's Shea Stadium on 13 October 1982. The band with Kenney Jones on drums are in fine fettle with several songs from the very recent *It's Hard* album mingled with some of their lesser-played tunes. A rousing 'Twist and Shout' brings the set to a satisfying conclusion.

Live in Hyde Park (2CD/DVD/Blu-ray: 6 November 2015)
A concert set in the green open spaces of inner London on 26 June 2015 as part of the extended 50th anniversary *The Who Hits 50!* tour. The staging is quite spectacular with giant screens providing the backdrop as the band storm effortlessly through their greatest hits and more. Guests include Paul Weller, the Kaiser Chiefs and Johnny Marr. Both picture and sound are excellent and

should be viewed on a large screen to share the experience enjoyed by the 50,000 strong crowd.

Live at the Isle of Wight Festival 2004 (2CD/DVD: 2 June 2017)

This captures The Who's heralded return to the Isle of Wight Festival on 12 June 2004 for the first time in 34 years. It was part of a string of dates that saw the band perform in the UK for the first time since the death of John Entwistle. They may be past their prime, but Daltrey, Townshend and co. were still able to demonstrate to the young pretenders at the festival how to put on a show. With the usual mix of '60's hits and a strong representation from *Tommy*, *Who's Next* and *Quadrophenia*, why fix what isn't broken.

Tommy Live at the Royal Albert Hall (2CD/3LP: 13 October 2017)

Another benefit concert at London's Royal Albert Hall in aid of the Teenage Cancer Trust. Recorded on 1 April 2017, it boasts The Who's first performance ever of *Tommy* in its entirety. As a result, this is a must have for fans of the rock opera in particular. The rest of the dates on the short *2017 Tommy & More* UK tour reverted back to the abridged version. With the rock opera occupying disc one of the CD package, disc two is the usual collection of hits, concluding with the inevitable 'Won't Get Fooled Again'.

Live at the Fillmore East 1968 (2CD/3LP: 20 April 2018)

A 50th anniversary souvenir of The Who's performance at New York's Fillmore East on 5 and 6 April 1968. They were touring in support of *The Who Sell Out* album at the time as part of The Who's concerted assault on America. Disc one of the 90-minute set features an eleven-minute 'A Quick One, While He's Away' and several cover versions including three Eddie Cochran tunes. Disc two consists of a rare 33 minute extended jam of 'My Generation'. Well worth investigating for fans of The Who's pre-*Tommy* period.

The Who's Tommy Orchestral (CD/2LP: 14 June 2019)

Although this is credited to Roger Daltrey and not The Who, as it's a recent release, I thought it was worthy of inclusion. In America, it entered the Billboard classical chart at number one. It was recorded in Budapest, Hungary and Bethel Woods, New York, during the 2018 tour. Daltrey is backed by the 'Who band' including Simon Townshend (vocals, guitar), Frank Simes (guitar), Scott Devours (drums), Jon Button (bass) and Loren Gold (keyboards). Keith Levenson conducts the Budapest Scoring Orchestra in a rousing 50th-anniversary celebration of Townshend's masterwork.

Woodstock 1969 – Live & Remastered (MP3/CD/Vinyl: 2 July 2019)

The Who's performance at Woodstock has gone down in rock history as one of the most iconic by any band, helped by the rising sun on that early morning of Sunday 17 August 1969. This is a 50th-anniversary release of the complete one hour set although it was first available as an MP3 download on 23 January 2018. Despite the remastered tag, the sound quality on the CD has come in for a good deal of criticism by fans. This release is not endorsed by the band.

Soundtracks

In addition to live albums, compilations and videos, *Tommy* and *Quadrophenia* have both inspired feature-length films. *The Kids Are Alright* is a rockumentary that spans the Keith Moon era. All three went on general release in cinemas and generated soundtrack albums released on vinyl and later, CD. The films themselves are available on DVD and Blu-Ray and occasionally are aired on terrestrial and satellite/cable TV. The documentary *Amazing Journey: The Story of The Who* was broadcast on television in many countries, including America and the UK and is available on DVD. The soundtrack is available on CD.

Tommy (2LP: 19 March 1975)

The *Tommy* soundtrack was recorded prior to filming which began on 22 April 1974 with writer and director Ken Russell at the helm. Originally scheduled for twelve weeks, shooting lasted eighteen weeks, requiring adjustments to the songs to match the timings of each scene. For Pete Townshend, it was a demanding and time-consuming undertaking, and the mixing was particularly arduous due to the different sound systems used in cinemas. The film is void of dialogue, relying on the songs and music, along with the visuals, to convey the narrative.

In addition to scoring the film and reworking most of the original material to clarify the plotline, Townshend introduced four new songs. He was also responsible for much of the instrumentation including the elaborate synthesised orchestrations. Roger Daltrey retained the lead role and guest singers include Tina Turner, Elton John, Eric Clapton and Paul Nicholas. Initially, The Who were to perform the entire score but Moon was far from working fit and rather than replace him, they brought in a cast of musicians for each song. Lead actors Oliver Reed and Jack Nicholson's shortcomings as singers were partly masked by backing vocals overdubbed at Ramport Studios. Tommy's mother Nora Walker played by Ann-Margret is given more prominence with several new songs including 'Champagne' and 'Mother and Son'.

Although the soundtrack was dismissed by a good proportion of the rock music press, it reached 21 in the UK chart and an impressive two in America. As musical director, Townshend was rewarded with an Oscar nomination for 'Best score adaptation'. He vowed never to do another film, even though he found the experience rewarding. It was later reissued as a double CD.

The Kids Are Alright (2LP: UK: 8 June 1979, USA: 24 June 1979)

Although a documentary, *The Kids Are Alright* is less a history of The Who and more a collection of live performances and interviews, interspersed with archive material of TV appearances, live footage and promotional films. It also attempts to show the daily life of the band members. It opens with the infamous American TV appearance on *The Smothers Brothers Comedy Hour* in 1967 and concludes with a show-stopping 'Won't Get Fooled Again' filmed at Shepperton Studios on 25 May 1978, Keith Moon's last stage appearance.

The 80-minute soundtrack album duplicates several live performances from the documentary including the *Tommy* medley from Woodstock. The 1968 performance of 'A Quick One, While He's Away' from *The Rolling Stones Rock and Roll Circus* is another highlight. Although it only managed 26 in the UK, it climbed to number eight on the Billboard chart, eventually achieving platinum status. An edited version was released on CD in the early '80s, but the full soundtrack was restored, remastered and reissued in 2000.

Quadrophenia (2LP: 5 October 1979)

Whereas the *Tommy* film belongs to the musical genre, *Quadrophenia* is essentially a drama that uses The Who's songs to accompany the gritty narrative and action scenes. Phil Daniels is superb as Jimmy and Sting a memorable and moody 'Ace Face'. Although she doesn't get to sing, look out for Toyah Willcox as Monkey, the girl spurned by Jimmy.

Although another double LP, the *Quadrophenia* soundtrack differs significantly from the original 1973 album. It includes ten key songs from the original, although they have been remixed and are sequenced differently. 'The Real Me' is used for the title sequence featuring a smiling Jimmy riding his Lambretta scooter. Side three of the vinyl discs includes three additional Townshend compositions to support the narrative. The fourth side is made up of classic Motown and R&B songs that would have been popular with Mods in the mid-'60s. Interestingly, The Who's 'My Generation' features diegetically in the film at a party gatecrashed by Jimmy and his friends but is not included on the soundtrack. Several other references to The Who are scattered throughout the film. The *Quadrophenia* songs were remixed by John Entwistle. Raphael Rudd, who shared Townshend's devotion to Meher Baba, arranged and conducted members of the London Philharmonic and the London Symphony Orchestra for parts of the soundtrack including the final scenes.

To coincide with the general release of the film, the album debuted in October 1979. Both did good business in the UK with the latter reaching 23 in the album chart, not bad for a soundtrack. Perhaps understandably given the distinctly regional subject matter, the album peaked at a lowly 46 in the *Billboard* chart. It was reissued on CD in 1993 and in 2000 with different tracklistings.

Amazing Journey: The Story of The Who (CD: 1 April 2008, 2DVD: 26 November 2007)

A sixteen track companion album to the excellent, two hour TV documentary *Amazing Journey: The Story of The Who*. The soundtrack CD includes just two live tracks, 'Summertime Blues' from *Live at Leeds* and 'Won't Get Fooled Again' from the 2001 *The Concert for New York City*. Otherwise it's the usual suspects of hit songs before concluding with 'Real Good Looking Boy' and 'Tea & Theatre'. The documentary itself is a better option and is available as a two-disc DVD box-set.

Compilations and Documentaries

This chapter includes LP and CD releases in the UK and USA. Where applicable, I've included the original UK release date. Video and DVD documentaries are also discussed. Numerous other made for television documentaries have been broadcast on terrestrial, cable and satellite networks around the world. Who songs have also been included on various artist compilations such as the 1969 *The House That Track Built*. Compilations of live recordings are included in the 'Live Albums and Videos' chapter.

Magic Bus: The Who on Tour (LP: September 1968)

In the fall of 1968, Decca in America had grown impatient at the lack of any new Who product. As a result, they released *Magic Bus: The Who on Tour*, the title of which was both exploitative and misleading. The Who had recently completed a successful summer tour of North America during which the 'Magic Bus' single had been a minor hit. The album wasn't a live recording as implied, but a collection of previously released tracks, some of which had already appeared on the two previous studio albums. In its favour, it does include single and EP tracks previously unavailable on a US album. It peaked at number 39 in the Billboard top 200 but failed to chart in Canada.

Direct Hits (LP: October 1968)

Released by Track Records, this was The Who's first UK compilation. It was rush-released in time for the Christmas market when it became evident that *Tommy* would not be available until the following year. Due to legal wrangles, the singles released in the UK on the Brunswick label are absent, including the classic debut trio 'I Can't Explain', 'Anyway, Anyhow, Anywhere' and 'My Generation'. The title is a misnomer considering only half of the twelve tracks were top 30 hits and some, including 'Bucket T', 'Doctor! Doctor!' and 'Mary Anne with the Shaky Hand' had not been released as singles in the UK.

Meaty Beaty Big and Bouncy (LP: 30 October 1971)

With the long-running legal issues with original producer Shel Talmy recently ended, The Who were able to release a compilation of the early singles including those recorded for the Brunswick label. Townshend once described it as – a little tongue in cheek perhaps – 'possibly the best ever Who album'. Kit Lambert didn't agree and tried to block the release because it wasn't chronologically sequenced and disagreed with the song selections. He's correct about the sequencing, the tracks would have made more sense in release date order, but it's hard to argue with the choice of songs.

It includes fourteen tracks, pretty decent for an LP at the time. More importantly, it showcases The Who at the peak of their powers as a singles band. With the exception of 'The Seeker' which closes side one, all the songs were recorded and released in the 1960s. Conspicuous by its inclusion is the single that never was, John Entwistle's 'Boris the Spider', the only non-Townshend song on the album. It remains one of The Who's best-selling compilations, reaching number nine and eleven respectively in the UK and American charts.

The Story of The Who (2LP: 24 September 1976)

This UK only collection was very popular in its time, reaching number two in the chart and was certified gold. It was helped by heavy TV promotion featuring an exploding pinball machine which was reproduced on the album cover. Released by Polydor, it combines classic singles with a generous selection of songs from *Who's Next*, *The Who by Numbers* and *Tommy*. The latter is represented by eight tracks that take up side three of the double LP. It provided a solid introduction to the band even though the first three singles and *Quadrophenia* are curiously overlooked.

Phases (9LP: May 1981)

For anyone that had let the Keith Moon era Who pass them by, this was a handsome box-set of the first nine albums including *Live at Leeds*. It was released in the UK and Germany only and each album is identical to the original release.

Hooligan (2LP: September 1981)

This focuses on singles and album tracks from the 1970s although 'I Can't Explain' and 'I Can See for Miles' – as well as 'Pinball Wizard' – are included as a reminder that The Who had a life before *Tommy*. Released by MCA in America only, it peaked at 52 in the Billboard chart and went onto achieve gold status.

Who's Greatest Hits (LP: 23 November 1983)

When The Who disbanded in 1983 and no new material on the horizon, the floodgates opened as far as compilations were concerned. Perhaps the most striking element of this LP – and later CD – is the artwork which replicates Townshend's union jack jacket. Otherwise, it's a patchy assortment of songs from MCA that somehow manages to omit most of The Who's best singles of the '60s. It still sold well for a compilation and was certified double platinum in the States.

Rarities Volume I (LP: 14 August 1983)
Rarities Volume II (LP: 14 August 1983)

Released as two separate LPs by Polydor in the UK, this is a collection of rare EP tracks and single B sides. As such, for fans, they were essential releases at the time even though they failed to capture the imagination of the general record buyers. *Volume I* covers the period 1966 to 1968 and *Volume II*, 1972 to 1973. In terms of content, *Volume II* is virtually identical to *Join Together – Rarities*, released in Australasia the previous year. They were later combined and reissued as a single CD *Rarities Volume I & Volume II*.

The Singles (LP: November 1984)
Released in the UK only by Polydor, this provides a better balance of '60s and '70s singles than *Who's Greatest Hits*. Again, however, the early pre-'Substitute' Shel Talmy produced singles are absent. Interestingly, the version of 'I Can See for Miles' here is taken from a BBC session. In 2011, it was reissued as a double CD in Japan with a far more comprehensive track selection.

Who's Missing (LP: 30 November 1985)
An ad hoc collection of rare and previously unreleased tracks. Townshend's compositions are outweighed by covers, two Entwistle tunes and a Daltrey obscurity 'Here for More'. Its highest chart placing was 44 in the UK. The Japanese CD reissue in December 2011 contains six bonus tracks of mostly Entwistle songs and was bundled with *Two's Missing*, originally released in 1987.

The Who Collection (2LP: 10 December 1985)
This is better, a complete roundup of the '60s and '70s singles on a double LP and later, double CD and mostly in chronological order. It includes a remix of 'Won't Get Fooled Again' and a few album tracks thrown in for good measure. Like *Who's Missing*, it peaked at 44 in the UK and was certified gold.

Two's Missing (LP: 11 April 1987)
Following the same format as *Who's Missing*, this contains EP and singles previously unavailable on LP. There is also the occasional cover version and previously unreleased live recording. The cover artwork depicting The Who from their '60s pop art period is one of its best assets.

Who's Better, Who's Best: This is The Very Best of The Who (2LP/CD: 18 March 1988)
Released on both sides of the Atlantic by Polydor and MCA. The singles are all present and correct and it contains an informative booklet with words by Who aficionado Richard Barnes. The quality of the mastering leaves a lot to be desired, however. It reached number ten in the UK and was certified gold on both sides of the Atlantic.

Who's Better, Who's Best (VHS: 1988)
A 60-minute video compilation that has a different track listing to *Who's Better, Who's Best: This is The Very Best of The Who* but still includes the principal hits from 1965 to 1978. Several songs feature the original promo video while others are backed by concert footage. The DVD version released several years later includes three additional promos from the early '80s.

Thirty Years of Maximum R&B (4CD: 5 July 1994)

Following the advent of CDs, there was a proliferation of boxsets in the early '90s and clearly, The Who were overdue for the deluxe treatment. This is a desirable item containing four CDs and a comprehensive booklet with an introduction from Pete Townshend. The tracks have all been remastered and remixed, and it's an excellent collection spanning the band's entire career at that point with singles, album tracks, previously unreleased live recordings and rarities. 'Substitute' is not the original but the 1970 *Live at Leeds* version, but then again, you can't have everything. It reached 48 in the UK album chart which was not bad for a boxset.

My Generation: The Very Best of The Who (CD: 27 August 1996)

Again released in Europe and North America by Polydor and MCA respectively, this is more modest fare. It does, however, contain all the remastered hits which, for many record buyers, is all they need. The songs are all in chronological order, and the release coincided with the reissue of the original albums on expanded and remastered CDs. It peaked at number eleven in the UK although surprisingly failed to chart in any other region.

20th Century Masters: The Millennium Collection: The Best of The Who (CD: 13 April 1999)

Many artists were subject to MCA's America only '20th Century Masters' collections, issued to commemorate the turn of the millennium. With only ten tracks of the most obvious hits, the content is pretty woeful.

Classic Albums: Who's Next (DVD: 22 October 2001)

This 60-minute documentary is part of Eagle Rock's extensive 'Classic Albums' series and chronicles the making of The Who's most popular album. It features previously unavailable live material including outtakes from Keith Moon's last stage appearance at Shepperton Studios on 25 May 1978.

The Ultimate Collection (2CD: 11 June 2002)

One of The Who's best-selling compilations that almost lives up to its title. With 40 tracks, it contains the majority of the singles plus choice album tracks. For reasons best known to the record companies, the American MCA release has fewer tracks and a different track sequencing to the Polydor edition released elsewhere. The 'Limited edition' contained a third disc of four additional tracks.

Then and Now (CD: 3 May 2004).

Although this greatest hits collection contains eighteen previously released singles – the 'Then' part of the title, the real reason for buying it was the inclusion of two brand new Who songs – the 'Now' part. They are 'Real Good

Looking Boy' and 'Old Red Wine'. Sales of this album soared following The Who's short set at *Live 8* on 2 July 2005 which was seen by nearly ten million British TV viewers. The 2007 reissue made a couple of track changes.

The 1st Singles Box (12CD: 25 May 2004)

A desirable collection, released for diehard UK fans only. It reproduces twelve of The Who's most popular singles, including the B sides, in CD format with 24 tracks spread over twelve discs. The inventive artwork for each disc reproduces the original sleeve as it appeared in different regions around the world.

In Their Own Words (DVD/Book: 29 August 2006)

The Who's story told by the band themselves, with additional insight from associates, fellow musicians and music pundits. These are combined with archive footage of live performances and television appearances. This one hour video is packaged with a 96-page book.

Greatest Hits (CD: 22 December 2009)
Greatest Hits & More (2CD: 13 February 2010)

Despite the unimaginative title – or perhaps because of it – this sold well on both sides of the Atlantic and must have filled many a Christmas stocking that year. As a single CD, it contained nineteen of the more popular singles and most recent releases. Two months later, it was bundled with tracks extracted from *Greatest Hits Live* and released as the two CD package *Greatest Hits & More* – another uninspired title.

Icon (CD: 5 April 2011)
Icon 2 (2CD: 5 April 2011)

In 2011, several artists featured in the 'Icon' series of compilations including the Moody Blues and this follows the established format. The single-disc *Icon* contains the absolute bare essentials with twelve hits from 'I Can't Explain' to 'Won't Get Fooled Again'. The 24 track *Icon 2* brings things more up to date, concluding with 'Real Good Looking Boy' and 'It's Not Enough'.

Pinball Wizard: The Collection (CD: 28 May 2012)

With the exception of a live version of 'I'm Free', the title track is the only song from *Tommy*. Otherwise, it mixes the occasional hit with less familiar offerings like 'Armenia City In The Sky', 'Circles' and 'Naked Eye'.

Sensation: The Story Of Tommy (DVD: 10 Mar. 2014)

This near, two-hour documentary unravels the story behind The Who's milestone work, from writing to recording and touring. Townshend, Daltrey and several others provide insightful commentary on the background behind the songs. The 33 minute DVD extra features the band's appearance on the

German TV show *Beat-Club* in 1969, previously released as *The Who Special EP* in 2003.

The Who Hits 50! (CD/2CD: 27 October 2014)

A superbly compiled release timed to commemorate The Who's 50th anniversary and support *The Who Hits 50!* tour. The two-disc edition includes almost all the UK and USA singles plus album tracks that are stage favourites. Given that the 2CD can be picked up at your local supermarket for a very modest price, the single-disc edition is dispensable. With 42 essential tracks, it's the ideal companion for a long car journey.

Lambert and Stamp (DVD: 2 November 2015)

The story of managers Kit Lambert and Chris Stamp who guided The Who through one of their most creative periods during the '60s and early '70s. At two hours, it's one of the best Who related documentaries available, highly recommended.

Bibliography

I'm indebted to the following books for providing a wealth of valuable – if occasionally conflicting – information.

Perry, J., *Classic Rock Albums: The Who Meaty Beaty Big and Bouncy* (Schirmer Books, 1998)

Ewbank, T., Hildred S., *Roger Daltrey: The Biography* (Piatkus Books Ltd, 2004)

Neil, A., Kent, M., *Anyway Anyhow Anywhere: The Complete Chronicle of The Who 1958 – 1978* (Virgin Books Ltd, 2005)

Cawthorne, N., *The Who and the Making of Tommy* (Unanimous Ltd, 2005)

Wilkerson, M., *Who Are You: The Life Of Pete Townshend* (Omnibus Press, 2009)

Townshend, P., *Who I Am* (Harper Collins, 2013)

Blake, M., *Pretend You're In A War – The Who & The Sixties* (Aurum Press Ltd, 2014)

Johns, G., *Sound Man* (Penguin Group, 2014)

Jones, K., *Let The Good Times Roll* (Blink Publishing, 2018)

Daltrey, R., *Thanks A Lot Mr Kibblewhite* (Blink Publishing, 2018)

Online Resources

https://www.thewho.com – Official Who website

https://www.thewho.net – Independent resource site for all things Who related

https://petetownshend.net – fan website

On Track series
Queen – Andrew Wild 978-1-78952-003-3
Emerson Lake and Palmer – Mike Goode 978-1-78952-000-2
Deep Purple and Rainbow 1968-79 – Steve Pilkington 978-1-78952-002-6
Yes – Stephen Lambe 978-1-78952-001-9
Blue Oyster Cult – Jacob Holm-Lupo 978-1-78952-007-1
The Beatles – Andrew Wild 978-1-78952-009-5
Roy Wood and the Move – James R Turner 978-1-78952-008-8
Genesis – Stuart MacFarlane 978-1-78952-005-7
JethroTull – Jordan Blum 978-1-78952-016-3
The Rolling Stones 1963-80 – Steve Pilkington 978-1-78952-017-0
Judas Priest – John Tucker 978-1-78952-018-7
Toto – Jacob Holm-Lupo 978-1-78952-019-4
Van Der Graaf Generator – Dan Coffey 978-1-78952-031-6
Frank Zappa 1966 to 1979 – Eric Benac 978-1-78952-033-0
Elton John in the 1970s – Peter Kearns 978-1-78952-034-7
The Moody Blues – Geoffrey Feakes 978-1-78952-042-2
The Beatles Solo 1969-1980 – Andrew Wild 978-1-78952-030-9
Steely Dan – Jez Rowden 978-1-78952-043-9
Hawkwind – Duncan Harris 978-1-78952-052-1
Fairport Convention – Kevan Furbank 978-1-78952-051-4
Iron Maiden – Steve Pilkington 978-1-78952-061-3
Dream Theater – Jordan Blum 978-1-78952-050-7
10CC – Peter Kearns 978-1-78952-054-5
Gentle Giant – Gary Steel 978-1-78952-058-3
Kansas – Kevin Cummings 978-1-78952-057-6
Mike Oldfield – Ryan Yard 978-1-78952-060-6
The Who – Geoffrey Feakes 978-1-78952-076-7

On Screen series
Carry On... – Stephen Lambe 978-1-78952-004-0
Powell and Pressburger – Sam Proctor 978-1-78952-013-2
Seinfeld Seasons 1 to 5 – Stephen Lambe 978-1-78952-012-5
Francis Ford Coppola – Cam Cobb and Stephen Lambe 978-1-78952-022-4
Monty Python – Steve Pilkington 978-1-78952-047-7
Doctor Who: The David Tennant Years – Jamie Hailstone 978-1-78952-066-8
James Bond – Andrew Wild 978-1-78952-010-1

Other Books
Not As Good As The Book – Andy Tillison 978-1-78952-021-7
The Voice. Frank Sinatra in the 1940s – Stephen Lambe 978-1-78952-032-3
Maximum Darkness – Deke Leonard 978-1-78952-048-4
The Twang Dynasty – Deke Leonard 978-1-78952-049-1
Maybe I Should've Stayed In Bed – Deke Leonard 978-1-78952-053-8
Tommy Bolin: In and Out of Deep Purple – Laura Shenton 978-1-78952-070-5
Jon Anderson and the Warriors - the road to Yes – David Watkinson
978-1-78952-059-0

and many more to come!

Would you like to write for Sonicbond Publishing?

At Sonicbond Publishing we are always on the look-out for authors, particularly for our two main series:

On Track. Mixing fact with in depth analysis, the On Track series examines the work of a particular musical artist or group. All genres are considered from easy listening and jazz to 60s soul to 90s pop, via rock and metal.

On Screen. This series looks at the world of film and television. Subjects considered include directors, actors and writers, as well as entire television and film series. As with the On Track series, we balance fact with analysis.

While professional writing experience would, of course, be an advantage the most important qualification is to have real enthusiasm and knowledge of your subject. First-time authors are welcomed, but the ability to write well in English is essential.

Sonicbond Publishing has distribution throughout Europe and North America, and all books are also published in E-book form. Authors will be paid a royalty based on sales of their book.

Further details are available from www.sonicbondpublishing.co.uk. To contact us, complete the contact form there or email info@sonicbondpublishing.co.uk